First World War
and Army of Occupation
War Diary
France, Belgium and Germany

49 DIVISION
Divisional Troops
Monmouthshire Regiment (Territorial Force)
3rd Battalion
and Machine Gun Corps 49 Battalion
1 November 1915 - 31 August 1916

WO95/2787/1

The Naval & Military Press Ltd
www.nmarchive.com
Published in association with The National Archives

Published by

The Naval & Military Press Ltd

Unit 10 Ridgewood Industrial Park,

Uckfield, East Sussex,

TN22 5QE England

Tel: +44 (0) 1825 749494

www.naval-military-press.com

www.nmarchive.com

This diary has been reprinted in facsimile from the original. Any imperfections are inevitably reproduced and the quality may fall short of modern type and cartographic standards.

© **Crown Copyright**
Images reproduced by permission of The National Archives, London, England, 2015.

Contents

Document type	Place/Title	Date From	Date To
Heading	WO95/2787 1915 Oct-1916 Sept 3rd Battalion Monmouthshire Regiment		
Heading	WO/95/2787/2 49 Battalion Machine Gun Corps		
Heading	Original War Diary Of 49th Battalion Machine Gun Corps From 1-3-18 To 31-3-18 Vol I		
War Diary		01/03/1918	31/03/1918
Operation(al) Order(s)	Operation Order No. 12 By Lieut-Colonel B.H. Badham Commanding 49th Battalion Machine Gun Corps.	13/03/1918	13/03/1918
Operation(al) Order(s)	Operation Order No 13. 49th Battalion Machine Gun Corps.	14/03/1918	14/03/1918
Operation(al) Order(s)	Operation Order No 14. 49th Battalion Machine Gun Corps.	14/03/1918	14/03/1918
Miscellaneous	Operation Order 49th Battalion Machine Gun Corps.	18/03/1918	18/03/1918
Miscellaneous	O.C. "A" Company.	18/03/1918	18/03/1918
Operation(al) Order(s)	Operation Order No 17.	19/03/1918	19/03/1918
Operation(al) Order(s)	Operation Order No 18.	22/03/1918	22/03/1918
Operation(al) Order(s)	D. Company. 49th Battn. M.G.C. Operation Order No. 25.	22/03/1918	22/03/1918
Operation(al) Order(s)	Operation Order No 19	24/03/1918	24/03/1918
Miscellaneous	Reference Operation Order No 18.	25/03/1918	25/03/1918
Operation(al) Order(s)	Operation Order No 20.	25/03/1918	25/03/1918
Operation(al) Order(s)	49th M.G. Batt. O.O. No 21.	27/03/1918	27/03/1918
Operation(al) Order(s)	Operation Order No 21A.	27/03/1918	27/03/1918
Operation(al) Order(s)	Operation Order No 22.	29/03/1918	29/03/1918
Operation(al) Order(s)	Operation Order No 23.	29/03/1918	29/03/1918
Heading	49th Divisional Troops 49th Battalion Machine Gun Corps April 1918 Battalion O.Os Attached.		
War Diary		01/04/1918	30/04/1918
Operation(al) Order(s)	Battalion Machine Gun Corps. Operation Order No. 24	01/04/1918	01/04/1918
Operation(al) Order(s)	Battalion Machine Gun Corps. Operation Order No. 25.	02/04/1918	02/04/1918
Operation(al) Order(s)	Battalion Machine Gun Corps. Operation Order No. 26.	05/04/1918	05/04/1918
Operation(al) Order(s)	Battalion Machine Gun Corps. Operation Order No. 27	05/04/1918	05/04/1918
Operation(al) Order(s)	Battalion Machine Gun Corps. Operation Order No. 28	08/04/1918	08/04/1918
Operation(al) Order(s)	Battalion Machine Gun Corps. Operation Order No. 29.	08/04/1918	08/04/1918
Operation(al) Order(s)	Battalion Machine Gun Corps. Operation Order No. 30.	09/04/1918	09/04/1918
Operation(al) Order(s)	Battalion Machine Gun Corps. Operation Order No. 31	09/04/1918	09/04/1918
Operation(al) Order(s)	Battalion Machine Gun Corps. Operation Order No. 32.	09/04/1918	09/04/1918
Operation(al) Order(s)	Battalion Machine Gun Corps. Operation Order No. 33.	18/04/1918	18/04/1918
Operation(al) Order(s)	Battalion Machine Gun Corps. Operation Order No. 34.	26/04/1918	26/04/1918
Operation(al) Order(s)	Battalion Machine Gun Corps. Operation Order No. 35.	26/04/1918	26/04/1918
Operation(al) Order(s)	Battalion Machine Gun Corps. Operation Order No. 36.	26/04/1918	26/04/1918
Operation(al) Order(s)	Battalion Machine Gun Corps. Operation Order No. 37.	26/04/1918	26/04/1918
Miscellaneous	O.C. "A" Company.	30/04/1918	30/04/1918
Miscellaneous	G 49th Division Technical & Tactical Report.	22/04/1918	22/04/1918
Heading	49th Division 49th Bn Mach. Gun Corps Apr 1918-Apr 1918 May		
Operation(al) Order(s)	49th Bn. Machine Gun Corps Order No. 93.	03/03/1918	03/03/1918
Heading	War Diary Of 49th Bn. M.G.C. For May 1918 Vol 3		
War Diary		01/05/1918	31/05/1918

Operation(al) Order(s)	49th Batt. M.G. Corps. Operation Order No. B/47		
Operation(al) Order(s)	Battalion Machine Gun Corps. Operation Order No 38	05/05/1918	05/05/1918
Operation(al) Order(s)	49th Battalion Machine Gun Corps. Operation Order No 39.	31/05/1918	31/05/1918
Heading	War Diary Of 49th Battn. M.G.C. From 1.6.18-30.6.18. Vol 4.		
War Diary		01/06/1918	30/06/1918
Operation(al) Order(s)	49th Battalion Machine Gun Corps. Operation Order No. 40.	01/06/1918	01/06/1918
Operation(al) Order(s)	49th Battalion Machine Gun Corps. Operation Order No. 41.	01/06/1918	01/06/1918
Operation(al) Order(s)	49th Battalion Machine Gun Corps. Operation Order No. 42.	02/06/1918	02/06/1918
Operation(al) Order(s)	49th Battalion Machine Gun Corps. Operation Order No. 43.	02/06/1918	02/06/1918
Operation(al) Order(s)	49th Battalion Machine Gun Corps. Operation Order No. 44.	03/06/1918	03/06/1918
Operation(al) Order(s)	49th Battalion Machine Gun Corps. Operation Order No 45	03/06/1918	03/06/1918
Operation(al) Order(s)	49th Battalion Machine Gun Corps. Operation Order No 46	08/06/1918	08/06/1918
Operation(al) Order(s)	49th Battalion Machine Gun Corps. Operation Order No. 47.	17/06/1918	17/06/1918
Operation(al) Order(s)	49th Battalion Machine Gun Corps. Operation Order No 48.	25/06/1918	25/06/1918
Operation(al) Order(s)	49th Battalion Machine Gun Corps. Operation Order No 49	27/06/1918	27/06/1918
Heading	War Diary Of 49th Battn. M.G.C. From 1.7.18. To 31.7.18. Vol. 5		
War Diary		01/07/1918	31/07/1918
Operation(al) Order(s)	49th Battalion Machine Gun Corps. Operation Order No 53	03/07/1918	03/07/1918
Operation(al) Order(s)	49th Battalion Machine Gun Corps. Operation Order No 54.	12/07/1918	12/07/1918
Operation(al) Order(s)	49th Battalion Machine Gun Corps. Operation Order No. 55.	16/07/1918	16/07/1918
Operation(al) Order(s)	49th Battalion Machine Gun Corps. Operation Order No. 57	18/07/1918	18/07/1918
Operation(al) Order(s)	49th Battalion Machine Gun Corps. Operation Order No. 58.	25/07/1918	25/07/1918
Operation(al) Order(s)	49th Battalion Machine Gun Corps. Operation Order No. 59.	26/07/1918	26/07/1918
Heading	Original War Diary 49th Battn. M.G.C. From 1.8.18.-31.8.48. Vol. 6.		
War Diary		01/08/1918	31/08/1918
Operation(al) Order(s)	49th Battalion Machine Gun Corps. Operation Order No 60.	03/08/1918	03/08/1918
Operation(al) Order(s)	49th Battalion Machine Gun Corps. Operation Order No 61.	11/08/1918	11/08/1918
Miscellaneous	Warning Order	16/08/1918	16/08/1918
Miscellaneous	Warning Order	17/08/1918	17/08/1918
Operation(al) Order(s)	49th Battalion Machine Gun Corps. Operation Order No. 62.	17/08/1918	17/08/1918
Operation(al) Order(s)	Administrative Instructions To Accompany Operation Order No. 62.	18/08/1918	18/08/1918

Miscellaneous	Amendment No. 1. To Administrative Instructions To Accompany Operation Order No. 62.	18/08/1918	18/08/1918
Miscellaneous	Table "A". 146th Infantry Brigade.		
Operation(al) Order(s)	49th Battalion Machine Gun Corps. Operation Order No 63	18/08/1918	18/08/1918
Operation(al) Order(s)	49th Battalion Machine Gun Corps. Operation Order No 64	19/08/1918	19/08/1918
Operation(al) Order(s)	49th Battalion Machine Gun Corps. Operation Order No 65	20/08/1918	20/08/1918
Miscellaneous	Amendment To Operation Order No. 65	20/08/1918	20/08/1918
Operation(al) Order(s)	49th Battalion Machine Gun Corps. Operation Order No. 66.	23/08/1918	23/08/1918
Miscellaneous	Amendment No 1. To Operation Order No. 66.	23/08/1918	23/08/1918
Operation(al) Order(s)	49th Battalion Machine Gun Corps. Operation Order No. 67.	27/08/1918	27/08/1918
Heading	Original War Diary 49th Battn. M.G.C. From 1.9.18.-30.9.18. Vol. 7.		
War Diary		01/09/1918	30/09/1918
Operation(al) Order(s)	49th Battalion Machine Gun Corps. Operation Order No. 68	01/09/1918	01/09/1918
Operation(al) Order(s)	49th Battalion Machine Gun Corps. Operation Order No. 70.	02/09/1918	02/09/1918
Operation(al) Order(s)	49th Battalion Machine Gun Corps. Operation Order No. 71.	11/09/1918	11/09/1918
Miscellaneous	49th Battn M.G.C. O.O. 72/2	20/09/1918	20/09/1918
Miscellaneous	Instructions Regarding Transport To Accompany 49th Battalion. M.G. Corps. Operation Orders Nos. 72 And 73	18/09/1918	18/09/1918
Miscellaneous	Amendment No. 1 To Operation Order No. 72.	18/09/1918	18/09/1918
Operation(al) Order(s)	49th Battalion, Machine Gun Corps. Operation Order No. 72	18/09/1918	18/09/1918
Miscellaneous	To All Recipients Of O.O. No. 73.	19/09/1918	19/09/1918
Operation(al) Order(s)	Amendment No. 1 To Operation Order No. 73.	18/09/1918	18/09/1918
Operation(al) Order(s)	49th Battalion, Machine Gun Corps. Operation Order No. 73	18/09/1918	18/09/1918
Operation(al) Order(s)	49th Battalion, Machine Gun Corps. Operation Order No. 74	18/09/1918	18/09/1918
Operation(al) Order(s)	49th Battalion, Machine Gun Corps. Operation Order No. 75	20/09/1918	20/09/1918
Miscellaneous	Table Accompanying O.O. 75.		
Operation(al) Order(s)	Administrative Instructions No. 1 (49th Battn. M.G.C.). To Accompany Operation Order No. 75	20/09/1918	20/09/1918
Operation(al) Order(s)	To O.C. "A" Company. (Adv. & Rear). 49th Division "G" (for Information).	23/09/1918	23/09/1918
Miscellaneous	49th Battalion. Machine Gun Corps. Amendment No. 1 To Operation Order No. 75.	23/09/1918	23/09/1918
Miscellaneous	Table Accompanying O.O. 75/1		
Operation(al) Order(s)	49th Battalion, Machine Gun Corps. Operation Order No. 76	22/09/1918	22/09/1918
Miscellaneous	Training Programme. 26.9.18 To 28.9.18	23/09/1918	23/09/1918
Miscellaneous	Training Programme.	29/09/1918	29/09/1918
Heading	War Diary Of 49th Bn. Machine Gun Corps October 1918 Vol 8		
Heading	Cover for Documents. Nature of Enclosures.		
War Diary		01/10/1918	31/10/1918

Type	Description	Start	End
Operation(al) Order(s)	49th Battalion Machine Gun Corps. Operation Order No. 78	08/10/1918	08/10/1918
Operation(al) Order(s)	49th Battalion Machine Gun Corps. Operation Order No. 79.	12/10/1918	12/10/1918
Miscellaneous	O.C. "C" Company (Rear)	14/10/1918	14/10/1918
Miscellaneous	49th Battalion Machine Gun Corps. Operation Order No. 80.	13/10/1918	13/10/1918
Operation(al) Order(s)	49th Battalion Machine Gun Corps. Operation Order No. 81.	17/10/1918	17/10/1918
Miscellaneous	March Table		
Operation(al) Order(s)	49th Battalion Machine Gun Corps. Operation Order No. 83	26/10/1918	26/10/1918
Operation(al) Order(s)	49th Battalion Machine Gun Corps. Operation Order No. 84.	28/10/1918	28/10/1918
Miscellaneous	Amendment To 49th Bn. M.G.C. Operation Order No. 84.	28/10/1918	28/10/1918
Operation(al) Order(s)	49th Battalion Machine Gun Corps. Operation Order No. 86	29/10/1918	29/10/1918
Miscellaneous	Addendum No. 1. To 49th Bn. M.G.C. Operation Order No. 86.	31/10/1918	31/10/1918
Miscellaneous	Addendum No. 2. To 49th Battalion Machine Gun Corps Operation Order No. 86.	31/10/1918	31/10/1918
Miscellaneous	Notes On The Rhonelle River.	30/10/1918	30/10/1918
Operation(al) Order(s)	49th Battalion Machine Gun Corps. Operation Order No. 87.	31/10/1918	31/10/1918
Miscellaneous	O.C. "A" Company.	28/10/1918	28/10/1918
Heading	Original War Diary From 1.11.18-30.11.18. Vol. 9.		
War Diary		01/11/1918	30/11/1918
Miscellaneous	A Form Messages And Signals.	04/11/1918	04/11/1918
Operation(al) Order(s)	49th Battalion Machine Gun Corps. Operation Order No. 88.	01/11/1918	01/11/1918
Miscellaneous	49th Battalion Machine Gun Corps. Operation Order No. 89.	01/11/1918	01/11/1918
Miscellaneous	Addendum No. 1. To 49th Bn. Machine Gun Corps. Operation Order No. 91.	06/11/1918	06/11/1918
Miscellaneous	49th Battalion Machine Gun Corps. Order No. 91.	04/11/1918	04/11/1918
Heading	War Diary Of 49 Bn M.G. Corps. December 1918		
War Diary	Auby	01/12/1918	04/12/1918
War Diary	Henin Lietard	05/12/1918	03/03/1919
War Diary	Douai	04/03/1919	30/04/1919
Heading	Pioneers 49th Division 3rd Monmouths November 1915		
War Diary	Elverdinghe	01/11/1915	30/11/1915
Heading	Pioneers 49th Div. 3rd Monmouths December 1915		
War Diary	Elverdinghe	01/12/1915	19/12/1915
War Diary	Canal Bank	20/12/1915	20/12/1915
War Diary	Elverdinghe	21/12/1915	27/12/1915
War Diary	Elverdinghe	15/12/1915	19/12/1915
War Diary	Elverdinghe	28/12/1915	29/12/1915
War Diary	Camp. 4. 28.A.8.	30/12/1915	31/12/1915
Heading	49. Div Troops. 3rd Monmouth Regt. Jan 1916 Vol IX Aug 1916		
War Diary	Reitveld	01/01/1916	04/02/1916
War Diary	Saisseval	05/02/1916	12/02/1916
War Diary	Ailly-Sur-Somme	13/02/1916	13/02/1916
War Diary	Molliens-Au-Bois	14/02/1916	14/02/1916
War Diary	Bouzincourt	15/02/1916	08/03/1916

War Diary	Forceville	09/03/1916	12/03/1916
War Diary	Bouzincourt	17/02/1916	29/02/1916
War Diary	Forceville	01/04/1916	12/04/1916
War Diary	Forceville	13/03/1916	31/03/1916
War Diary	Forceville	13/04/1916	31/05/1916
Heading	49th Divisional Pioneers Pioneers 1/3rd Battalion Monmouthshire Regiment June 1916		
Miscellaneous	D.A.G. 3rd Echelon Base	05/07/1916	05/07/1916
War Diary	Forceville	01/06/1916	25/06/1916
War Diary	Rubempre	26/06/1916	27/06/1916
War Diary	Contay	28/06/1916	28/06/1916
War Diary	Harponville	29/06/1916	30/06/1916
Heading	Pioneers. 49th Div. War Diary 1/3rd Battn. The Monmouthshire Regiment. July 1916		
War Diary	Bouzincourt	01/07/1916	10/07/1916
War Diary	Hedauville	11/07/1916	31/07/1916
Miscellaneous	D.A.G. 3rd Echelon Base.	10/10/1916	10/10/1916
War Diary	Hedauville	01/08/1916	07/08/1916
War Diary	Forceville	08/08/1916	09/08/1916
War Diary	Capelle	10/08/1916	27/08/1916
War Diary	Rouen	01/09/1916	09/09/1916
War Diary	Hesdin	10/09/1916	10/09/1916
War Diary	Rouen	11/09/1916	16/09/1916
War Diary	Hesdin	17/09/1916	18/09/1916
War Diary	Rouen	19/09/1916	20/09/1916
War Diary	Hesdin	21/09/1916	21/09/1916
War Diary	Rouen	22/09/1916	30/09/1916
War Diary	Hesdin	28/08/1916	31/08/1916
Heading	WO95/Stray/ZZZ		

PUBLIC RECORD OFFICE

Group/Class WO 95
Piece 2787

1915 OCT — 1916 SEPT

3RD Battalion Monmouthshire Regiment

MISSING WITHIN DEPARTMENT.

(date)...
(Signed)....................................

wo/95/2787/2

49 Battalion Machine Gun Corps

CONFIDENTIAL Vol I

ORIGINAL

WAR DIARY

OF

49TH BATTALION, MACHINE GUN CORPS

FROM 1-3-18 TO 31-3-18

Vol I

Army Form C. 2118.

WAR DIARY
or
INTELLIGENCE SUMMARY.

(Erase heading not required.)

Instructions regarding War Diaries and Intelligence Summaries are contained in F. S. Regs., Part II, and the Staff Manual respectively. Title pages will be prepared in manuscript.

Place	Date	Hour	Summary of Events and Information	Remarks and references to Appendices
	1.3.18.		Wallaceroth at 15.53 and 15.41, 15.20 altered so as to obtain a better field of fire for close defence purposes. Enemy tried to raid our lines after a French Mortar bombardment but was repulsed leaving 3 prisoners.	(1)M/18 (W)M/18
	2.3.18.		The 146th, 147th, 148th, 25th Machine Gun Companies become "A" "B" "C" "D" Companies 49th Battalion Machine Gun Corps.	(2)M/18
	3.3.18.		"B" Company was relieved in the Right Sub-sector by "C" Company. "B" Company on relief proceed to MATAWAI Camp. The horses of "D" Company placed in isolation by the D.A.D.V.S. owing to the animal occupants of the stables having Christie Lampho ——.	(3)M/18
	5.3.18.		Relieving times carried out as per Divisional Harassing Fire Programme. Capt. HANSON assumes command of "B" Company vice Capt. J. H. MUHLIG (to 30th Division)	(4)M/18

Army Form C. 2118.

WAR DIARY
or
INTELLIGENCE SUMMARY.
(Erase heading not required.)

Place	Date	Hour	Summary of Events and Information	Remarks and references to Appendices
	7.3.18		Disposition in line as for 6.3.18. Special shoots were asked for by 37th Division on our right. POLDERHOEK CHAU was consequently kept under continuous fire during the night by guns at J.10.b.26.30 - J.10.b.35.30 - J.10.b.50.30 - J.10.b.55.30. No of rounds fired in harassing fire 23,000 rounds	(MW)
	8.3.18		Disposition as for 7.3.18. SOS signal was sent up on the 37th Divisional front on our right at 5.45 pm. - Guns at J.10.b.26.30 - J.10.b.35.30 - J.10.b.50.30 - J.10.b.55.30 opened fire on POLDERHOEK CHAU on their SOS lines from J.16.d.14 to J.22.b.05.80. This was repeated at 6.45 pm. The enemy succeeded in occupying a small portion of the front line, but was ejected on the morning of the 9.3.18. All through the night a rate of 50 rounds per gun per hour was left up on POLDERHOEK CHAU. "C" Company suffered two casualties at No. 1 position. Total No rounds fired during the SOS. 60,000 rounds.	(MW)
	9.3.18		Very little hostile shelling during the morning. Counter preparation	(MW)

D.D.&L., London, E.C.
(A7853) Wt W8.9/M1672 350,000 4/17 Sch 52a Form/C/2118/14

WAR DIARY or INTELLIGENCE SUMMARY

Army Form C. 2118.

Place	Date	Hour	Summary of Events and Information	Remarks and references to Appendices
			Shoot ordered for 9pm for a duration of 45 minutes on the Right Brigade front. "B" Company relieved "A" Company in the left Sub-Sector. "A" Company occupy posts # 5, 5a, 6, 7 & 9 in the Corps Line. Lieut. Smith of "A" Company wounded in the shoulder. A report was received by the 34th Division stating how very effective his barrage had been and was mainly instrumental in breaking up further attacks. Battalion Canteen opened at CAFE BELGE.	
	10.3.18		Counter Preparation Shoots carried out on Right Brigade front 5.15 & 5.45am. Neighbourhood of ZONNEBEKE church shelled. An assistant Transport Officer (Lt Thomas "D" Company) appointed. "C" Company transport moved to WAKATU lines. 13,000 rounds fired in harassing fire during the night 10/11th.	
	11.3.18		Counter Preparation shoots at 3.30pm and 4.45 am. The front of the Division on our right was subjected to a sharp & intense bombardment at 7.0 pm. The headquarters of the	

WAR DIARY
or
INTELLIGENCE SUMMARY.
(Erase heading not required.)

Army Form C. 2118.

Instructions regarding War Diaries and Intelligence Summaries are contained in F. S. Regs., Part II. and the Staff Manual respectively. Title pages will be prepared in manuscript.

Place	Date	Hour	Summary of Events and Information	Remarks and references to Appendices
			Battalion were moved from the Ramparts to the Post Office - YPRES. On the whole a very quiet day. No. of rounds fired in harassing fire & counter preparation shoots on night 11/12th 33,000 rounds. Casualties NIL.	YPRES
	12.3.18		Lieut. W.J. Hall M.C. attached to Battalion Headquarters as Intelligence Officer & assistant Adjutant. Recreation room at MATAWAI camp opened. Enemy artillery active throughout the day. Vicinity of camps at MATAWAI shelled during the night. no damage done. YPRES shelled lightly at intervals during the evening. 31,000 rounds fired harassing fire - Casualties NIL.	
	13.3.18		A raid was carried out by the 6th West Riding Regt. & H.L. West Riding Regt. at 3.30 am and 7am. the objectives of the raids were on pill-box near Tank at I.14.a.42.60 and post at I.6c.7.8. - Our Machine Guns co-operated from positions at I.10.b.5.6. - I.10.b.50.55 - I.10.b.50.85 - I.10.b.50.90 - I.11.a.50.40 - I.5c.00.30. - D.26c.8.2. - D.28c.8.3. - D.28c.65.60. - D.28c.55.40.	

WAR DIARY
or
INTELLIGENCE SUMMARY.
(Erase heading not required.)

Army Form C. 2118.

Place	Date	Hour	Summary of Events and Information	Remarks and references to Appendices
			Rate of fire etc as per attached operation order. The Raid at 3.30 am was not successful owing to our troops on entering the enemy lines, finding the enemy were not in the post. The raid at 7am was entirely successful, we brought in a total of 37 prisoners. 25,000 rounds fired in all, including rounds fired in conjunction with raid & counter preparation shoot. Lieut. H. SMITH of "B" Company leaves the Battalion to take up 6 months home duties. Casualties Nil.	O.O. 13
	14.3.18		The front line of 144th Infantry Brigade (on the right) was subjected to heavy shelling throughout the morning, probably in retaliation for our unsuccessful raid. Machine Guns at J.10.b.25.30 - J.10.b.35.30 - J.10.b.50.30 - J.10.b.53.30 fired in support of a raid carried out by the 34th Division on our right. Their targets were J.22.b.10.90. to J.22.b.10.10. Times of fire 9-20 pm to 9-40 pm. No. of rounds fired...	

Place	Date	Hour	Summary of Events and Information	Remarks and references to Appendices
	15.3.18		harassing fire 14,450 rounds. 2/Lieut C ALLCOCK & 2/Lieut P BROUGH arrived as reinforcements & posted to A & C Companies respectively. - Digging of horses completed. "A" Company relieves "C" Company in the right sub-sector in accordance with Operation Order No. 12. "C" Company occupy the posts in the Botha line on relief. Our lines protected by the G.O.C. Division in the afternoon. No of rounds fired in harassing fire 14,450 - Casualties NIL	O.O No 12 O.O No 12
	16.3.18		Capt. Allen. R.A.M.C joined the Battalion as Medical Officer. Nos 1 & 4 Sections "D" Company relieve 2 & 3 Sections "D" Company in Barrage positions near the Butte in accordance with "D" Company O.O No 2. No of rounds fired in harassing fire 8,500. Heavy shelling on the whole Divisional front during the day & night. Gas shells fell about the Battalion during the evening. 11,000 rounds were fired in harassing fire during the night. Casualties, 1 OR killed & 1 OR wounded.	O.O No 2#

Army Form C. 2118.

WAR DIARY
or
INTELLIGENCE SUMMARY.
(Erase heading not required.)

Instructions regarding War Diaries and Intelligence Summaries are contained in F. S. Regs., Part II. and the Staff Manual respectively. Title pages will be prepared in manuscript.

Place	Date	Hour	Summary of Events and Information	Remarks and references to Appendices
	17.3.18		Church Parade for details at Camp at BELGIAN BATTERY CORNER in the morning. One also held there for transport in afternoon. Considerable harassing of back areas throughout the day. Enemy machine guns caused trouble throughout the day & night. An enemy Machine Gun was spotted at J.23a 85.60 - 11,000 rounds were fired in harassing fire during the night. Casualties 2 O.R. wounded (gas shell) Capt. N.F. KINDER "B" Company is appointed 2nd in command of "D" Company	
	18.3.18		A Counter preparation shoot was carried by the Artillery opposite the 39th Division front machine Guns at J.10.b. 25.30 - J.10.b. 35.30 - J.10.b. 50.30 and J.10.b. 55.30 co-operated by firing on their S.O.S lines. The whole area was subjected to gas shelling throughout the night. Ypres was a very marked increase in Artillery activity throughout the day against our forward and rear areas. YPRES came in for shelling during the morning & night. The machine gun at J.6.c. 15.15 was moved to a new position at	

Army Form C. 2118.

WAR DIARY
or
INTELLIGENCE SUMMARY.
(Erase heading not required.)

Instructions regarding War Diaries and Intelligence Summaries are contained in F. S. Regs., Part II. and the Staff Manual respectively. Title pages will be prepared in manuscript.

Place	Date	Hour	Summary of Events and Information	Remarks and references to Appendices
			T.6.00.40 - No of rounds fired in harassing fire 16,000 rounds. Casualties NIL.	
	19.3.18		A very quiet day on the whole front owing to very bad weather and poor visibility. In the evening orders were received regarding a special shoot to take place the next day, consequently the guns in the forps line were re-inforced by "C" Company. The back areas came in for considerable shelling - YPRES was shelled in the early morning. Lieut. HARRIS reported for duty as Quartermaster to the Battalion. At 9.50 p.m. movement was observed by one of our gun teams in the wire about T.11.d.05.20. On investigation it was found that there were two wounded Germans there, immediately after another German rose up & surrendered. 18,000 rounds were fired in harassing fire. - Casualties NIL.	(Sgd)
	20.3.18		Machine Guns fired in conjunction with the Artillery on targets etc. as per operation order No /7. Enemy retaliation	(Sgd) OO.17

WAR DIARY
or
INTELLIGENCE SUMMARY.

(Erase heading not required.)

Army Form C. 2118.

Place	Date	Hour	Summary of Events and Information	Remarks and references to Appendices
	21.3.18		very slight. Enemy fairly active with gas shells throughout the night. Still considerable activity in shelling of back areas. Lieut. A PAWSON taken on the strength of this Battalion and posted to "C" Company. 2/Lt C ALLCOCK transferred from "C" Company to "B" Company. Considerable artillery activity with gas shelling throughout the day. "C" Company relieve "B" Company in the left sub sector in accordance with OO No 12. Capt. V.L. BATTEN. R.A.M.C. posted to the Battalion vice Capt. T.W. ALLEN to 2nd W.R. Field Ambulance. No of rounds fired in harassing fire 40,000 rds. Casualties NIL	WS
	22.3.18		Artillery activity in forward area much quieter than on preceding days, but still fairly active on back areas. Arrangements made with 1st/8th Infantry Brigade regarding a proposed raid. 3,000 rounds fired in harassing fire. Casualties: 1 OR wounded (shell) : 1 OR wounded (gas).	WS

WAR DIARY
or
INTELLIGENCE SUMMARY.
(Erase heading not required.)

Army Form C. 2118.

Place	Date	Hour	Summary of Events and Information	Remarks and references to Appendices
	23.3.18		Quiet day. Occasional shelling of back areas. Nos 2, 3, "D" Company relieve Nos 1 & 4 Sections in barrage positions in accordance with "D" Company OO 25. All preparations for raid by 148th Inf. Brigade OO 25 completed. Preliminary orders issued for redistribution of the line, take place on the 25/26. 6,300 rounds fired in harassing fire. - Casualties NIL.	D Coy OO 25
	24.3.18		Fairly quiet day in the forward areas, back areas again came in for considerable attention. No of rounds fired in harassing fire 10,000 rounds. - Casualties 1 OR.	
	25.3.18		Line redistributed as follows. Guns at ZONNEBEKE CHURCH and at D.29a.40.78. - D.23c.35.20. and D.23c.70.45. were relieved by the 33rd Machine Gun Battalion and 5 guns at J.15b.25.30. - J.15b.22.40. - J.15b.50.72. J.10c. central - J.9a.85.95. of the 34th Machine Gun Battalion in accordance taken over from the 34th Machine Gun Battalion in accordance with Operation Order No 19. The 148th Inf. Brigade carried out a raid against enemy strong points at J.12a.4.2. and J.11d.3.0. at 9.0 p.m. Our machine guns and those of the 234th Machine Gun Bn.	OO 19

WAR DIARY
or
INTELLIGENCE SUMMARY.
(Erase heading not required.)

Army Form C. 2118.

Place	Date	Hour	Summary of Events and Information	Remarks and references to Appendices
			Both recoperated in accordance with Operation Order No 18. One of the raids carried out was entirely successful, four prisoners & two Machine guns being captured. Our casualties were Nil. No. of rounds fired in Co-operation with raid 40,350. No fired in harassing fire Nil.	OO No 18
	26.3.18		Very quiet day on the whole front. At 11.0 pm preliminary orders were issued ordering "B" Company & "D" Company to take over the whole 34th Divisional Sector on the 28th owing to the 34th Division being ordered to reinforce our line further South. Casualties Nil. Rounds fired in harassing fire 13,000.	(1)
	27.3.18		16 Guns of "B" Company relieved Guns on the left Sub-Sector of the 34th Divisional Front & 8 guns of "D" Company relieved guns in the Right Sub-sector of the 34th Divisional front. "B" Company (ult) Headquarters at JACKDAW POST J13c 70.30 and "D" Company Advanced Headquarters at Hill 60 Defectors.	(1)

taken up are shown on attached map. This necessitated
all guns in the Corps line of old sector being withdrawn. No 15 gun at
D 29 a.8.1 was relieved by a gun of the 33rd Battalion
Machine Gun Corps in accordance Operation Order No 21.
The boundaries of the Division become as shown on Map A, the
49th Division having taken over the whole of the 37th
Divisional front (on our right) and giving up to the 33rd Division
the front held by the right Company, 146th Brigade.
Capt. J.A. Husband of "C" Company reported the Battalion having
be recalled from leave. 2/Lt. A.G. Grimes joined the Battalion as a
reinforcement & posted to "D" Company. Transport lines at
MATAWAI CAMP were shelled in the afternoon, but no damage
done. The back areas and YPRES came in for considerable
shelling during the day. Quiet in the forward area.
Casualties NIL. No. of rounds fired in harassing fire.— 13,000.

Army Form C. 2118.

WAR DIARY
or
INTELLIGENCE SUMMARY.
(Erase heading not required.)

Instructions regarding War Diaries and Intelligence Summaries are contained in F. S. Regs., Part II. and the Staff Manual respectively. Title pages will be prepared in manuscript.

Place	Date	Hour	Summary of Events and Information	Remarks and references to Appendices
	28.3.16		Guns at I.15.b, I.15.d, I.9.b.80.00 and I.3.c.0.3 were withdrawn and sent to I.14.b.15.30 (Corps Res: No 1) and are reinforced by one Gun of "C" Company - The four guns of "C" Company in reserve, were sent to take up a barrage position at KLEIN ZILLEBEKE. 2/Lt 6 Allcock badly wounded in face & head. One other rank wounded.	
	29.3.16		Quiet day on whole sector. Officers of 61st Battalion Machine Gun Corps reconnoitred the eleven left guns on the Divisional front prior to taking them over on the night of the 31st March.	

Army Form C. 2118.

WAR DIARY
or
INTELLIGENCE SUMMARY.
(Erase heading not required.)

Instructions regarding War Diaries and Intelligence Summaries are contained in F. S. Regs., Part II. and the Staff Manual respectively. Title pages will be prepared in manuscript.

Place	Date	Hour	Summary of Events and Information	Remarks and references to Appendices
	30.3.18		Quiet day, nothing to report. — Casualties NIL. Rounds fired in harassing fire 14,800	SW
	31.3.18		One company of the 6th Battn. Machine Gun Corps relieve the following guns of "B" Company in the left sector - J.5.b.3.1 - J.5.b.45.20. - J.5.b. 18.25 - J.5.a. 90.98 - D.29.c.80.20 - J.4.b.85.13 and 4 guns at D 28.c. 45.35. Also gun at J.3.c. 85. 45. "B" Company after this relief, relieve "A" Company in the following positions J.11.c.25.45 - J.11.b.40.80 - J.11.b.49.95 - J.5.d.50.20. - J.6.c.15.15 - J.10.c.55.35. - J.10.a.0.2. and two guns at J.11.a.00.65. "A" Company occupy on relief of above guns by "B" Company. Both lots. 4, 5, 5a, the remaining 5 guns going into reserve. All in accordance with Operation order 22. The one company of the 6th Battn. Machine Gun Corps comes under orders of 49th Division. Casualties NIL	AW O.O 22

SECRET.   Copy No. 10.

OPERATION ORDER NO. 12
by
Lieut.- Colonel B.H.Badham
Commanding 49th Battalion Machine Gun Corps.

1. "A" Coy will relieve "C" Coy in the RIGHT SUB-SECTOR on the night 15/16th March 1918.

2. All Details of Reliefs will be arranged between O.C.Coys concerned.

3. Lists of Stores handed over will be forwarded to this Office.

4. Completion of relief will be wired to this Office using the word "TIN".

5. "A" and "C" Companies to acknowledge.

                                            Capt. & Adjt.
                                    49th Battn. Machine Gun Corps.

13.3.18.

Copies to:-

    No.1. "A" Coy.
       2. "C" Coy.
       3. "B" Coy.
       4. "D" Coy.
       5. 146th Inf. Brigade.   ⎫
       6. 147th Inf. Brigade.   ⎬ For information.
       7. 148th Inf. Brigade.   ⎪
       8. 49th Division   "G".   ⎪
       9. C.M.G.O. XXII Corps.   ⎭
       10 War Diary.
       11. ⎫
       12. ⎭   Retained.

Issued at _Bofem_

SECRET.

OPERATION ORDER NO 13.
49th Battalion Machine Gun Corps.

14.3.18.

1. The Machine Guns at R2. R3. R4. R5. will fire in support of a raid of the 37th Division on the night 14/15th instant.

2. Target J22 b 10 90 to J22 b 10 10 as on attached tracing.

3. Rate of fire 75 rounds per gun per minute.

4. Guns will open fire at 9-20 p.m. and cease at 9-40 p.m. The actual times will be taken from the Artillery Fire.

5. ACKNOWLEDGE.

                                         Lt.- Colonel.
14-3-18   Commanding 49th Battn. Machine Gun Corps.

\# No tracing.

Issued at........

Copies to:@ 2.

    O.C. Right Group.
    37th Battn. Machine Gun Corps   For
    "G" 49th Division.   information.
    War Diary.

SECRET

OPERATION ORDER NO 14.
49th Battalion Machine Gun Corps.

1. No.8 Corps Post in the Line will be occupied on the same scale as the posts already occupied in the Corps Line.

2. O.C."C" Company. will arrange to occupy the above post on the night 15/16th March 1918 in addition to those now occupied

3. Completion will be reported to this Office using the Code word "COPPER".

4. "C" Company to acknowledge.

                                                    Capt. & Adjt.
                                    49th Battn Machine Gun Corps.

Issued at.......

14.3.18.

Copy No....10.

Copies To:-
1. "C" Company.
2. "A" Company.
3. "B" Company.
4. "D" Company.
5. 146th Infantry Brigade.
6. 147th Infantry Brigade.
7. 148th Infantry Brigade.
8. 49th Division "G".
9. C.M.G.O. XX11 Corps.
10 War Diary.
11. "
12. Retained.

War Diary.
*****

SECRET
OPERATION ORDER
40th Battalion Machine Gun Corps.

18.3.18.

1. "C" Company will relieve "B" Company in the left sub-sector on the night 21/22nd March 1918.
"B" Company will take over the posts in the Corps Line now occupied by "C" Company.

2. Details of relief will be arranged between Companies concerned.

3. Handing over lists of Trench stores will be forwarded to this office.

4. Requirements for train arrangements will reach this office not later than 4-0 p.m. 19th instant.

5. Completion of relief will be wired to this office using Code Word "BRASS".

6. "B" and "C" Companies will acknowledge.

B.H. Basham   Lt.- Colonel.
Commanding 40th Battalion Machine Gun Corps.

18-3-18

Issued at ....

Copy No. 11

Copies to :-

1. O.C. "B" Company.
2. O.C. "C" Company.
3. O.C. "A" Company.
4. O.C. "D" Company.
5. XXII C.M.G.O.
6. 40th Division "Q".   } For
7. 146th Infantry Brigade. } information.
8. 147th Infantry Brigade. }
9. 148th Infantry Brigade. }
10. 23rd M.G.Battalion.
11. War Diary.
12. War Diary.
13. Retained.

SECRET   OPERATION ORDER   NO 16
49th Battalion Machine Gun Corps.

Reference Machine Gun   18.3.18.
Defence Scheme Map.

1. No 5 Machine Gun will move to a position at J 6c 00 40.

2. The emplacement will be made for an angle of fire of 50°. Primary line of fire will be grid bearing of 58°.

3. The position and line of fire have been pointed out to the Right Group M.G. Commander.

4. The position will be altered by 12-0 midnight 18/19th instant.

5. ACKNOWLEDGE.

B.H.Basham.
Lt.- Colonel,
Commanding 49th Battalion Machine Gun Corps

18-3-18

Issued at 5-0.p.m.

Copy No. 9

Copies to:-

    1. "A" Company.
    2. "B" Company.
    3. "C" Company.
    4. "D" Company.
    5. 146th Infantry Brigade.   }
    6. 147th Infantry Brigade.   } For
    7. 148th Infantry Brigade.   } information.
    8. 49th Division "G".
    9. War Diary.
   10. War Diary.
   11. Retained.

SECRET

Reference Operation Order No 10 in para 2.
For "grid bearing 36° " ʳᵉᵃᵈ
grid bearing of 147½°".

[signature]
Lt.- Colonel
Comdg. 40th Bn. Machine Gun Corps.

O.C. "A" Company.
O.C. "B" Company.
O.C. "C" Company.
O.C. "D" Company.
War Diary.

13.1.18.

Reference Map:-   OPERATION ORDER NO 17.   Copy No. 9.
ZONNEBEKE
1/10,000
                                                                 19.3.18.
BECELAERE
1/10,000

1. The following programme has been arranged for the 20th instant to inflict loss on the enemy.
Machine Guns re-inforced with guns from the Corps Line will fire on the following objectives:

Gun	Target.
R.1. re-inforced with gun in Corps Line Post No. 4.	J. 17c.10.75.
R 2. R 3. R 4. R 5. guns from Corps Post No. 5 to near R 10. & R 11. Positions.	J. 18c.2.6. to J 18a. 6.0.
R 6. R 7. R 8. R 9. R 10. R 11.	J.18a.8.9. and area within 150 yds.
R 16. R 17.	J. 6d.35.05. to J.6d.90.35.
Nos. 7 & 9 will move to about J.4b. 9.4.	K. 7a. 5.1.
Guns in Corps Line post No. 6 move to about J.10a. 37.50.	J. 12c.70.60.
R 15. re-inforced by gun in Corps Post No 5a.	J. 12d. 05. 65 to J.12d.55.00.
R 14. re-inforced by R 13.	J.6d..00.90. to J. 6b. 35 10.

2. Rate of fire 100 rounds per gun per minute.

3. Time of fire ZERO to ZERO + 15 MINUTES.
Time to be taken from the opening of the artillery.

4. Guns in temporary positions will move back to their permanent positions on completion of firing.
The additional personnel will return to their Company Headquarters.

5. Guns to be in position ready to fire at 5-0 p.m. on the 20th inst. This will be reported to Battalion Headquarters by the code word "TULIP".

6. ZERO hour will be at 7-0 p.m.

7. A.B.C.& D Companies to acknowledge.

Issued at 10.30 P.M.

Lt.- Colonel.
Commanding 49th Battn. Machine Gun Corps.

19-3-18

-2-

Copies To:-
1. "D" Company.
2. "A" Company.
3. "B" Company.
4. "C" Company.
5. 49th Division-"G".)
6. 146th Infantry Brigade)
7. 147th Infantry Brigade.) For
8. 148th Infantry Brigade.) information.
9. War Diary)
10. War Diary/
11. Retained

SECRET

OPERATION ORDER NO 18.   Copy No... 7

22.3.18.

1. Enemy posts will be raided opposite the 148th Infantry Brigade front at a time and date to be notified later.

2. Co-operation will be given by Machine Guns as under:-

   Left Group

   Guns Nos. R 16. R 17. R 18. R 19. to fire on targets as shewn on attached tracing, from emplacements to be made about R 16 position.

   Right Group

   Guns Nos. R 10. R 11. R 13. and R 15. to fire from their existing emplacements on to targets as shewn on attached map.

   Guns R 2. R 3. R 4. and R 5. to fire on their S.O.S. lines.

   Guns R 6. R 7. R 8. and R 9. to fire on the targets as shewn on attached map.

3. Machine Guns of the 37th Division will also co-operate by firing on to line running from J. 17a. 80.75. to J. 17b. 90.72.

4. All preparations will be completed by the evening of the 23rd.

5. Places to be raided, date and time of raid, and rate of fire will be notified later.

6. Acknowledge.

Issued at... 8.0 A B.H. Badham Lt.- Colonel.
                  Commanding Battn. Machine Gun Corps.

Copies to:-

   1. O.C. Left Group.
   2. O.C. Right Group.
   3. O.C. "D" Company.   )
   4. 148th. Infantry Brigade.)
   5. 37th Machine Gun Battn.)   For information.
   6. "G" 49th Division.   )
   7. War Diary. ✓
   8. War Diary.
   9. Retained.

"D" Company. 49th Battn. M.G.C.
Operation Order No. 25.

SECRET. Copy No. 5.
Ref. Map. Sheet 28. 1/40.000.   22nd March 1918.

1. (a). Nos. 2. and 3. Sections will relieve Nos. 1. and 4. Sections in positions R2. R3. R4. R5. R6. R7. R8. & R9 on the morning of the 23rd inst.
   (b) Nos. 2 & 3. Sects will leave Hdqrs. at 4.0. a.m.

2. Tripods and belt boxes will be handed over. Each ingoing team will carry in two filled belt boxes, & each outgoing team will carry out 2 filled belt boxes.

3. All trench stores, maps, and gun charts will be handed over.

4. Receipts for (2) and (3) will be sent to Company Headquarters immediately after relief.

5. Relieving Sections will proceed via OVERSEAS AVENUE and RESERVE LINE.

6. Relief complete will be wired to Coy. Hdqrs. Code word "SCYLLA".

7. Nos. 2. and 3. Sections to acknowledge.

Issued at. 9.0. a.m.

for Commanding "D". Coy. 49th Bn. M.G.C.   W. Kinder Capt.

Copy No. 1 to No 2. Section
  "   "   2 " " 3   "
  "   "   3 " " 1   "
  "   "   4 " " 4   "
  "   "   5 " 49th Bn. M.G.C. For information.
Copies. 6 & 7. Spare.

SECRET   OPERATION ORDER NO 19   Copy No 6

1. The following re-distribution of the line will be carried out on the night 25/26th March.

2. "C" Company will hand over the following positions to the 33rd Battalion Machine Gun Corps — 13. 14. 15. R 20 R 21.
After relief these guns and teams will relieve "A" Company in positions 7. 8. 9. R 14. R 15.

3. O.C. "C" Company will meet an Officer of the 33rd Battalion Machine Gun Corps at DEVILS CROSSING (D.27a.0.4.) at 7-0 a.m. 25th instant, and arrange details of relief. The relief will commence at 7-0 p.m. 25th instant.

4. After relief by "C" Company, "A" Company will take over the following five positions from the 37th Battalion Machine Gun Corps. — J. 15b. 28.25. — 2 guns. J. 15b. 55.65.   J. 10c.55.45.   J. 9d. 90.90.

4. O.C. "A" Company will meet an Officer of the 37th Battalion Machine Gun Corps at GLENCORSE DUGOUTS in J. 14b.20.60. at 7-0 a.m. 25th instant to arrange all details of relief.

6. Completion of relief will be reported to this office by the code word "SLIP".

7. ACKNOWLEDGE.

24.3.18   B.H.Basham   Lt.- Colonel.
                                     Commanding Battn. Machine Gun Corps.

Issued at 5-30 p.m.

Copies to:—
    1. O.C."A" Company.
    2. O.C."C" Company.
    3. O.C."B" Company.
    4. O.C."D" Company.
    5. 146th Inf. Brigade.   For information.
    6. 147th Inf. Brigade.
    7. 148th Inf. Brigade.
    8. "G" 49th Division.
    9. 37th Battn. M.G.C.
    10. 33rd Battn. M.G.C.   P.T.O.

Copies To:-

11. War Diary
12. War Diary.   } For information.
13. Retained.

SECRET.

War Diary

143th Brigade G. 148/13/ 2.
49th Battalion M.G.C. - M36.G 2

Reference Operation Order No 18.

1. ZERO DAY. — Twenty - Fifth instant.
2. ZERO HOUR. — Nine p.m.
3. Please acknowledge.

[signature]
Lt.- Colonel.
Comdg. 49th Battalion Machine Gun Corps.

25.3.18.

Copies to all recipients of O.O. 18.

SECRET   OPERATION ORDER NO 20.   COPY. No. 9

1. "B" Company will relieve "A" Company in the RIGHT Sub-sector on the night of 27/28th instant.

2. "A" Company will take over the posts now occupied by "B" Company. in the Corps Line.

3. Details of relief will be arranged between O.C. Companies concerned.

4. Train requirements will be wired to this office at once.

5. Handing over lists will be forwarded to this office.

6. Completion of relief will be wired to this office using code word "IRON".

7. "A". "B". "C" and "D" Companies. to acknowledge.

                                                  Lt.- Colonel.
                         Commanding - Battn. Machine Gun Corps.

25.3.18.

Issued at 5.0 pm

Copies to:-

1. "A" Company.
2. "B" Company.
3. "C" Company.
4. "D" Company.
5. 146th Infantry Brigade.
6. 147th Infantry Brigade.   For
7. 148th Infantry Brigade.   information.
8. "G" 49th Division.
9. War Diary.
10. War Diary.
11. Retained.

SECRET. 49th M.G. Batt. O.O. No. 21.

1. No 15 guns will be relieved by the guns of the 33rd Division tonight.

2. This will take place about dusk.

3. All details to be arranged between O.C. C Coy & O.C. Coy of 33rd Div. whose Headquarters are at DEVILS CROSSING D27.a.0.4.

4. Completion of relief will be wired to H.Q. using code word IRON.

5. Tripods will be taken out by you.

6. Acknowledge by bearer.

Issued at 2.50 p.m.
27-3-18

O.C. C Coy.

W/M Spindler Capt. for M.O.
Cmdg. 49th Bn. M.G. Corps

Capt. W.
Wm Irving

OPERATION ORDER NO 22.A

Copy No... 3

O.C. "A" Company.

Guns No1. R2. and R 15 will be with-drawn without relief tonight and sent to J. 14 b. 15.30. (Corps Post No 1.) They will be re-inforced by one gun of "C" Company which is placed under your orders.
S.O.S. Line as per attached tracing.

Guns to be in position by 9-0 a.m. 28.3.18.

O.C. "C" Company.

Your four guns at present in reserve will go to I. 36b.35.20. (KLEIN ZILLEBEKE).
S.O.S.Lines as per attached tracing. Guns to be in position by 9-0 a.m. 28.3.18.

Your gun No 15 being relieved by 33rd Division will proceed on relief to Corps Post No 1. J. 14b.15.30. and come under the orders of O.C. "A" Company.
Gun to be in position by at 9-0 a.m. 28.3.18.

Lt.- Colonel.
- Battn. Machine Gun Corps.

27.3.18.

Issued at.. 5-0.p.m.

Copies to :
1. "A" Company.
2. "C" Company.
3. War Diary.
4. War Diary.   For information.

SECRET

OPERATION ORDER NO 22.

Copy No. 7

The 6th Battalion Machine Gun Corps will relieve the following guns of "G" Company on the night 30/31st March at Nos. 10. 11. 12. 13. 14. R17. R18. R19. R20. R21. and the following gun of "A" Company. R14.
Time will be notified later.
After this releif "C" Company will relieve "A" Company at the following positions:-

Numbers 5. 6. 7. 8. 9. R1. R3. R12. R13.

"A" Company gun No 3. at JERK HOUSE will change positions with "C" Company gun in Corps Post No 1.

After relief "A" Company will leave 1 gun in Corps Post No 4. 2. guns in Corps Post No.5. and 2 guns in Post 5a.
These guns will be manned by 2 men only.
The remaining guns and personnel will return to the Company Lines at CAFE BEIGE.
Arrangements will be made by O.C.Companies concerned.

The attached map shows the numbering of gun positions for the purposes of xxx this relief.

Acknowledge.

29.3.18.

B H Barham Lt.- Colonel,
Commanding - Battn. Machine Gun Corps.

Issued at................

Copies to:-

       1."A" Company.
       2."B" Company.   #
       3."C" Company.
       4."D" Company.   #
       5. 6th Battan. Machine Gun Corps. #
       6. "G" 49th Division.
       7. War Diary. ✓
       8. War Diary.   #
       9 Retained.

No map.

OPERATION ORDER NO 23.   Copy. No. 7.

Reference Operation Order No 22, for night 30/31st March,
read night 31st March/ 1st April.

                                            Lt.- Colonel.
                                Commanding 49th Battn. Machine Gun Corps.

Issued at.. 5 pm

29.3.18.

Copies to:-

       1. "A" Company.
       2. "B" Company.
       3. "C" Company.
       4. "D" Company.
       5. 6th Battn. Machine Gun Corps.
       6. "G" 49th Division.
       7. War Diary.
       8. War Diary.
       9. Retained.

49th Divisional Troops

49th BATTALION

MACHINE GUN COMPANY *Corps*

APRIL 1918.

Battalion O.Os attached.

Army Form C. 2118.

WAR DIARY
or
INTELLIGENCE SUMMARY.

(Erase heading not required.)

Place	Date	Hour	Summary of Events and Information	Remarks and references to Appendices
	APRIL 1		Nothing of interest to report. Casualties Nil. Number of rounds fired in harassing fire 12,000	
	2		The personnel of the four companies move to BRISTOL CAMP at H.35.d.3.0. Transport of A.B. and C. Coys move to MIDDLESEX CAMP at H.32.d.3.1. Transport of D Coy remain at K'MOUDA CAMP. Two Companies 6th M.G. Battalion move into MATAWA CAMP. H.Q. of Battalion remain at YPRES. All moves done in accordance with O.O. 24. Casualties 1 killed and 1 wounded. 12,500 rounds fired in harassing fire	O.O. 24
	3		H.Q. of the Battalion move to BRISTOL CAMP, 6th Bn. M.G. Corps taking over the Headquarters at POST OFFICE, YPRES, the area N of the POLYGONBEEK comes under the orders of the G.O.C. 69th Division. H.Q. 49th DIVISION move	

WAR DIARY
or
INTELLIGENCE SUMMARY.

(Erase heading not required.)

Army Form C. 2118.

Instructions regarding War Diaries and Intelligence Summaries are contained in F. S. Regs., Part II. and the Staff Manual respectively. Title pages will be prepared in manuscript.

Place	Date	Hour	Summary of Events and Information	Remarks and references to Appendices
	APRIL 3 (con)		At CHATEAU SEGARD. 2ND LIEUT W.P.BOADEN and 2ND LIEUT A.H.WINTLE joined the Battalion as reinforcements and are posted to B Coy. Casualties Nil. Number of rounds fired in harrassing fire 11,000	
	4		The 6th Battalion M.G. Corps relieve all guns of the 49TH Bn. M.G. Corps North of the POLYGONBEEK. All interCompany reliefs carried out in accordance with O.O. No.25. "C" Company came out to rest. Casualties NIL. Number of rounds fired in harrassing fire 7000 rounds.	6.0.25
	5		One gun A Company taken over A.A. defence north from X th Corps Heavy Arte. Gun at J14.a.6.0. in accordance with 6.0.26. Quiet day for the whole front. Casualties 1 O.R. Wounded.	6.0.26

Army Form C. 2118.

WAR DIARY
or
INTELLIGENCE SUMMARY.
(Erase heading not required.)

Instructions regarding War Diaries and Intelligence Summaries are contained in F. S. Regs., Part II. and the Staff Manual respectively. Title pages will be prepared in manuscript.

Place	Date	Hour	Summary of Events and Information	Remarks and references to Appendices
	APRIL			
	6		Two guns were placed in Corps Post No 3 and two in position at J.19.c.6.6. 6,500 rounds fired in harassing fire. Casualties NIL.	0.0.27
	7		Some heavy shelling during the day about CLAPHAM JUNCTION. 4,500 rounds fired in harassing fire. Casualties NIL.	
	8		Information received that the 21st Bn M.G.Corps are to relieve all guns South of the MENIN ROAD at an early date. The guns of D Company 9,10,11,12 change positions with the guns of B Coy at R.9, R.10, No.5 and No.6 positions in accordance with O.O No.28. 7000 rounds were fired in harassing fire during the night. Casualties NIL.	0.0.28
	9		The 6th Battalion MG Corps relieve the following guns. Two at Corps Pot 3. One at JERK HOUSE J.15.b.60.70. 2 guns at CARLISLE FARM	

WAR DIARY
or
INTELLIGENCE SUMMARY.
(Erase heading not required.)

Army Form C. 2118.

Place	Date	Hour	Summary of Events and Information	Remarks and references to Appendices
	APRIL 9		at J.15.b. 25.30. The remaining 18 guns of "A" and "B" Coys. are relieved by 21st Battn. M.G. Corps. Personnel of all guns relieved proceed to BRISTOL CAMP. "C" Coy. hurried off to embus at "ANZAC CAMP" at midnight, for an unknown destination. Transport to go to "LA CRECHE". "C" Coy comes under direct orders of 147th Inf. Bde. Casualties :- 1 O.R. wounded.	O.O.29.
	10.4.18.		"A" Coy proceed by Light Railway at 10.0 a.m. to GODWAERSVELDE Area to join 146th Inf. Bde. Group. "B" Coy two to DRANOUTRE to join the 148th Inf. Bde. group & come under orders of 148th Inf. Bde. Hdqrs. of the Battn. move to WESTOUTRE. "D" Coy. are relieved by a Coy. of the 21st M.G. Battn. & proceed to CHIPPEWA CAMP by train after relief. "A" Coy. recalled from GODWAERSVELDE Area & sent to CHIPPEWA CAMP. "A" Coy. called out at midnight & ordered to proceed to PARRAT Fm. near WYTCHAETE at midnight & come under Orders of O.C. 1/7th W. Yorks. Regt. Report of "C" Coys operations. "C" Coy embused at ANZAC CAMP & debused 3 kilos S. of NEUVE EGLISE at 7. a.m. They were then met by the Transport	(O.O.30.) O.O.31. O.O.32.

Army Form C. 2118.

WAR DIARY
or
INTELLIGENCE SUMMARY.
(Erase heading not required.)

Instructions regarding War Diaries and Intelligence Summaries are contained in F. S. Regs., Part II. and the Staff Manual respectively. Title pages will be prepared in manuscript.

Place	Date	Hour	Summary of Events and Information	Remarks and references to Appendices
	10.4.18	about 9.0 a.m.	The whole Coy then moved to within about a kilo of NIEPPE. Eight guns went into the NIEPPE LINE. Situation very obscure. "D" Coy. had 1 O.R. killed and 11. O.Rs. gassed.	
	11.4.18		"A" Coy. sent 4 guns to PLATEAU Fm. (N.18.b. 50.60.) and 2 in O.2.d. 30.55. and O.2.d 60.60. The remaining guns remained in reserve at Coy. H.Q. at N.11.d. 8 guns to the Line; 4 under 2/Lt. Coates to L'alouette; 4 under 2/Lt. Watts & 2/Lt. Boaden, forward of NEUVE EGLISE. Lt. H.S. Boocer left to command "C" Coy. "C" Coy. found that the Infantry in front of them had commenced to withdraw; & after a heavy shelling & M.G. bombardment it became evident that they had no Infantry in front of them. During the morning the enemy was seen putting an Outpost line about 600 x from our line. About 7.15. a.m. the Infantry on the right were seen to retire, & the enemy were known to have crossed to BAILLEUL - ARMENTIERES railway from the South. 2/Lt. Marshall was sent with 2 guns to protect this flank just South of the Mill in B.8.C. H about 8.0. a.m.	

WAR DIARY
or
INTELLIGENCE SUMMARY.

(Erase heading not required.)

Army Form C. 2118.

Instructions regarding War Diaries and Intelligence Summaries are contained in F. S. Regs., Part II. and the Staff Manual respectively. Title pages will be prepared in manuscript.

Place	Date	Hour	Summary of Events and Information	Remarks and references to Appendices
	11.4.18		Lt. Marshall with his 2 guns advanced by short rushes under heavy fire & drove the enemy over the railway, where they dug in. It was during this advance that Capt. T. S. Husband, commanding "C" Coy was mortally wounded. At 7.30 p.m. the Brigade began to withdraw. The guns withdrew with the Infantry without much trouble except that 2/Lt. Jones was for a short time cut off with his section & had to fight his way out. The Coy. then assembled at a point one mile S.E. of Nr. BAILLEUL – ARMENTIERES. ROAD. "D" Coy. "D" Coy. were ordered to take up the defence of KEMMEL HILL together with the 19th Bn. Lancs. Fusiliers & one Coy. of R.E's. The whole defence to come under the orders of Lt. Col. BOUSFIELD C.M.G. D.S.O. After reconnaissance it was decided to place these sections on the Eastern & Southern slopes of the hill & to keep one section in reserve. The H.qrs. were established in the R.F.C. range at N.19. c. 9.0. Lt BOXER was taken from "B" Coy & placed in command of "C" Coy. Casualties :- T.S. Husband died of wounds; 2/Lt H.P. Gardner wounded, & 4 O.R. wounded.	

WAR DIARY
or
INTELLIGENCE SUMMARY.
(Erase heading not required.)

Army Form C. 2118.

Place	Date	Hour	Summary of Events and Information	Remarks and references to Appendices
	12.4.18		"A" Coy. Two guns were put into position at N.18.c.30.85. Two at O.1.d.20.10. 8 4 guns in crater at SPANBROEKMOLEN N.30.c.60.80. Four guns remained in reserve at LINCOLN CAMP. 9.0 p.m. Enemy attack commenced. 9.30 p.m. Withdrawal commenced. All 8 guns in action. During night 2 guns knocked out on left. Two made one stand. These then knocked. All right hand section missing. Both officers killed. H.Q. moved with Bde. to T.1.d.7.9. All guns stood to on line of Railway (T.1.2.3.) "C" Coy. The Coy remained in billets at S.27. central, when a very heavy Area shoot was put up by the Enemy, the ammunition dumps in the vicinity being set on fire. At this time the 6th & 7th W.R.Regts. advanced astride the Road running S.W. from J.17. central. Two guns were sent forward with the 6 & W.R.Regts. 2 guns with the 7th W.R.Regt. At about 5.30 p.m. it was reported that enemy cavalry patrols were in the S.W. part of BAILLEUL. Three guns were immediately put in position, commanding the BAILLEUL - ARMENTIERES	

Army Form C. 2118.

WAR DIARY
or
INTELLIGENCE SUMMARY.

(Erase heading not required.)

Instructions regarding War Diaries and Intelligence Summaries are contained in F. S. Regs., Part II. and the Staff Manual respectively. Title pages will be prepared in manuscript.

Place	Date	Hour	Summary of Events and Information	Remarks and references to Appendices
	12.4.18.		Road about S.27.a. central. Two guns were detailed to fire the Road about S.27.a. central. Two guns were detailed to fire the Gap known to exist to the S.W. of BAILLEUL on the right of the Bde. Where right flank rested on the railway at about S.25.b. central. The O.C. Coy went to a farm at S.25.b.8.8. & was able to observe the enemy occupying the Signal box in the railway about 800x S.W. of this point. A gun was sent forward to this point with 2. Corp. of the 4th W.R. Regt. & cleared the Signal box. "D" Coy. Final dispositions arranged on the KEMMEL DEFENCES. Casualties 14/P. W.J. Watts killed. Lt. J. WARD & Lt. J.L. OLIVER wounded. 8. O.R. killed. 11. O.R. wounded & 9. O.R. missing.	
	13.4.18.		"A" Coy. 16 guns in line. 4 guns (N.29.c.50.50.) 2 guns VANDENBERGE FARM. (N.18.c.15.80.) 2 guns VANDAMME FARM (N.18.c.35.70.) 2 guns N.18.b.50.60. 2 guns SOMER FARM (O.14.c.90.25) 4 guns SPANBROEKMOLEN (N.30.c.6.8.). Heavy shelling of guns at (N.30.c.6.8.) Section H.Q. & one gun blown up. "B" Coy. No. 3. Sect. under 2/Lt. HAMES went up & replaced No. 1. relieving	

Army Form C. 2118.

WAR DIARY
or
INTELLIGENCE SUMMARY.
(Erase heading not required.)

Place	Date	Hour	Summary of Events and Information	Remarks and references to Appendices
	13.4.18.		2/Lt. COATES in the firing line. No 1. Section under Lt. BURNIE & 2/Lt. WINTLE took positions in reserve in part of railway. Lt. ELLIS. M.C. joined for duty as 2nd in Command vice Lt. BOXTER. "C" Coy. Situation of guns. 4 guns on left of BAILLEUL - HAZEBROUCK Railway. 2 guns on right of railway about 500* in advance of the Station, and 1 gun at Cross Roads 300* outside BAILLEUL on the BAILLEUL - METEREN RD. Situation quiet until 3 p.m. when enemy started shelling with guns of large calibre. At 5 p.m. the O.C. Coy. received first intimation of an attack by the enemy by a demand from Lt Wood for more belt boxes. 3 guns were sent forward to support our Infantry. O.C. Coy. took remaining gun & placed himself at disposal of O.C. 6th Bn. W.R. Regt. The Infantry withdrew & all guns kept their ground & covered the withdrawal. 2/Lt. CALDWELL was wounded in the first 5 minutes after the attack. The disposition of the guns at 12. M.N. was :- 9 guns in line ; 4 in reserve; 2 guns were without tripods or teams. Casualties :— 2/Lt. BORDEN killed; 2/Lt. W.G. CALDWELL wounded.	

Army Form C. 2118.

WAR DIARY
or
INTELLIGENCE SUMMARY.
(Erase heading not required.)

Instructions regarding War Diaries and Intelligence Summaries are contained in F. S. Regs., Part II. and the Staff Manual respectively. Title pages will be prepared in manuscript.

Place	Date	Hour	Summary of Events and Information	Remarks and references to Appendices
	13.4.18.		3. O.R. killed: 12. O.R. wounded, & 10. O.R. missing.	
	14.4.18.		"A" Coy. Two guns from O.2.d.30.55. and O.2.d.00.60. moved to DOME HOUSE. One gun stood up. Otherwise no change.	
			"B" Coy. Position unchanged during day. 2 guns went to positions on DRANOUTRE - NEUVE EGLISE Rd. in T.7.d.	
			"C" Coy. At midnight 13/14 Adv. Coy. H.Q. was in a house on the BAILLEUL - ARMENTIERES RD. about 1/4 mile out of BAILLEUL. At 1.30 p.m. orders for withdrawal were received & Adv. H.Q. was moved to X 11.c.7.0. & the guns withdrew with the Infantry. Disposition was then as under: - One gun at X Rds. on METEREN - BAILLEUL RD. 2 guns on BAILLEUL - STEAM MILL Dys about S.19.a.3.3. One gun at S.19.a.0.1. One gun at S.25.b.3.3. 2 guns at S.25.b.9.7. 2 guns on Ry. line East of Station. The enemy attacked about 5 p.m. & pressed on to STEAM MILL & after a very heavy bombardment succeeded in capturing it. The team then fired practically all their ammunition, & when the Infantry withdrew	

WAR DIARY
or
INTELLIGENCE SUMMARY.
(Erase heading not required.)

Army Form C. 2118.

Place	Date	Hour	Summary of Events and Information	Remarks and references to Appendices
	14.4.18		endeavoured to get away, the enemy being only about 50 yds away from them. Only 2 men survived of the gun and tripod were lost. The guns in the forward position were forced to withdraw & it was during this withdrawal that 2/Lt. WOOD shewed great initiation by covering the left flank. 2/Lt. JONES with 2 guns at S.25.b.9.8. engaged two different enemy Field Artillery batteries & is believed to have silenced them at a range of 1500 yds. Our Casualties were as follows:- 2/Lt. W.A. HAWES wounded. 4 O.R. killed. 18 O.R. wounded. 6 O.R. missing.	
	15.4.18		"A" Coy dispositions as noted:- 4 guns about IRISH HOUSE. 2 guns in VANDAMME FM. 2 guns VANDENBERGHE FM; Otherwise no change in disposition. A party of 50 of the enemy were fired on in PHEASANT WOOD at about 600 yds. range & most of the party were put out. On the night of 15th. The Infantry were withdrawn from the line in front of SPANBROEKMOLEN to line approx STORE FM. N.29.a.80.20. 8 men running due South. The section in the line was not informed of this withdrawal, but managed to get back safely. "A" Coy. H.Q. & Transport move to CAMBRIDGE CAMP	

Army Form C. 2118.

WAR DIARY
or
INTELLIGENCE SUMMARY.
(Erase heading not required.)

Place	Date	Hour	Summary of Events and Information	Remarks and references to Appendices
near BEAVER CORNER.	15.4.18		"B" Coy. No 3. Section under 2/Lt. HAWES in the continued enemy attack was almost completely wiped out & lost 2 guns by bombing and 2/Lt. HAWES was wounded. 4 guns under Lt. BURNIE and 2 under 2/Lt. COATES went forward to positions in S.12. c.7.d. These guns withdrew with the Norfolks and Leicesters respectively to a point which was established round front of DRANOUTRE & KEMMEL HILL. H.Q. moved with Bde. to H.31. d.2.1. in afternoon. All guns withdrawn from Railway line to LINDENHOEK – DRANOUTRE RD. In the night H.Q. moved with Bde. to N.30. d.2.6. "C" Coy. Adv. H.Q. were moved back to ST. JANS CAPPEL, and the whole Coy. came out of the line and reorganised. At about 6.0.p.m. orders were received to take up positions about the front line. Nothing of importance happened during the day. "D" Coy. The Reserve Section was moved to positions in a field about N.31. c.7.9. as it appeared that the vulnerable point in the Hill Defences	

Army Form C. 2118.

WAR DIARY
or
INTELLIGENCE SUMMARY.
(Erase heading not required.)

Instructions regarding War Diaries and Intelligence Summaries are contained in F. S. Regs., Part II. and the Staff Manual respectively. Title pages will be prepared in manuscript.

Place	Date	Hour	Summary of Events and Information	Remarks and references to Appendices
	15.4.18		was the S.W. and S.E. slopes owing to the advance made by the enemy on the previous day. The shelling of the hill was much heavier during the day. Casualties :- 1. O.R. killed & 6. O.R. wounded.	
	16.4.18		"A" Coy. Two guns which had been placed about COMET FARM, 8" MGR teams were captured together with their Section Officer (2/Lt. LAMONT). During a heavy bombardment at 5.30.a.m. 2/Lt. BENTLEY & his Section Sergeant set out to visit guns in the crater, & on arriving there found the Boche in possession. The Officer and Sergt. returned to the Section H.Q. followed by the Boche, got out his servant and runners & fought their way back to our line, taking back with them one prisoner who was handed over to the H.Q. of the WELSH REGT. at PARRAIN Fm. 2/Lt. SPENCER was transferred from "A" Coy. to "C" Coy. 9th Bn. M.G.C. Coy. H.Q. at N.15.a. 00.10. Transport moved to MILLEKRUISSE. "B" Coy. Positions unchanged. We came under 71st Bde. No further developments. Fairly quiet, except in valleys, which were badly shelled by enemy Batteries. "C" Coy. Two reserve sections were sent up to hill in S.1.d. in order to bring	

Army Form C. 2118.

WAR DIARY
or
INTELLIGENCE SUMMARY.
(Erase heading not required.)

Instructions regarding War Diaries and Intelligence Summaries are contained in F. S. Regs., Part II. and the Staff Manual respectively. Title pages will be prepared in manuscript.

Place	Date	Hour	Summary of Events and Information	Remarks and references to Appendices
	16.4.18.		Harassing fire to bear on the Enemy's Range. One Section was moved out of the front line to reserve line. At 2.30.p.m. the enemy put down his usual bombardment, which, owing to the mist & poor observation, did very little damage. At 4.30.p.m. he attempted to attack. The Gun at S.2.c.2.9. which up to this time had been doing harassing fire on BAILLEUL engaged a large party of the enemy at 600. yds.range, good observation was obtained, the strike of the bullets being seen right in the middle of the party. Heavy casualties were caused. The one gun of No. 2 Sect. remaining in the front line in a position S.7.b.5.8. engaged a party of enemy at 500 yds.range, causing them to withdraw hastily, leaving dead. At 4.30.p.m. this gun engaged a party of enemy with a M.G. who advanced from the house at S.7.b.6.4.16 a hedge about 150 yds.from our front line. The enemy got his gun into action & fired, & then our gun got into action. A party went out afterwards & collected 1 light M.G. 6 unwounded prisoners, 12 wounded prisoners, including an Officer, & 25.enemy dead	

Army Form C. 2118.

WAR DIARY
or
INTELLIGENCE SUMMARY.
(Erase heading not required.)

Instructions regarding War Diaries and Intelligence Summaries are contained in F. S. Regs., Part II, and the Staff Manual respectively. Title pages will be prepared in manuscript.

Place	Date	Hour	Summary of Events and Information	Remarks and references to Appendices
	16.4.18		were counted. Prisoners were SAXONS of the 107th Regt. At about 4.p.m. a gun of No. 4. Sect. at X. 12. a. 1. 4. engaged a party of the enemy who were trying to get a Light M.G. into action. The party withdrew, leaving one man wounded & the man at the gun dead. Meeting with strenuous resistance the enemy abandoned his attempts & remained "doggo" for the remainder of the day. "D". Coy. KEMMEL HILL was subjected to an intense bombardment & the defences had assumed the character of the British Front line. Two more guns were moved to N. 31. a. 3. 9. to prevent the enemy working round to the West. Casualties 1. O.R. killed and 6. O.R. wounded. 2/Lt. LAMONT missing; 28 O.R. missing.	
	17.4.18.		"A". Coy. No change. The Boche did considerable sniping during the day. "B". Coy. 71st Bde. H.Q. moved to M. 28. d. 6. 7. Coy. H.Q. unchanged. "C". Coy. The enemy artillery was very active over the Bde. Area throughout the morning, but quieter later. One of our Machine guns in front line opposite ST. JANS - BAILLEUL Rd. fired on a party of enemy who	

WAR DIARY
or
INTELLIGENCE SUMMARY.
(Erase heading not required.)

Army Form C. 2118.

Place	Date	Hour	Summary of Events and Information	Remarks and references to Appendices
	17/4/18		good results. Harassing fire on BAILLEUL was kept up during the night. "D" Coy. Exceptional concentration of Enemy artillery on KEMMEL HILL. Followed by Infantry attacks, strength estimated at between one & two Battalions. They were driven off by rifle & M.G. fire. They succeeded in reaching DONEGAL FARM. The method of advance was as follows:- M.G. teams pushed forward along dead ground, hedges, and ditches, followed by snipers & parties by Sections of Infantry. Many good targets were presented to our M.G. & Telescopic observation shewed that heavy casualties were inflicted, probably between two and three hundred. The consternation caused could be distinctly seen. One party, with M.G. tried to come into action & direct fire was turned on to it at 1200 yds. One of the crew was killed and 3 wounded. The Casualties in the Coy. were pretty heavy, & one gun was completely smashed. Bn. H.Q. moved from WESTOUTRE to ABEELE & Div. H.Q. moved to L.25.d.9.1. "D" Coy's transport moved from FERMOY FARM to CHIPPEWA CAMP, having been gassed at 7 a.m. & shelled out at 10 a.m. Casualties:- 2 O.R. killed; 17 O.R. wounded. 2 O.R. missing.	

WAR DIARY
or
INTELLIGENCE SUMMARY.
(Erase heading not required.)

Army Form C. 2118.

Place	Date	Hour	Summary of Events and Information	Remarks and references to Appendices
	18.4.18.		"A" Coy. 2/Lt. SPENCER rejoined Coy. Fairly quiet day. Nothing further to report.	
			"B" Coy. French troops arrived in the line & took over from most of the Infantry there. Orders were issued that "B" Coy would be relieved by "D" Coy owing to the French taking over KEMMEL HILL. This order was subsequently cancelled.	
			"D" Coy. Several good targets were obtained, especially in the neighbourhood of DONEGAL FARM. When this was shelled by our Artillery the enemy left the farm & provided excellent opportunities of engaging them with M.G. fire. Only 13 guns are intact. In the evening the French took over command of the defences. The Coy. remained on the Hill in their present positions at the request of the French & came under their orders. Casualties 1 O.R. killed; 6 O.R. wounded.	
	19.4.18.		"A" Coy. No change. Heavy indirect fire was kept up on WYTSCHAETE WOOD.	
			"B" Coy. The French relieved "B" Coy. in accordance with "B" Coy's O.O. H.M.2. H.M.2. & moved to Camp at G.18. arriving there about 3.0.a.m. 24.4.18.	

WAR DIARY
or
INTELLIGENCE SUMMARY.
(Erase heading not required.)

Army Form C. 2118.

Place	Date	Hour	Summary of Events and Information	Remarks and references to Appendices
	19.4.18.		"D" Coy. Heavy shelling of KEMMEL HILL continued. Nothing further to report. Casualties 2.O.R. killed & 1.O.R. wounded.	O.O. 33 Cancelled
	20.4.18.		"A" Coy. Two guns No. 3 Sect. at DOME HOUSE relieved by 2 guns of 9th Bn. M.G.C. The Tank Corps placed 10 Lewis guns in support of No. 2 Sect. at VANDENBERGHE FARM and VANDAMME FARM.	
			"B" Coy. moved to Camp at BRANDHOEK CROSS ROADS.	
			"C" Coy. are relieved by the French & come out to their transport lines near MONT DES CATS. Casualties NIL.	
	21.4.18.		"A" Coy. No. 2 Sect. relieved by 9th Bn. M.G.C.	
			"B" Coy. at BRANDHOEK CAMP.	
			"C" Coy. Move from their transport lines near MONT DES CATS to BIRD CAGE CAMP near POPERINGHE STATION.	
			"D" Coy. KEMMEL HILL. Casualties 1 O.R. wounded.	
	22.4.18.		"A" Coy. All "A" Coy. relieved & concentrated at WARBURG CAMP at H. 32. d. 0. 3.	
			"B" Coy. at Brandhoek.	

WAR DIARY
or
INTELLIGENCE SUMMARY.
(Erase heading not required.)

Army Form C. 2118.

Place	Date	Hour	Summary of Events and Information	Remarks and references to Appendices
	22.4.18.		"C" Coy. at BIRD CAGE CAMP near POPERINGHE.	
			"D" Coy. at KENNEL HILL under orders of the French.	
			Casualties:- 1. O.R. wounded.	
	23.4.18.		Battn. H.Q. move from ABEELE to ERIE CAMP & are joined here by the whole of "B" and "C" Coys.	
			"A" Coy. shell in rest at WARBOURG CAMP.	
			"D" Coy. shell at KENNEL HILL. Casualties:- 1 O.R. wounded.	
	24.4.18.		LT. HALL M.C. appointed to command "A" Coy. & to be Acting Major.	
			Dispositions same as for 23.4.18. Casualties.- NIL.	
	25.4.18.		Enemy launched strong attacks on KENNEL HILL & northwards. From information received it appears that KENNEL HILL has been surrounded & taken, which involves the whole of "D" Coy. Stragglers returning from "D" Coy. in the afternoon report that the Hill is cut off & that the last seen of "D" Coy. was that they were engaged in hard fighting. The line in the evening ran:- LOCRE – FERMOY FARM. – LA CLYTTE, along CHEAPSIDE and RIDGE WOOD. "C" Coy. was ordered	

WAR DIARY
or
INTELLIGENCE SUMMARY.
(Erase heading not required.)

Army Form C. 2118.

Place	Date	Hour	Summary of Events and Information	Remarks and references to Appendices
	25.4.18.		to join the 147th Infy. Bde. who were concentrating in OUDERDOM, and "B" Coy to stand by in readiness to move. "B" Coy. were sent up to OUDERDOM later in the day to join the 148th Infy. Bde. The Transport of "D" Coy. who were in CHIPPEWA CAMP were shelled out & joined the Bn. at ERIE CAMP. Major W.F.M. SPROULLE M.C. over command of "B" Coy. temporarily for Major H.D. HANSON at OUDERDOM. "C" Coy. went into the line with 147th Infy. Bde. in the afternoon, taking up positions about MILLEKRUISSE to N.14.a.5.5. "B" Coy. were ordered to reconnoitre & take up positions for the defence of the CHEAPSIDE RD. Sector at dawn on the 26th. In the evening the line ran as stated on G.A. 172. Casualties:- Killed 1 O.R. Wounded 6 O.R. Missing:- Major W. MILNE; Capt. M.F. KINDER; Lt. A.K. STEEL; Lt. J.B. BROWN; 2/Lt. A.H. CLARKE; 2/Lt. F.S.S. DAWKINS.	G.A. 172.
	26.4.18.		"B" Coy. went into the line & took up positions as follows:-	

Army Form C. 2118.

WAR DIARY
or
INTELLIGENCE SUMMARY.
(Erase heading not required.)

Instructions regarding War Diaries and Intelligence Summaries are contained in F. S. Regs., Part II. and the Staff Manual respectively. Title pages will be prepared in manuscript.

Place	Date	Hour	Summary of Events and Information	Remarks and references to Appendices
	26.4.18.		Two guns at N.9.b.9.c. Two guns about N.9.d.3.1. Two guns in H.8.b.9.1. Four guns near HALLEBAST CORNER. It was found hard to definitely fix the guns owing to the dense fog prevailing.	
			"C" Coy's dispositions are as follows:- N.15.a.90.40. N.9.c.70.40. N.14.b.80.70.	
			An attack by the 147th & 148th Bels. in conjunction with the French Kts in the early hours 26th was not very successful, our line remained unchanged. The enemy kept up very heavy shelling throughout the day, causing a great number of Casualties. Two O.R. from "D" Coy. rejoined the Bn. The 11th M.M.G. Battery is held as Div. reserve at OUDERDOM G.20.C. in accordance with O.O. No. 35. The 4th M.M.G. Battery takes up positions to strengthen the left flank of the Div. as per O.O. No. 36. Casualties 3. O.R. Killed 3. O.R. wounded	O.O.35 O.O.36
	27.4.18.		The Command of the 9th Divn. Front from LA CLYTTE to the VIERSTRAAT - HALLEBAST RD. passed to G.O.C. 79th Divn.	

Army Form C. 2118.

WAR DIARY
or
INTELLIGENCE SUMMARY.
(Erase heading not required.)

Instructions regarding War Diaries and Intelligence Summaries are contained in F. S. Regs., Part II. and the Staff Manual respectively. Title pages will be prepared in manuscript.

Place	Date	Hour	Summary of Events and Information	Remarks and references to Appendices
	27.4.18.		At 11 a.m. consequently all M.G. Coys. came under the orders of 49th Bn. M.G.C. The enemy was considerably quieter throughout the day, & this enabled a thorough reconnaissance of the sector to be made.	M.G. 39.
			"A" Coy sent up 4 guns to the following positions :- N.8.a.4.5. N.8.a.5.5. N.2.d.8.0. & N.8.a.80.97, with Section H.Q.	O.O.34.
			at N.2.a.8.0. in accordance with O.O.No. 37. These guns come under the tactical command of O.C. "C" Coy. The 11th & 4th M.M.G. Batteries come under the tactical command of 49th Bn. M.G.C.	O.O. 37.
			5. O.R. from "D" Coy rejoined the Bn. Coy. Casualties 1 O.R. killed. 2 O.R. wounded.	
	28.4.18.		"B" Coy's advanced H.Q. move from OUDERDOM Village to G.24.W. c. Central. Adv. Bn. H.Q. move to same place. Two subsections of "C" Coy. are sent to KLEINE VIERSTRAAT and N.3.d.7.1. & come under tactical command of O.C. "B" Coy. Two guns at	

WAR DIARY
or
INTELLIGENCE SUMMARY.
(Erase heading not required.)

Army Form C. 2118.

Place	Date	Hour	Summary of Events and Information	Remarks and references to Appendices
	28.4.18.		HALLEBAST CORNER take up positions in N.14.c. I come under orders of O.C. 4th M.M.G. Battery. A gun of "C" Bty. engaged a party of the enemy who were endeavouring to get a M.G. into action about N.14.d, & caused several casualties. The enemy artillery throughout the day was exceptionally quiet until the evening, when at about 8.15.p.m. the enemy opened a heavy bombardment on the whole front. About 15 minutes later our S.O.S. went up several times & was immediately responded to by our Artillery. A very heavy barrage was put down on the entire front, but no Infantry action developed. Casualties :- 3 O.R. killed ; 6. O.R. wounded.	
	29.4.18.		At 3.0.a.m. the enemy opened a very heavy artillery barrage on the front of the Division, & also on the 25th Div, & French on our right & 21st Div. on our left. At 5.0.a.m. our S.O.S. who went up & was immediately responded to by our Artillery. The enemy did not appear to attack our immediate front, although	

WAR DIARY
or
INTELLIGENCE SUMMARY.

(Erase heading not required.)

Army Form C. 2118.

Place	Date	Hour	Summary of Events and Information	Remarks and references to Appendices
	29.7.18.		it was ascertained later that the 148th Inf. Bde. was attacked 3 times, the Infantry repelling each assault. The shelling was very heavy until the evening, when it quietened down somewhat. Considering the intensity of the barrage our casualties were exceedingly light, consisting of O.P. killed 9. O.P. wounded. The rear Bn. H.Q. were shelled out of ERIE CAMP & moved to near ABEELE L.26.b.6.8. "A" Coy to MUD FARM G.27.a.9.3. in accordance with B.S.137. Casualties :- 6 O.R. killed. 14 O.R. wounded.	B.S.137.
	30.7.18.		Quiet day on the whole Divisional Front. "A" Coy relieve "B" Coy. on the left subsector. "B" Coy on relief proceed to MUD FARM at G.27.a.9.3. Lt. H.C.V. THOMAS appointed 2nd. in Command of "D" Coy, & to be Acting Captain whilst so employed. Major H.D. HANSON resumed Command of "B" Coy. The 148th Inf. Bde. were relieved in the left subsector by the 74th. Inf. Bde. Casualties :- 2 O.R. wounded.	

WAR DIARY
or
INTELLIGENCE SUMMARY.
(Erase heading not required.)

Army Form C. 2118.

Place	Date	Hour	Summary of Events and Information	Remarks and references to Appendices
			The following telegrams & messages were received from the Commander in Chief and the Army Commander, congratulating the Division on its work during the recent operations:-	
			From Commander in Chief:- 29.4.18. I desire to express my appreciation of the very valuable and gallant service performed by troops of 49"P. Div. since the entry of 147"'Bde. into the battle north of ARMENTIERES. The courage & determination shewn by this Division has played no small part in checking the enemy's advance, and I wish to convey to General CAMERON and to all officers & men under his command my thanks for all that they have done.	
			From Army Commander to XXII. Corps. 29.4.18. The Army Commander wishes to congratulate you & wishes you to convey his congratulations to all Divisions of your Corps engaged today on the splendid defence they have made & the results achieved by them.	
			The Corps Commander has also had a visit from the COMMANDER-in-CHIEF who desired him to express to the Divisions his high appreciation of their	

Army Form C. 2118.

WAR DIARY
or
INTELLIGENCE SUMMARY.
(Erase heading not required.)

Place	Date	Hour	Summary of Events and Information	Remarks and references to Appendices
			gallantry and the manner in which they have repulsed the German attack today.	
			Extract from IX Corps letter 19.4.18 :- The G.O.C. 34th Div. reports that the undermentioned Units have specially distinguished themselves in the recent fighting :-	
			49½ Bn. M.G. Corps.	

[signatures]

SECRET

* Battalion Machine Gun Corps.
OPERATION ORDER NO.24

Copy No. 9

1.4.18.

Reference Warning Orders issued 31.3.18. Companies will move to BRISTOL CAMP tomorrow 2.4.18.

1. O.C. "A" "B" "C" and "D" Companies (Rear) will each detail 1. N.C.O. and 9 men to report at BRISTOL CAMP at 7-30 a.m. for work under Major SPROULE.
These men will take their equipment etc, and will not return to present Camp.

2. Companies will move complete with Transport (except "D" Company, whose transport remain in present stables), from present lines as follows:-

"A" Company. 1-0 p.m.
"B" Company. 1-15 p.m.
"C" Company. 1-30 p.m.
"D" Company. 1-45 p.m. (less Transport)

3. A party of 1 N.C.O. and 4 men will be left behind in present Camp to clean the camp and huts.
O.C.Companies and Transport Officer will ensure that all Huts, Cookhouses, and outbuildings are left clean.

4. The Regimental Quarter Guard will move to the new camp at 1-30 p.m. under instructions to be issued by the Regimental Sergeant Major.

5. Battalion Quarter Masters Stores will be established at Bristol Camp by 2-0 p.m.

6. All work-shops will be established in BRISTOL CAMP by 2-0 p.m. under instructions to be issued by the Quarter Master.

7. The Canteen and Recreation Room will be moved under instructions to be issued by the Transport Officer.

8. "D" Company's Guard will mount in BRISTOL CAMP by 6-0 p.m. 1.4.18, and will patrol the camp to prevent any stores or the contents of the huts being removed.

9. Gun Limbers will be kept at the Camp ,and other Limbers at the Transport Lines.
Headquarters will move to BRISTOL CAMP on 3rd instant, and open there at 12-0 noon.

Capt. & Adjt.
- Battn. Machine Gun Corps.

Issued at... 5.30 p.m.

P.T.O.

Copies to:-
1. "A" Company.
2. "B" Company.
3. "C" Company.
4. "D" Company.
5. Q" 49th Division.
6. Transport Officer.
7. Quartermaster.
8. War Diary.
9. War Diary.
10. Filed.

SECRET.   Battalion Machine Gun Corps.   Copy No. 10
                          OPERATION ORDER NO 26

                                                            Tuesday 2.4.18.

1.   The following reliefs will take place on the 4/5th instant
     at a time to be notified later.
     "B" Company, 6th Battalion Machine Gun Corps will relieve
     the guns of "C" Company numbers 38 & 18.

2.   "A" Company, 6th Battalion Machine Gun Corps will relieve
     the guns of "D" Company, numbers R.27. R.28/ R.29 R.30.
     R.33. R34. R35. R36.
     "A" Company, 6th Battalion Machine Gun Corps will relieve
     the guns of "C" Company, numbers 31.15.16.17. R.26. R.28
     R.31. R32.

3.   On relief "D" Company's guns will relieve:
     "C" Company in positions 12. R.3. R.4. R.5. R.6.
     "A" Company at Nos 10 & 11.
     "B" Company at No 9.
     "B" Company's guns No 9 will form a pair with No 8
     and be called 8a.

4.   "A" Company will retain the Battery R.16. R.17. R.18.
     R.19 and will in addition place 2 guns in Corps P st No 3
     and Corps Post J. 14.1. Guns in Corps Post 4.5. and 5a
     will be withdrawn.

     All details of relief will be arranged between Companies
     concerned.

     On completion of this relief:
     "A" Company retain 8 in reserve and 8 guns in the line.
     "B" Company retain 16 guns in the line.
     "C" Company retain 16 guns in reserve.
     "D" Company retain 16 guns in the line.

     Acknowledge.
                                   (sd) B.H.Bedham   Lt.- Colonel.
                                   Commanding 49th Battn. Machine Gun
                                                                Corps.
     Issued at.   4-0

     Companies:-
            1. "A" Company.
            2. "B" Company.
            3. "C" Company.
            4. "D" Company.
            5. "G" 49th Division   )
            6. 146th Infantry Brigade.)
            7. 147th Infantry Brigade.)
            8. 148th Infantry Brigade.)   For information.
            9. 6th Battn. Machine Gun Corps)
           10. War Diary.
           11. War Diary.
           12. Retained.

SECRET   Battalion Machine Gun Corps.
                      OPERATION ORDER NO 26.

                                5.4.18.

1.   One gun of "A" Company will take over the A.A.Defence work
        from Xth Corps School Lewis Gun at J.14a.6.0.

2.   The gun for this purpose will be furnished by R.19.

3.   The gun will do A.A. work by day and be relayed at dusk
        on its Barrage line.

4.   Handing over lists will be forwarded to this office.

5.   Relief to be complete by 7-45 a.m. tomorrow 6th instant.

6/   Completion of relief will be wired to Battalion Headquarters
        using code word " BADGE".

7.   Acknowledge by bearer

                                              Capt. & Adjt.
                                        - Battn. Machine Gun Corps.

        Issued at 9-25 p.m.

        Copies to:-

                        1. O. ."B" Company.
                        2. ~~"C" 40th Division.~~
                        3. War Diary.   } For information.
                        4. War Diary.   }
                        5. Retained.

COPY   Copy No.

SECRET

Battalion Machine Gun Corps.
OPERATION ORDER NO 27.

5.4.18.

1. One gun of "A" Company will take over the A.A.Defence work from Xth Corps School Lewis Gun at J.14.a.6.0.

2. The gun for this purpose will be furnished by R.19.

3. The gun will do A.A. work by day and be relayed at dusk on its barrage lines.

4. Handing over lists will be forwarded to this office.

5. Relief to be complete by 7-45 a.m. tomorrow 6th instant.

6. Completion of relief will be wired to Battalion Headquarters using code word "BADGE".

(Sd). W.Bates Capt. & Adjt.
40th Battn. Machine Gun Corps.

Issued at 9-25 p.m.

Copies to:

1. O.C. "A" Company.
2. War Diary.   } For information.
3. War Diary.
4. Retained.

Copy No. 3

SECRET.   Battalion Machine Gun Corps.
                         OPERATION ORDER NO 28.
                         ==========================

                                            Monday. 8.4.18.

1.   The guns of "D" Company, 9, 10, 11, 12, will change positions
        with the guns of "B" Company at R.9. R.10. and No.5. and 6.

2.   Change to be complete by 12 midnight 8th instant.

3.   Acknowledge.

                                        H. Bradshaw
                                            Capt. & Adjt.
                                        Battn. Machine Gun Corps.

Issued at 4.30 pm

Copies to:-
            1. "B" Company.
            2. "D" Company.
            3. War Diary. ✓   ) For information.
            4. War Diary.   )
            5. Retained.

SECRET.   Battalion Machine Gun Corps.
                 OPERATION ORDER NO 29.

                                                    Copy No. 8

                                          Monday. 8.4.18.

1.   The following guns will be relieved by 6th Battalion
     Machine Gun Corps on the night of 9/10th April. 1918.

     2. Guns No.3. Corps Line Post J.9c.50.30.
     1. Gun JERK HOUSE J.15b.60.70.
     2. Guns CAMILLE FARM J.15b.25.50.

     The remaining 16 guns will be relieved by 21st Battalion
     Machine Gun Corps on the night of 9/10th April.

2.   O.C."B" Company will detail 2 Guides to be at BIER CROSS
     ROADS at 9-15 a.m. 9th instant, to conduct two Officers
     round his sector, and O.C."D" Company will also detail two
     Guides to conduct two Officers round his guns (also to be at
     BIER CROSS ROADS at 9-15 a.m.)

3.   O.C."B" and "D" Companies will each detail two Guides
     to be at BIER CROSS ROADS at 4-0 p.m. 9.4.18. to act as
     guides for the relief.

4.   All previous instructions regarding this relief are
     cancelled.

5.   Handing over lists will be forwarded to this Office.

6.   Completion of relief will be wired to this Office using
     code word "SILVER".

7.   Acknowledge. ("B" & "D" Companies by bearer).

                                          Capt. & Adjt.
                                          Battn. Machine Gun Corps.

Issued at 8.0 p.m.

Copies to:-

     1. "B" Company.
     2. "D" Company.
     3. "A" Company.
     4. "C" Company.
     5. "G" 40th Division.   )
     6. 6th Battn. Machine Gun Corps.) For
     7. 21st Battn. Machine Gun Corps) Information.
     8. War Diary.   )
     9. War Diary.   )
     10. Retained.   )

SECRET.   Battalion Machine Gun Corps.   Copy No. 3
                         OPERATION ORDER NO. 30.

                                                                Tuesday. 9.4.18.

1.   The 21st Battalion Machine Gun Corps will relieve "D" Company
     49th Battalion Machine Gun Corps in the line on the 10/11th April.

2.   Guides will meet the incoming Company at ZYLEBEKE CHURCH
     at 2-30 p.m. on 10th.

3.   All guns possible will be relieved by day.

4.   On relief "D" Company will return to BRISTOL CAMP.

5.   All details of relief will be arranged between Companies
     concerned.

     Issued at 2.30 p.m.
                                                       Lt.-Colonel.
                                            Commanding - Battalion Machine Gun C

     Copies to:

                1. "D" Company.
                2. 21st Battn. M.G.Corps.   }
                3. War Diary.   }   For
                4. War Diary.   }   information.
                5. Retained.

SECRET   Battalion Machine Gun Corps   Copy No. 10
                OPERATION ORDER NO X1.

Ref: Maps 27 & 28 1/40,000   Tuesday, 9.4.18.

1. The Battalion will leave BRISTOL CAMP on 10th instant as under:

"A" Company by route march starting at 8-30 a.m. to OOSTHAEGHELDE Area. via WESTOUTRE Cross Roads R. 16c.3.7. where they will be met by their billeting Officer and conducted to billets.

"B" Company to join 147th Brigade at WIPPEN HOEK area by route march at 8-45 a.m. Route via HAIRIBAST, RENINGHELST, Cross Roads in G.22f. V.W. Cross Roads in L.34d.1.3.

"C" Company to join 148th Brigade in WESTOUTRE Area by route march starting at 9-0 a.m. Route via HAIRIBAST, LA CLYTTE and Cross Roads H.17c central.

"D" Company to Divisional Area at HOOGRAAF. Details will be issued later.

2. Transport will join their respective Companies under Transport Officer's arrangements.

3. Each Company will send an officer to report to the Brigade Headquarters and Area Commandants and ascertain his exact billets.

He will take over billets and meet his Company on the line of march and lead them to their billets.

4. On arrival in billets Companies will notify the Brigades to whom they are attached.

5. All extra Regimental Employed men will be returned to their Companies forthwith.

6. Rations will be carried for 10th instant, after which they will be drawn under Brigade arrangements.

7. All Ordnance Stores will be drawn from Battalion Headquarters

                                                 Lt. Colonel.
                                  Commanding 49 Battn. Machine Gun
                                                        Corps

Issued at 3 pm
Copies to:-
1. "A" Company.
2. "B" Company.
3. "C" Company.
4. "D" Company.
5. Transport Officer.
6. 146th Inf. Brigade.
7. 147th Inf. Brigade.
8. 148th Inf. Brigade.
9. "G" 49th Division.
10. War Diary.
11. War Diary.
12. Retained.

                                                                                 For information.

SECRET.   Battalion Machine Gun Corps.   Copy No 9.
                           OPERATION ORDER NO 32.

Reference Map.   Tuesday 9.4.18.

        Reference Operation Order No 31:

        The Battalion will leave BRISTOL CAMP on 10th instant
        as under:-

1.   "A" Company to proceed by Light Railway from CAFE BELGE at
        10-0 a.m. where they come under the orders of G.O.C.
        146th Brigade to whom they will report their arrival
        in Camp. Detrain at RUDY SIDING.

2.   "B" Company will be attached to 147th Infantry Brigade
        in WIPPEN HOEK area by Route March starting at 8-45 a.m.
        Route via HALLEBAST, RENINGHELST, CROSS ROADS in G. 32d, CROSS
        ROADS in L. 34d. 1.3.

3.   "C" Company will be attached to 148th Brigade in
        WESTOUTRE AREA by Route March starting at 9-15 a.m. Route
        via HALLEBAST, LA CLYTTE, and CROSS ROADS H. 17o. Central.

4.   "D" Company will move to the Divisional Area at HOOGRAFT.
        Details to be issued later.

5.   "A" Company's transport will march to GODEWAERSVELDE.

6.   "B" "C" and "D" Companies Transport march with their
        respective Companies.

7.   Usual intervals will be kept on the line of march.

8.   Headquarters Staff as detailed by the Adjutant will
        march to DICKEBUSCH and will be conveyed in Lorries
        to the new area under the command of Lt. W.J.Hall.

9.   Para. 1. of Operation Order No 31. is cancelled.

10.   Para. 2. of Operation Order No 31. will be read in conjunction
        with paras. 5 & 6 of this order.

        Acknowledge.
                                                        Capt. & Adjt.
Issued at 7.30 p.m   Battn. Machine Gun Corps.
Copies to :-
            1. "A" Company.
            2. "B" Company.
            3. "C" Company.
            4. "D" Company.
            5. Transport Officer.
            6. 146th Inf. Brigade.   )
            7. 147th Inf. Brigade.   )   For
            8. 148th Inf. Brigade.   )   information.
            9. "G" 49th Division.   )
            10. War Diary.
            11. War Diary.

SECRET.   — Battalion Machine Gun Corps.   Copy No. 8
OPERATION ORDER NO 33.

Thursday 18.4.18.

1. On the night 19/20th April "D" Company 49th Battn. Machine Gun Corps will relieve 8 guns of the 25th Battn Machine Gun Corps, and 8 guns of "B" Company 49th Battn. Machine Gun Corps.

2. O.C."D" Company, 49th Battn. Machine Gun Corps will report to General Brown at M.28d.7.8, when relief is complete and live at his Headquarters.

3. O.C."B" Company will detail one officer to report to General Green-Wilkinson at M.28d.1.2.

4. Relief will commence at 8-0 p.m. 19th instant.

5. The Company officers concerned will meet at 10-0 a.m. 19th instant at Farm in M.30d.2.4. to arrange details of relief.

6. O.C."D" Company will report completion of relief to this Office using code word "ZINC".

7. After relief the whole of "B" Company 49th Battn. Machine Gun Corps will occupy the camp vacated by "D" Company 49th Battn. Machine Gun Corps.

8. ACKNOWLEDGE.

Capt. & Adjt.
— Battn. Machine Gun Corps.

Issued at... 7.30 pm

Copies to:-
1. "B" Company.
2. "D" Company.
3. 25th Battn. Machine Gun Corps through "B" Company 49th Bn. M.G.C.
4. 148th Infantry Brigade.
5. General Browns Force   ) For
6. "G" 49th Division.   ) information.
7. Major Sproulle   )
8. War Diary.
9. War Diary.
10. Retained.

Cancelled

SECRET.   Battalion Machine Gun Corps.   COPY. No. 5
OPERATION ORDER NO 34.

Ref. Sheets 20.N.E. & S.E. 1/20,000   Friday, 24.4.18.

1.   The two guns at present in H.22.A. will be moved and placed
        in a position about H. 4.d. central.

2.   The guns at present in position in H.3.d. and H.9.c. will
        be placed in position about dawn 27th April as follows:-

        2 Guns in the vicinity of PETIT VIERSTRAAT CABARET in H.30.c.
        and 2 guns in the vicinity of DICKEBUSH PARK in H.4.c.

        The gun positions in H.3.d. and H.9.c. will be occupied later
        by 4 guns of "A" Company.

3.   Major H.J.H.Sproule, M.C., will supervise the movement of
        the guns as set out in (2) above.

4.   "B" and "C" Companies to acknowledge by Bearer.

5.   "A" Company to acknowledge.

                                                Capt. & Adjt. &c
                                            Battn. Machine Gun Corps.

Copies to:-
        1. "A" Company.
        2. "B" Company.
        3. "C" Company.
        4. "D" 49th Division.
        5. War Diary.
        6. War Diary.   For Information.
        7. Retained.

SECRET.　　　　　　　Battalion Machine Gun Corps.　　　　　Copy No. 2
　　　　　　　　　　　OPERATION ORDER NO 35.

Sheet 28 N.W.　　　　　　　　　　　　　　　　　　Friday 26.4.18.

1.　　The 11th M.M.G.Battery will be held as Divisional reserve
　　　at OUDERDOM G.30.c.

2.　　11th M.M.G. Battery will proceed to location set out in (1)
　　　and report exact map reference to 49th Battn. Machine Gun
　　　Corps whose Headquarters is as follows:-

　　　Until 1-0 p.m. 27th instant ERIE CAMP G. 11.c.6.2.
　　　After 1-0 p.m. 27th instant G 30.c.15.70.

3.　　11th M.M.G.Battery to acknowledge by bearer.

　　　　　　　　　　　　　　　　　　　　　　　　　Capt. & Adjt.

　　　Copies to :-

　　　　　　1. 11th M.M.G.Battery.
　　　　　　2. War Diary.
　　　　　　3. War Diary　　　　　　　　　For information.
　　　　　　4. Retained.

SECRET.   Battalion Machine Gun Corps.   Copy No.....
OPERATION ORDER NO 36.

Ref. Sheets 28. N.W.& S.W.   Friday. 26.4.18.

1. The 4th Mortor Machine Gun ~~Company~~ Battery will place guns as follows to strengthen the left flank of the Division,

    2 guns about N. 3.d.5.9.
    2 guns about N.3.d.0.8.
    2 guns about H.32.d.7.5.

2. Time guns in position and exact map location will be forwarded as early as possible to 49th Batth. Machine Gun Corps (Headquarters which are as follows:

    Until 1-0 p.m. 27th instant ERIE CAMP G.11.c.6.2.
    After 1-0 p.m. 27th instant G. 30.c.15.70.

3. 4th M. M.G.Battery to acknowledge by bearer.

                                            Capt. & Adjt.
                                   49th Batth. Machine Gun Corps.

Copies to:-

1. 4th H.M.G. Battery.
2. War Diary.   )
3. War Diary.   ) For information.
4. Retained.   )

SECRET   Battalion Machine Gun Corps.   Copy No. 2
OPERATION ORDER NO 37.

will cause   **Friday 26.4.18.**

1. O.C. "A" Company the following guns to be placed in position forthwith.

         2 guns in N.2.d.
         2 guns in N.3.a.

2. The remainder of "A" Company will move to ERIE CAMP on the morning of 27th instant. Arrangements for accomodation will be made by the Adjutant.

3. Acknowledge.

                                             Capt. & Adjt.
                           49th Battn. Machine Gun Corps.

Copies to :-

1. "A" Company.
2. War Diary.
3. War Diary.   }   For information.
4. Retained.

SECRET

O.C. "A" Company.
O.C. "B" Company.
O.C. "C" Company.
O.C. "D" Company.
4th M.M.G.Battery.
11th M.M.G.Battery.
Major [illegible] M.C.
Transport Officer.

} Through Advanced H.Q.

40TH MACHINE GUN BATTALION. ORDERLY ROOM.
No. BS.137
Date 30 [illegible] 18.

---

1. "C" COMPANY. Half of "C" Company will be in the line and half will be at Rear Battalion Headquarters Sheet 27. L.30.[illegible].

All transport, except that required for fighting, will be at Rear Battalion Headquarters. Section reliefs will be arranged by O.C. C Company.

2. "A" COMPANY. (16 guns in line). All personnel not actually required for fighting and all transport not required for fighting will be at Rear Battalion Headquarters Sheet 27. L.30.[illegible].

"A" Company will be relieved periodically, under Battalion arrangements by "B" Company.

3. "B" COMPANY. 10 guns will be maintained in the Forward Reserve Line, Sheet 28 [illegible] with sufficient personnel and transport for fighting purposes.

The remainder of "B" Company will be at Rear Battalion Headquarters Sheet 27. L.30.[illegible].

Major [illegible] will resume command of "B" Company taking over from Major [illegible] M.C., after the relief on night 30th April/1st May 1918.

This Company will be re-organised by Major [illegible].

4. "D" COMPANY. This Company will be under Capt. [illegible] appointed 2nd-in-command, and will be gradually re-organised.

For this purpose [illegible] of all drafts will be posted to this Company. Should, however, "A" "B" and "C" Companies be over 100 Other Ranks in strength a larger proportion of drafts will be posted to "D" Company.

Capt. [illegible] will have two guns in Rear Reserve at Rear Battalion Headquarters manned by the remaining personnel of "D" Company.

5. The following will then be the distribution of fighting and reserve guns.

"A" Company.	16 guns in line.	
"B" Company.	10 guns in close reserve.	
"C" Company.	8 guns in line.	
"C" Company.	8 guns in Rear Reserve	Re-organising
"D" Company.	2 guns in Rear Reserve	Re-organising
4th M.M.G.Battery.	7 guns in line.	
11th M.M.G.Battery.	6 guns in Reserve at [illegible].	

A motor cyclist orderly will be maintained at 40th Division Headquarters by O.C. 11th M.M.G.Battery.

..Over.

-2-

O.C. 112th H.M.G. Battery will notify this Battalion of any move ordered by Division.

6. Lt. F.H.P.-- will hold himself in readiness to proceed to the line to relieve and officer to be detailed by O.C. "C" Company under arrangements already made.

7. Acknowledge.

                                                    [signature]
                                                    Capt. & Adjt.
                                                    42th Bttn. Machine Gun Corps.

30.4.18.

"G".
49th Division.

TECHNICAL & TACTICAL REPORT.

TACTICAL. — The following are lessons learnt during the recent fighting.

1. Strong gun teams are essential and guns must be protected on the flanks by snipers, at least one sniper being on each flank.

2. Guns should never be worked in less than pairs.

3. It is absolutely necessary to select positions in rear, to which the guns may withdraw if necessary, and these positions should, if possible, be supplied with a small amount of ammunition ready packed in belts.

   The importance of having S.A.A. ready in filled belts was again brought out. It is suggested that filled belts should be packed in S.A.A. boxes.

4. Machine Guns should not be placed in front line. They should not be nearer than 800 yards. If this is carried out they cannot be swamped before being able to open fire. All Infantry should be warned where Machine Gun fire will open in case of attack, whether they are near the bands of fire or not, it being found that Machine Gun fire has too often been rendered useless owing to the withdrawal of our Infantry.

   In some instances, Infantry ordered guns forward of the front line in spite of the lessons learnt during the Somme fighting, which proved that if an attack is made in a mist it is impossible for Machine Guns to become effective even if loaded and laid for action. At least six gun teams of this Battalion were swamped owing to this and are missing, without, so far as is known, having fired a single shot.

5. With regard to Reserves:- As Machine Gun work in open fighting is very trying, it is therefore better to have a fair proportion in a central reserve, than to put the whole force into the fight.

6. The importance of co-operation with, but at the same time, freedom of action from the Infantry was once again brought out as were also the use of ground and cover from view.

   Few persons appear to realise that it is worth while to go a short distance out of ones way, in order to keep hidden from view.

TECHNICAL. — It is suggested that 16 barrels, no longer fit for overhead Machine Gun fire, be retained on Battalion establishment for the purposes of range work, this will effect a great saving of barrels.

It has been found that it would be preferable to replace half of the Binoculars Prismatic by Telescopes Signalling, unless a marksmans sight, - as at present used on the German Machine Guns, - can be fitted to our Machine Guns.

(Sd) B.L. Badham

Lt.- Colonel.
Commanding 49th Battn. Machine Gun Corps

22.4.18.

49TH DIVISION

49TH BN MACH. GUN CORPS
APR 1918- APR 1919
MAY

40th Bn. Machine Gun Corps Order No. 93.
-----------oOo-----------

Copy No. 14.

Reference Map : Sheet 44.a.   HENIN 3.3.19.
1/40,000.

1.   The 40th Bn. M.G.C. will move from HENIN HIETARD to
        billets in DOUAI on the morning of the 4th by route march.

2.   Battalion Headquarters, "A" and "B" Companies will pass
        starting point F.28.d.0.0. at 1000 hrs. "C" and "D"
        Companies at 1400 hrs.
        DRESS :   Marching Order.

3.   The usual march intervals will be maintained.

4.   Billeting parties from Companies will meet Major ....
        Spruille.B.C. at the Divisional Reception Camp, DOUAI at
        1000 hrs.

5.   Transport Officer will make the necessary arrangements
        for transport on arrival in DOUAI.

6.   Two lorries will be placed at the disposal of the Quartermaster
        at 1200 hrs.
        The S.S. Wagon and M.A. limber at the disposal of Transport
        Officer. Company limbers at the disposal of Companies.
        The Mess Cart will report to Bn. Headquarters at 0845 hrs.
    Education Officer will arrange for the Bn. Library to be packed
        ready for loading at the Quarter Guard at 1400 hrs. on the
        3rd.

7.   Companies will ensure that billets are left in a clean and
        sanitary condition. Capt Ross will meet the Area Commandant
        at "A" Company Headquarters at 1430 hrs, and obtain receipts
        to that effect.

8.   Headquarters will close at HENIN LIETARD at 1400 hrs on the
        4th and re-open at 69, BOULEVARD PASTEUR, DOUAI at the
        same hour.

9.   ACKNOWLEDGE   (Companies and Area Commandant only)

Issued at.../130hrs.   Caswell
                                        Capt. & Adjt.
                                        40th Bn. M.G.C.

Copies to :
        1. O.C. "A" Company.
        2. O.C. "B" Company.
        3. O.C. "C" Company.
        4. O.C. "D" Company.
        5. Quartermaster.
        6. Transport Officer.   (3)
        7. Education Officer
        8. O.C. Signals.
        9. Area Commandant, HENIN LIETARD.
       10. War Diary.
       11. War Diary.
       12. Office.

War Diary Vol 3

Hq'rs Bn for M.G.C.

March 1917

Sheet 1.

Army Form C. 2118.

WAR DIARY
or
INTELLIGENCE SUMMARY.
(Erase heading not required.)

Instructions regarding War Diaries and Intelligence Summaries are contained in F. S. Regs., Part II. and the Staff Manual respectively. Title pages will be prepared in manuscript.

Place	Date	Hour	Summary of Events and Information	Remarks and references to Appendices
	1.5.18.		"B" Coy arrive in Camp at MUD FARM (G 27. a. 9.3) at 3.30 a.m. after having been relieved in the line by "A" Coy. "B" Coy. move from MUD FARM to Hagro. near ABEELE in the afternoon. Enemy's artillery was exceptionally quiet in the whole of the front area throughout the day. The two guns of "A" Coy. in reserve near HALLEBAST CORNER were moved to about N.3.c.9.8.	
	2.5.18.		Our Artillery was fairly active throughout the day; the enemy seemed to concentrate more on roads. 2000 rounds were fired in harassing fire. Dispositions in the line remained unaltered.	
	3.5.18.		An increase of artillery was noticeable during the day. A heavy barrage was put down by the Enemy at 4.45 a.m. & lasted until 6.10 a.m. No Infantry action followed. The French take over the right sub-sector, but the Machine guns remain in the line with them. "B" Coy. are ordered to assemble at MUD FARM at full Coy. strength at 9.30 p.m. at 8.25 p.m. the S.O.S.	

Army Form C. 2118.

Sheet 2.

WAR DIARY
or
INTELLIGENCE SUMMARY.
(Erase heading not required.)

Place	Date	Hour	Summary of Events and Information	Remarks and references to Appendices
	3.5.18.		Went up in the direction of MONT ROUGE & a heavy S.O.S. Barrage was put down lasting until 9.45.p.m. The Artillery was very active throughout the night	
	4.5.18.		"A" Coy. (less one Sub-section) are relieved by the 30th (Bn Batt.) M.G.C. and "C" Coy. withdraw from the line. Both Coys. assemble at Hagrs. near ABEELE. All in accordance with O.O. No. B/47. "B" Advance Hqrs. close at OUDERDOM & open at ABEELE. "B" Coy. rejoin the Bn. from MUD FARM (G.27.a.9.3.) Information received that the Baths. will move to N. Camp near ST-JAN-TER-BIEZEN on the 6th. The day was spent in cleaning up & bathing.	B/47.
	5.5.18.		One of "A" Coys. Limbers was hit near OUDERDOM while bringing out two gun teams, the driver being wounded & one horse being killed & the other wounded. Carvalho M.M.G. Batteries Nos. 4. 6. 7 and 11. come under command of O.C. Corps Mounted Troops at 9.0.a.m.	

Army Form C. 2118.

Sheet 3.

WAR DIARY
or
INTELLIGENCE SUMMARY.
(Erase heading not required.)

Instructions regarding War Diaries and Intelligence Summaries are contained in F. S. Regs., Part II, and the Staff Manual respectively. Title pages will be prepared in manuscript.

Place	Date	Hour	Summary of Events and Information	Remarks and references to Appendices
	6.5.18.		The whole of the 49th Battn. M.G.C. move from their Camp near ABEELE to new Camp at F.27.a.2.6. in accordance with Operation Order No 38. Two guns of "A" Coy. & one gun of "B" Coy. rejoin the Battn. from the line. The following Officer reinforcements arrived & were posted to Coys. as under :- 2/Lt. W.F.M. Gilchrist to "C" Coy. 2/Lt. F.N. Peach to "B" Coy. 2/Lt. J.R. Lawson to "C" Coy. 2/Lt. B. Thomson to "C" Coy. Lt. C.H.A. Sturge & Lt. F.T.R. Ives to "B" Coy. Lt. A. Batt and 2/Lt. F. Dudley to "B" Coy. 2/Lt. F.R. Plews to "A" Coy. The day was spent in improving Camp arrangements.	38.
	7.5.18.		Battn. training; Special attention being paid to musketry.	
	8.5.18.		Battn. training. Inspection of "A" Coy. by the C.O. The Battn. was ordered to be ready to move off at two hours notice.	
	9.5.18.		Battn. training. Inspection of "B" Coy. by C.O.	
	10.5.18.		Battn. training. Sports held in the Football field in the afternoon. 29 Reinforcements reported.	
	11.5.18.		Battn. in training. Capt. A.M.R.Bain reported as reinforcement &	

Army Form C. 2118.

Sheet 7.

WAR DIARY
or
INTELLIGENCE SUMMARY.
(Erase heading not required.)

Instructions regarding War Diaries and Intelligence Summaries are contained in F. S. Regs., Part II. and the Staff Manual respectively. Title pages will be prepared in manuscript.

Place	Date	Hour	Summary of Events and Information	Remarks and references to Appendices
	11.5.18.		posted to command D "Coy. Draft of 97 men arrived.	W. Mulholland
	12.5.18.		Church Parade ordered & Cancelled owing to wet weather.	W. Mulholland
			Shooting match, officers & Sergeants on range in evening.	W. Mulholland
	13.5.18.		Battn. in training.	W. Mulholland
	14.5.18.		Battn. in training. Draft of 40 O.R.s joined the Battn. as reinforcements.	W. Mulholland
	15.5.18.		Battn. in training. The first case of fever broke out.	W. Mulholland
	16.5.18.		Battn. in training.	W. Mulholland
	17.5.18.		Battn. in training. "A" & "B" Coys. with their transport inspected by the G.O.C. Division. Ten Officer reinforcements arrived & posted to Coys. as under.	W. Mulholland
			Lt. H.H.E. Keen "D" Coy. Lt. C.V. Hancock "B" Coy.	
			Lt. S.A. Russell "D" " Lt. F. James "D" "	
			Lt. R. Tasker "C" " Lt. W.R. Harwood "D" "	
			Lt. A.J. McLean "B" " 2/Lt. A.C. Whatley "D" "	
			2/Lt. E.D. Barrett "D" " 2/Lt. D.T. Williams "D" "	W. Mulholland

Army Form C. 2118.

WAR DIARY
or
INTELLIGENCE SUMMARY.

Sheet 5.

(Erase heading not required.)

Instructions regarding War Diaries and Intelligence Summaries are contained in F. S. Regs., Part II. and the Staff Manual respectively. Title pages will be prepared in manuscript.

Place	Date	Hour	Summary of Events and Information	Remarks and references to Appendices
	17.5.18		Two O.R. reinforcements also arrived.	
	18.5.18		Battn. in training. Inspection of "C" Coy. "D" Coy. & Hdqrs. will	
	19.5.18		their transport by G.O.C. Division.	
	20.5.18		Battn. in training. Transport inspected by O.C. Divisional Train.	
	21.5.18		Battn. in training. Draft of 38. O.R's joined the Bn. as reinforcements.	
	22.5.18		Battn. in training.	
	23.5.18		(do) Draft of 20. O.R's joined the Bn. as reinforcements.	
	24.5.18		(do)	
	25.5.18		(do) Draft of 6. O.R's joined " " "	
	26.5.18		(do)	
	27.5.18		(do)	
	28.5.18		(do)	
	29.5.18		(do) Draft of 17. N.C.O's joined the Battn. as reinforcements.	
	30.5.18		(do) Orders received from 291st Bri. to take over from the 21st Sert. M.G.C.	
	31.5.18		in accordance with Operation Order No. 39.	39.

Secret.   Copy No 2

49th Batt. M.G. Corps

Operation Order No B/47

1. On the night 4/5th inst
"A" Company less 1 Subsection will march on relief to Rear H.Q. near ABEELE

2. "B" Company less 1 gun will remain in reserve at MUD FARM (G 27. a. 4. 6)

3. "C" Company will withdraw all guns now in the line in the Right Sector to Rear H.Q. at ABEELE

4. The guns of "C" Company in the left sub-sector will be relieved and march to ABEELE under orders of O.C. "A" Coy.

5. At 9 am on the 5th inst "B" Company will march to Rear H.Q. near ABEELE

6. 1 Coy. M.M.G. and 3 guns of 49th Bn will be withdrawn on the night 5/6th and join their Units near ABEELE.

7. Advanced Battalion H.Q. will close at G 24 c. 5. 6. and open at Rear H.Q. at the same hour.

Issued at 12 noon.

Copies to:-
 Rear H. Qrs. 2
 G. 49th Division.
 O.C. "A" Coy.
 O.C. "B" Coy.
 O.C. "C" Coy.

B.B. Bartram Lt. Col.
Commanding 49th Bn. M.G. Corps

SECRET   Battalion Machine Gun Corps.
                        OPERATION ORDER No 38.

Ref: Map Sheet. 27.   Sunday. 5.5.18.

1.   The 49th Battalion Machine Gun Corps will move from its present Camp to N Camp at F.27.a.50.30. tomorrow 6th instant.

2.   Companies will move complete with all their transport at the following times:

       "A" Company. - 9-0 a.m.;   "B" Company. - 9-15 a.m.

       "C" Company 9-30 a.m. ;   "D" Company. - 9-45.a.m.

       Headquarters personnel and Headquarters transport will march with "D" Company under arrangements to be made by the Regimental Sergeant Major and Transport Officer respectively.

3.   The following route will be adhered to:- L.17.b.4.2. - IN DE HOOGE CABERET (L.4.b.80.20.) - F.27.b.60.90. and the usual distances will be maintained on the march. All men will march in Full Marching Order and will carry their blankets.

4.   Guides will be at F.27.b.60.90. to guide Companies into the Camp.

5.   Transport Officer will arrange for the G.S.Wagon to be at Headquarters at 9-15 a.m. to load up with 20 tents.
This wagon will proceed with "D" Company.
Remaining tents will be carried by Companies as follows:

       "A" Company.- 7. ; "B" Company. - 8. ; "C" Company. - 8.
"D" Company will carry 9 bivouacs.
The Regimental Sergeant Major will arrange for all tents and bivouacs to be struck and dumped at the entrance of the Camp by 8-30 a.m.

6.   Each Company will detail an advance party of one N.C.O. with bicycle to report to Major SPROULLE at Orderly Room at 8-0 a.m.

7.   Battalion Headquarters will close at present Camp at 10-0 a.m. and will open at the new Camp at the same hour.

8.   The guard will dismount at present Camp at 9-45 a.m. and will march with "D" Company.
This guard will remount at new Camp on arrival.

9.   A motor lorry will be at the Camp at 8-0 a.m. This will load up with tubs from the Bath House and will then proceed to the Quartermaster's Stores and be at the disposal of the Quartermaster.

                                                                              -Over-

The Quartermaster will have one man at Headquarters at 8-0 a.m. to guide this lorry to the stores after loading up with the tubs

10/ All Quartermaster Stores will move under the Quartermaster's arrangements and will be clear of their present camp by 10-0 a.m.

11. ACKNOWLEDGE.

[signature]

— Battn. Machine Gun Corps.

Copies To:-

1. O.C. "A" Company.
2. O.C. "B" Company.
3. O.C. "C" Company.
4. O.C. "D" Company.
5. Quartermaster.
6. Transport Officer.
7. Signalling Officer.
8. 2/ Lt. D.T. Jones.
9. R.S.M.
10. War Diary.
11. War Diary.   } For information.
12. File.

SECRET   49th Battalion Machine Gun Corps.   Copy No. 12

OPERATION ORDER NO 39.

REF Map... Sheet 27528   Friday. 31.5.18.

1. "A" Company will relieve the Machine Gun Company of the 41st Battalion Machine Gun Corps in the RIGHT SECTOR of the 41st Division on night of 2nd/3rd June 1918.

2. "B" Company will relieve the Machine Gun Company of the 41st Battalion Machine Gun Corps in the LEFT SECTOR of the 41st Division on the night 3rd/4th June 1918.

3. "C" and "D" Companies will relieve two Companies of 41st Battalion Machine Gun Corps on 3rd June 1918.

4. O.C."A" Company and 2nd in command of "B" Company will each proceed by Lorry as follows, to reconnoitre line and positions to be taken over:

"A" Company with 147th Infantry Brigade (time and place of departure will be notified as early as possible).

"B" Company with 148th Infantry Brigade lorry starting from SCHOOL CAMP (Sheet 27 L.2.d.) at 9-30 a.m. 1.6.18.

5. ACKNOWLEDGE. (A,B,C, and D, Companies only)

                                               Capt. & Adjt.
                        49th Battn. Machine Gun Corps.

Issued at.. 11.30/a.m.

Copies to :-

     1. O.C."A" Company.
     2. O.C."B" Company
     3. O.C."C" Company.
     4. O.C."D" Company.
     5. Signal Officer.
     6. Quartermaster.
     7. 49th Division "G"
     8. 41st Battalion Machine Gun Corps.
     9. 146th Infantry Brigade.
   10. 147th   do   } For information/
   11. 148th   do
   12. War Diary
   13. War Diary
   14. Retained

Confidential
War Diary
of
49th Battn. M.G.C.
From 1.6.18. – 30.6.18.
Vol 4.

Army Form C. 2118.

Sheet 1.

WAR DIARY
or
INTELLIGENCE SUMMARY.
(Erase heading not required.)

Place	Date	Hour	Summary of Events and Information	Remarks and references to Appendices
	1918 June 1.		Battalion in training.	
	2.6.18.		Church Parade. G.O.C. Division attended. Half of A.Coy. Half of B. Coy. & 6 guns of D. Coy. proceeded by light railway from REMY SIDING to MACHINE GUN SIDING (Sheet 28. H.12.a) The two half Coys of A and B. relieve a Coy. of the 41st. Battn. M.G.C. in the forward area, & the 6 guns of D. Coy. relieve 6 guns of the 36th Battn. M.G.C. in the KRAIE defences in accordance with Operation Orders Nos. 39, 40, and 43. Casualties NIL.	O.O.39. 40. 41. 43.
	3.6.18.		C. Coy. & 10 gun teams of D. Coy. leave PUGWASH (PROVEN) & proceed to HALLE by light railway in accordance with O.O.42. The dispositions of the Battn. are as under :— A. Coy. H.Q. at I.8.b.0.4. Two sections in forward positions & two sections in the Ramparts YPRES; Transport at H.26.a.0.5. B. Coy. H.Q. at I.8.b.0.4. Two sections in forward positions & two sections in the Ramparts YPRES. Transport at H.26.a.0.5. C. Coy in support. H.Q. H.2.b.1.6. Eight guns in positions in the	O.O.42. O.O.44.

WAR DIARY
or
INTELLIGENCE SUMMARY.

Army Form C. 2118.

Sheet 2.

Place	Date	Hour	Summary of Events and Information	Remarks and references to Appendices
	3.6.18.		BRIELEN line 9: eight guns in the VLAMERTINGHE defences. Transport at A.A.b.7.0. D. Coy. Sios guns in the KAAIE defences 8: 10 guns in reserve at A.29.b.5.2. Transport at A.29.b.5.2. During the night there was considerable gas shelling about YPRES resulting in a number of casualties to B. Coy. Casualties:— Coy. Sergt. Major B. Coy. & 32. O.R. (all gas)	
	4.6.18.		Battn. H.Q. move from N. Camp to CHATEAU LOVIE. F.16.d. central. The Q.M. stores, 2nd line transport & Coy. rear H.Q. all move to (O.D.45) F.18.a.7.3. Dispositions in the line remain the same. A class for training N.C.O's to become Instructors is commenced at rear H.Q. Fairly heavy shelling of back areas. Front area fairly quiet. Casualties NIL.	
	5.6.18.		Dispositions remain unaltered. 10. O.R. wounded. Gas.	
	6.6.18.		Casualties 2. O.R. killed (Shell) 2. O.R. wounded (Shell). 1. O.R. wounded (Gas).	

Army Form C. 2118.

Sheet 3.

WAR DIARY
or
INTELLIGENCE SUMMARY.
(Erase heading not required.)

Place	Date	Hour	Summary of Events and Information	Remarks and references to Appendices
	7.6.18.		Hostile Artillery quiet throughout the day. 1. O.R. wounded (Gas) 2/LT. A.C. WHATELEY evacuated to Hospital (accidentally injured through playing football).	
	8.6.18.		Our Heavy Artillery active all day. Hostile Artillery quiet. Casualties:- 3. O.R. wounded (Gas) C. Coy. Rear H.Q. established at Sheet 27. F.18.a.8.4. Lt. PAWSON left Bn. to join Indian Army.	
	9.6.18.		Hostile Artillery active during the day cutting our wire in Support lines. Casualties:- 7. O.R. wounded (Gas).	
	10.6.18.		Artillery on both sides quiet. Aircraft active in the evening. Engaged on both sides by heavy A.A. fire. B. Coy. took over 6 guns in KAAIE defences from D. Coy. as per this Office letter. The 6 guns of D. Coy returned to Reserve with their H.Q. Casualties 1. O.R. wounded (Shell).	
	11.6.18.		Harassing fire from Artillery & M.G. during night. Cloth Hall at YPRES evidently registration mark. Casualties NIL. D. Coy relieved C. Coy. in support as per O.O. No. 46.	

WAR DIARY
or
INTELLIGENCE SUMMARY.
(Erase heading not required.)

Army Form C. 2118.

Sheet 4.

Place	Date	Hour	Summary of Events and Information	Remarks and references to Appendices
	11.6.18.		C. Coy relieved A. Coy. in the Right Sector.	
			A. Coy moved to Reserve in location previously occupied by D.	
			Coy. as per O.O. No. 46.	O.O.46.
	12.6.18.		Medical Officer proceeded to DeadEnd YPRES to take over duties of R.E. M.O. The Rear Bn. H.Q. & Transport personnel under the M.O. under Hq N.& of the R.E. Casualties NIL.	
	13.6.18.		Enemy shelling MENIN GATE. Bombs were dropped on INFANTRY BARRACKS. Casualties NIL.	
	14.6.18.		Casualties NIL.	
	15.6.18.		Hostile Artillery very active during early morning on the right of Divisional Front. Casualties NIL.	
	16.6.18.		Shelling of back areas above normal. The following Officers and N.C.O.s were granted decorations as under :-	
			Military Cross.	
			T/2/Lt. W.A. HAWES.	
			T/2/Lt. D.T. JONES.	
			D.C.M.	
			15664 A/Sgt. H. LUFFRUM.	
			44626. Sgt. J.J. KENNEDY.	

WAR DIARY or INTELLIGENCE SUMMARY

Army Form C. 2118.

Sheet 5.

Place	Date	Hour	Summary of Events and Information	Remarks and references to Appendices
	16.6.18.		Military Cross.	
			2/Lt. R.E. BENTLEY.	
			T/2/Lt. S.F.H. WOOD.	
			D.C.M.	
			59214. 4/Cpl. C. BARRETT.	
			24612. Sgt. A. WALKER.	
			20247. Sgt. F.J. JACKSON.	
			The 2 guns on East bank of "Moat" near LILLE GATE moved to emplacements in the Ramparts. Casualties 1. O.R. wounded (Shell)	
	17.6.18.		Lt. BARRETT left the Battn. to join Indian Army. Casualties NIL.	
	18.6.18.		Coy. Sergt. Major Clegg A.J. posted to the Battn. as a reinforcement. New emplacements for guns in I.13.a. commenced. Artillery activity on both sides very quiet.	
			One O.R. wounded (Shell) G.I. O.R. wounded (remained at duty)	
	19.6.18.		Artillery activity quiet. Casualties NIL.	
	20.6.18.		The 4th Duke of Wellington's Regt. carried out a Minor Operation against the enemy front North of ZILLEBEKE Lake with the purpose of capturing prisoners. Two guns at I.9.c. 05.00 & 3 guns at I.9.c.40.20. put up a barrage in support of the operation about	

WAR DIARY
or
INTELLIGENCE SUMMARY.

Army Form C. 2118.

Sheet 6.

Place	Date	Hour	Summary of Events and Information	Remarks and references to Appendices
	20.6.18		I.17.d. LT. KEENE with 2 guns followed a platoon of the 4th Duke of Wellington at 50 yards interval. Route followed was round the North of YPRES, down the Ramparts, out through LILLE GATE, WARRINGTON ROAD, C.3 light railway, to point of Assembly. On reaching about I.8.d.1.5. the limber was unloaded & guns man handled to about I.15.d.8.0. which was reached at 11.15. p.m. The Infantry moved forward at 12 midnight, the gun teams following at 50 yards distant. Great trouble was experienced in keeping in touch. The Sergt. on one gun was held up by a Machine gun on the edge of the lake to his front, which he attempted with the help of a Lewis gun to silence. Great trouble was experienced in getting back, owing to the smoke from our Artillery barrage blowing back. This made signals almost invisible. The withdrawal was further hampered owing to the long grass making movements of heavily loaded men very difficult. Eleven prisoners & one	

Army Form C. 2118.

Sheet 7.

WAR DIARY
or
INTELLIGENCE SUMMARY.
(Erase heading not required.)

Place	Date	Hour	Summary of Events and Information	Remarks and references to Appendices
	20.6.18		Machine Gun were Captured in the operation.	
			B. Coy. were relieved in the forward area by D. Coy. A. Coy. relieve D. Coy. in support of B. Coy. come out to reserve, all in accordance with Operation Order N° 47. One of C. Coy's. guns moved into position in the SALLY PORTE. 24.250 rounds were fired in support of the raid. Casualties NIL.	0.0.47.
	21.6.18.		Enemy shelled H.4.b. 8ᵗʰ H.A.A. from 1.0.p.m. till dark. B 30. b. shelled with gas shells at 4.0.p.m. until 4.30.p.m. otherwise shelling quiet. Casualties NIL.	
	22.6.18.		The 2 guns moved to DRAGOON FARM from I.4.c.1.2. to fire in a S.E. direction. Reinforcement of 13. O.R. reported.	
	23.6.18.		Quiet day on the whole front with the exception of the VLAMERTINGHE area, which was shelled from the direction of KEMMEL, necessitating the H.Q. of the Reserve Bde. moving to BRAKE CAMP. 500 rounds were fired in harassing fire.	
	24.6.18.		Enemy Artillery more active than usual during the night with	

Army Form C. 2118.

Sheet 8.

WAR DIARY
or
INTELLIGENCE SUMMARY.
(Erase heading not required.)

Instructions regarding War Diaries and Intelligence Summaries are contained in F.S. Regs., Part II. and the Staff Manual respectively. Title pages will be prepared in manuscript.

Place	Date	Hour	Summary of Events and Information	Remarks and references to Appendices
	24.6.18.		4.2. shells in I.1.c. REIGERSBURG shelled heavily with 5.9.0. from 10.0.a.m to 11.0.a.m. 750 rounds fired in harassing fire on DORMY HOUSE. I.16.d. 7.0. Casualties 1. O.R. wounded (shell).	
	25.6.18.		Back areas shelled in the neighbourhood of VLAMERTINGHE 8" a considerable reply to our barrage at 12.30.a.m. A few gas shells on the Powder Magazine YPRES at 1.30.a.m. Hostile artillery quiet on the forward areas. 750 rounds fired in harassing fire. Casualties NIL.	
	26.6.18.		About midnight enemy put down a 5.9. barrage about I.19.a.3.5. Goldfish Chateau & Vlamertinghe shelled during the day. 7000 rounds fired in harassing fire. Casualties NIL.	
	27.6.18.		Hostile Artillery registering on the Ramparts during the morning. 7.000 rounds were fired by C. Coy. in support of raid & a total of 12.700 rounds in all were fired during the night. Casualties NIL.	
	28.6.18.		Relief of Coys. postponed owing to the 148th Infantry Bde. carrying	

WAR DIARY
or
INTELLIGENCE SUMMARY.

(Erase heading not required.)

Army Form C. 2118.

Sheet 9.

Instructions regarding War Diaries and Intelligence Summaries are contained in F. S. Regs., Part II. and the Staff Manual respectively. Title pages will be prepared in manuscript.

Place	Date	Hour	Summary of Events and Information	Remarks and references to Appendices
	28.6.18.		out a raid in which 6 guns of C. Coy. cooperated with harassing fire, firing 13,500 rounds. The raid was a failure owing to smoke drifting over own raiding party. Casualties 1. O.R. wounded (shell). Reinforcement of 444 reported Bn. H.Q.	
	29.6.18.		Very quiet throughout the day. A. Coy. relieved C. Coy in the forward area on the night. B. Coy. relieved A. Coy. & C. Coy. came out into support, all in accordance with operation orders 448 & 49. Casualties NIL.	O.O.48. O.O.49.
	30.6.18.		Hostile artillery activ in the back areas, but quiet forward. Casualties NIL.	

Copy No. 13

SECRET.
40th Battalion Machine Gun Corps.
* OPERATION ORDER NO. 40. *

REF MAPS Sheet 27 & 28.   Saturday. 1.6.18.

In continuation of Operation Order No 39.

1. The relief by "A" Company will commence from Headquarters of the Company to be relieved at 10-0 p.m. 2.6.18.

2. The relief by "B" Company will commence from Headquarters of the Company to be relieved at 10-0 p.m. 3.6.18.

3. The RIGHT Company ("A" Company) will relieve the working party detailed to work under the Tunnellers and will be responsible that the working party is formed as directed.

4. Guides for relief will be arranged by O.C. Companies concerned.

5. Two Belt Boxes per gun will be taken into the line with the guns. The remaining belt boxes will be taken over.

6. Rations will be sent from rear Headquarters starting at 8-0 p.m. daily.

7. "C" Company will be in support at ORILLIC CAMP Sheet 28 H.3.b.1.6.
O.C. "C" Company will detail two Officers to report at ORILLIC CAMP tomorrow 2.6.18. to reconnoitre the YELLOW line.

8. "D" Company will be in reserve at the Camp at Sheet 28 A.29.b.5.3.
O.C. "D" Company will detail one Officer to report to the above Camp tomorrow 2.6.18 to reconnoitre the Reserve Line.

9. Fighting Limbers will go forward with each Company. Remaining transport will remain at Battalion Headquarters.

10. Location of Battalion Headquarters will be notified in due course.

11. Time of entraining on Light Railway will be notified as soon as possible. Probable place of entrainment RELY SIDING.

12. "A", "B", "C", and "D" Companies and Transport Officer to acknowledge.

Capt. & Adjt.
40th Battn. Machine Gun Corps.

Issued at.....5.30 p.m.

-Over-

Copies to :-

1. O.C. "A" Company.
2. O.C. "B" Company.
3. O.C. "C" Company.
4. O.C. "D" Company.
5. Transport Officer.
6. Signal Officer.
7. Quartermaster.
8. 49th Division "G"
9. 41st Battn. Machine Gun Corps.
10. 146th Infantry Brigade.
11. 147th do
12. 148th do
13. War Diary.
14. War Diary
15. Retained

For information.

Copy. No. 6

SECRET.

49th Battalion Machine Gun Corps.
OPERATION ORDER NO. 41.
------------------oOo------------------

Ref Maps. Sheet 27. & 28.   Saturday. 1.6.18

In continuation of Operation Order No. 40.

1. Train conveying "A" Company will leave REMY SIDING Sheet 27/ L.23.a. at 7-15 p.m. 2nd June 1918. under orders to be issued by Staff Captain 148th Infantry Brigade.

2. Company will detrain at FORWARD DUMP SIDING Sheet 28 H.6.c.

3. Company will march off from TUNNELLERS CAMP at 5-15 p.m. arrive REMY SIDING 7-0 p.m.

4. Transport will meet Company at detraining point under arrangements to be made by O.C."A" Company.

5. Completion of relief will be wired to this office using code word "VIOLET".

6. "A" Company to acknowledge.

                                                    Capt. & Adjt.
                                            49th Battn. Machine Gun Corps.

Issued at......

Copies to:-
1. O.C."A" Company.
2. 148th Infantry Brigade.
3. 49th Division "G".   )   For
4. 41st Battn. Machine Gun Corps.   )   information.
5. War Diary.
6. War Diary. ✓
7. Retained.

Copy No. 11

SECRET.   49th Battalion Machine Gun Corps.
* OPERATION ORDER NO 42. *

Ref. Maps: Sheets 27 & 28.   Sunday. 2.6.18.

In continuation of Operation Orders No. 39 & 40.

1. One train conveying "C" Company and 10 gun teams of "D" Company will leave PUMWASH (PROVEN) at 6-0 a.m 3.6.18. Detraining place HAGLE Sheet 27 G.6.a.

2. Details as above will march off from TUNNELLERS CAMP at 6-30 a.m.

3. Transport will meet Companies at Detraining point under arrangements to be made by O.C. Companies concerned.

4. Completion of relief will be wired to this Office using code word "ROSE".

5. Location of Headquarters of Companies and Forward Transport Lines will be forwarded to this Office as early as possible.

6. "C" and "D" Companies to acknowledge.

                                Capt. & Adjt.
                                49th Battn. Machine Gun Corps.

Issued at......

Copies to:-

    1. "C" Company.
    2. "D" Company.
    3. Signal Officer.   3a. Transport Officer)
    4. Quartermaster.
    5. 41st Battn. Machine Gun Corps. ⎫
    6. "Q" 49th Division.   ⎪
    7. 146th Infantry Brigade.   ⎬ For
    8. 147th   do   ⎪ information
    9. 148th   do   ⎭
    10. War Diary.
    11. War Diary.
    12. File.

SECRET   49th Battalion Machine Gun Corps.   Copy No....

OPERATION ORDER NO 43.

Ref Maps Sheet 27 & 28   Sunday 2.6.18.

In continuation of Operation Order Nos. 39 & 40.

1. Train conveying "B" Company and 6 gun teams of "D" Company will depart from REMY SIDING (Sheet 27 L.23.a.) at 7-15 p.m. 3.6.18. Detraining Place MACHINE GUN SIDING. (Sheet 28 H.12.a.)

2. The six guns of "D" Company will relieve the six guns of 36th Battalion Machine Gun Corps. in the KAAIE Defences under arrangements made by O.C."D" Company.

3. Details as above will march from FUSILIERS CAMP at 5-0 p.m. arrive REMY SIDING 7-0 p.m. O.C."B" Company will detail one officer to go in advance to REMY SIDING to arrive there at 6-30 p.m. to make entraining arrangements.

4. Transport will meet Companies at Detraining Point under arrangements to be made by O.C.Companies.

5. Completion of relief will be wired to this Office using code word "BUTTERCUP".

6. Map location of Headquarters of Companies and Forward Transport Lines will be forwarded to this office as soon as possible

7. "B" and "D" Companies to acknowledge.

                                                 Capt. & Adjt,
                                    49th Battn. Machine Gun Corps.

Issued at.....

Copies to :-

       1. O.C."B" Company.
       2. O.C."D" Company.
       3. Transport Officer.
       4. Signal Officer.
       5. Quartermaster.
       6. 36th Battn.M.G.C.)
       7. "G" 49th Division.
       8. 146th Infantry Brigade.   For
       9. 147th   do   information.
    10. 148th   do
    11. War Diary.
    12. War Diary.
    13 File
    14. 41st Battn. Machine Gun Corps.)

SECRET.

Copy. No. 12

49th Battalion Machine Gun Corps.
OPERATION ORDER No 44.
------------------Oo------------------

Ref Maps.

Monday. 3.6.18.

Reference Operation Order No. 3. of 2.6.18.

1. The detraining station will now be MISSION JUNCTION (Sheet 28 B.27.c.9.3.) and not MACHINE GUN SIDING as previously ordered.

2. Transport arrangements will be made accordingly.

3. ACKNOWLEDGE. ("B", "D" Companies and Transport Officer)

Capt. & Adjt.
49th Battn. Machine Gun Corps.

Issued at. 2 p.m.

Copies to :-

1. O.C. "B" Company.
2. O/C. "D"   "
3. Signal Officer.
4. Transport Officer.
5. Quartermaster.
6. 36th Battn. M.G.C.
7. 41st Battn. M.G.C.
8. "Q" 49th Division.
9. 146th Infanrty Brigade.
10. 147th   do
11. 148th   do
12. War Diary.
13. War Diary.
14. Retained.

} For information.

SECRET.   49th Battalion Machine Gun Corps.   Copy. No. 13
                  *OPERATION ORDER NO 45 *
                  ---------------oOo---------------

Ref Maps.   Monday. 3.6.18.

1.   Rear Company Headquarters will move to F. 18 a.7.5.
      (Sheet 27) tomorrow 4.6.18.

2.   Companies less Transport will march under the Adjutant
      to new Camp.

3.   Companies will parade on ground South on Tents ready to
      march off at 8-30 a.m.

4.   Transport and remainder of Battalion Headquarters
      (less Signals) will move under Transport Officer at 8-45 a.m.

5.   Quartermaster will arrange with Transport Officer for
      removal of all stores.

6.   Signals will move under orders of Signalling Officer.

7.   The Transport Officer will detail the Cooks Cart and
      Headquarters Limber to report to H.Q. Officers Mess
      and Battalion Orderly Room respectively at 8-0 a.m.
      All Headquarters Officers Kits will be packed and dumped
      outside Battalion Orderly Room by 7-45 a.m.

8.   Battalion Headquarters will close at 8-30 a.m. at present
      camp and re-open as soon after as possible at Sheet 27
      F.16.d. 20.40.

9.   Signalling Officer will arrange for one Runner to remain
      at present Headquarters until 12 noon 4.6.18. to collect
      any messages that may arrive.

10.   Companies are responsible for leaving the Camp and
      Transport Lines clean.

11.   All tents will be left correctly pitched.

12.   Quarters will be allotted by Major. W.J.M.Sproulle. M.C.
      on arrival at the new Camp.

13.   The R.S.M. will detail the Headquarters personnel
      according to instructions issued.

14.   ACKNOWLEDGE.

                                            Capt. & Adjt.
                                       49th Battn. Machine Gun Corps.
      Issued at.......

                                                        -Over-

Copies to:-

1. O.C."A" Company.
2. O.C."B" Company.
3. O.C."C" Company.
4. O.C."D" Company.
5. Quartermaster
6. Signalling Officer.
7. Transport Officer.
8. R.S.M.
9. "G" 49th Division.
10. "A"   do
11. "Q"   do
12. War Diary.
13 War Diary.
14. File.

For information.

SECRET. 49th Battalion Machine Gun Corps.   Copy. No.....
OPERATION ORDER NO 46
———————————oOo———————————

Ref Sheet 27. 118 Saturday. 8.6.18.

1. "C" Company will relieve "A" Company in the RIGHT Sector on the night of 11th/12th June 1918.

2. "D" Company will relieve "C" Company in support on the morning of 11th June 1918. Relief to be complete by 12 noon.

3. "A" Company, on completion of relief by "C" Company will be held in reserve in the position now occupied by "D" Company.

4. Mutual arrangements for relief will be made between O.C.Companies concerned.

5. No concentration of troops will be allowed in YPRES. Attention is directed to this Office letter S.T. 301/23 dated 7.6.18.. The largest party to be kept together will be one Sub - Section.

6. Handing over lists will be forwarded to reach this Office not later than 24 hours after completion of relief.

7. O.C."D" Company will leave a party of 1. Officer, 1. N.C.O. and 8 men in his present Camp until it has been taken over by "A" Company.

8. Reference paras 1 & 2 above. After relief by "D" Company, "C" Company will remain in the vicinity of VLAMERTINGHE CHATEAU until moving to relieve "A" Company.

9. Train to convey "A" Company to reserve Camp will be arranged if possible . O.C."A" Company will wire by 6-0 p.m. 8.6.18. the approximate time relief will be complete, and state train accommodation required.

10. All rear Company H.Q., to be composed of the personnel laid down in this Office letter S/T. 151/8 of today, will be established at Sheet 27. F.18.a. (present rear H.Q. of "A". "B" and "D" Companies).

11. Completion of reliefs will be wired using code words as follows:-

   "C" Company relieves "A" Company.   "DAISY"
   "D"   "   "   "C"   "   "MIMOSA"
   "A"   "   "   "D"   "   "PRIMROSE"

12. ACKNOWLEDGE. (A.B.C. and "D" Companies only).

Issued at 12.3...

Capt. & Adjt.
49th Battn. Machine Gun Corps.

-Over-

Copies to:-

1. O.C,"A" Company.
2. O.C."B" Company.
3. O.C,"C" Company.
4. O.C."D" Company.
5. Quartermaster.
6. Transport officer.
7. Signal Officer.
8. "G" 49th Division.
9. 146th Inf. Brigade.
10. 147th do
11. 148th do
12 War Diary.
13. War Diary.
14. File.

For information.

SECRET.

Copy No. 12

49th Battalion Machine Gun Corps.
* OPERATION ORDER NO. 47. *

Ref Maps.: Sheets 27 & 28.   Monday. 17.6.18.

1. "D" Company will relieve "B" Company in the LEFT Sector on the night of 20/21st. June 1918.

2. "A" Company will relieve "D" Company in Support on the morning of 20th June 1918. Relief to be complete by 12 noon.

3. "B" Company, on completion of relief by "D" Company will be held in Reserve in the position now held by "A" Company.

4. Mutual arrangements for relief will be made between O.C. Companies concerned.

5. NO CONCENTRATION OF TROOPS IN YPRES will be allowed. Attention is directed to this Office letter S.T. 301/23 dated 7.6.18. The largest party to be kept together will be one Sub-section.

6. Handing over lists will be forwarded to reach this office not later than 24 hours after completion of relief.

7. O.C."A" Company will leave a party of 1 Officer, 1. N.C.O. and 8 men in his present Camp until it has been taken over by "B" Company.

8. Reference 1 & 2 above, after relief by "A" Company, "D" Company will remain in the vicinity of VLAMERTINGHE CHATEAU until moving to relieve "B" Company.

9. Train to convey "B" Company to Reserve Camp will be arranged if possible.
O.C."B" Company will wire by 6-0 p.m. 18.6.18 the approximate time relief will be complete and the number to be entrained.

10. The working party at present supplied to the RIGHT Sector by "D" Company will be supplied by "A" Company from and including Midnight 19th/20th June 1918.

11. Completion of Reliefs will be wired to this office using code words as follows:

    "D" Company relieves "B" Company.   "STOCK".
    "A"   "   "   "D"   "   "SWEET PEA"
    "B"   "   "   "A"   "   "PANSY".

12. ACKNOWLEDGE. (A.B.C. and D Companies only).

Capt. & Adjt.
49th Battn. M.G.C.

Issued at.......

-2-

Copies to:

1. O.C."A" Company.
2. O.C."B" Company.
3. O.C."C" Company.
4. O.C."D" Company.
5. Quartermaster.
6. Transport Officer.
7. Signalling Officer.
8. "G" 49th Division.
9. 146th Infantry Brigade.
10. 147th   do
11. 148th   do
12. War Diary.
13. War Diary.
14. Retained.

For information.

SECRET.

Copy No. 13

49th Battalion Machine Gun Corps.
* OPERATION ORDER NO 48. *

Ref Maps.   Tuesday 25.6.18.

1. "A" Company will relieve "C" Company in the RIGHT Sector on the night of 28th/29th June 1918.

2. "B" Company will relieve "A" Company in support on 28th June 1918. Relief to be complete by 12 noon.

3. "C" Company, on completion of relief by "A" Company, will be held in Reserve in the position now held by "B" Company.

4. Mutual arrangements for relief will be made by O.C. Companies concerned.

5. NO CONCENTRATION OF TROOPS IN YPRES will be allowed. Attention is directed to this Office letter S.T. 301/23 dated 7.6.18.
    The largest party to be kept together will be one Sub-Section.

6. Handing over lists will be forwarded to reach this Office not later than 24 hours after completion of relief.

7. O.C. "B" Company will leave a party of 1 Senior N.C.O. and 8 men in his present Camp until it has been taken over by "C" Company.

8. Reference 1 & 2 above, after relief by "B" Company, "A" Company will remain in the vicinity of VLAMERTINGHE CHATEAU until moving to relieve "C" Company.

9. Train to convey "C" Company to Reserve Camp will be arranged if possible.
    O.C. "C" Company will wire by 6.0 p.m. 26th June 1918 the approximate time relief will be complete and the number to be entrained.

10. Completion of reliefs will be wired to this Office using code words as follows:

    "A" Company relieves "C" Company   -   "VIOLA"
    "B"   "   "   "A"   "   -   "SNOWDROP"
    "C"   "   "   "B"   "   -   "MARGUERITE".

11. ACKNOWLEDGE.   (A.B.C. and D Companies only.)

                                                    Capt. & Adjt.
                                                  49th Battn. M.G.C.

Issued at 3-45 p.m.

-Over-

Copies to:-

1. O.C."A" Company.
2. O.C."B" Company.
3. O.C."C" Company.
4. O.C."D" Company.
5. Quartermaster.
6. Signalling Officer.
7. Transport N.C.O. (L/Sgt. ABBOTTS)
8. "G" 49th Division.
9. 146th Infantry Bde,
10. 147th   do
11. 148th   do
12. War Diary.
13. War Diary.
14. Retained.
15. RETAINED.

For information

Copy. No. 14

SECRET.   49th Battalion Machine Gun Corps.
           * OPERATION ORDER NO 49 *

Ref Maps.   Thursday 27.6.18.

1.   Reference Operation Order No 48 dated 25.6.18. the
     following amendments will be made.

2.   "A" Company will relieve "C" Company on the night of
     29th/30th June 1918.

3.   "B" Company will relieve "A" Company in Support 29th June
     1918. Relief to be complete by 12 noon.

4.   ACKNOWLEDGE by wire (A.B.C. and D. Companies only).

                                        Capt. & Adjt.
                                      49th Battn. M.G.C.

     Issued at.......

     Copies to:-
               1. O.C."A" Company.
               2. O.C."B" Company.
               3. O.C."C" Company.
               4. O.C."D" Company.
               5. Quartermaster.
               6. Signalling Officer.
               7. Transport N.C.O. (L/Sgt. ABBOTTS.) ⎫
               8. "G" 49th Division.   ⎬ For
               9. 146th Infantry Brigade.   ⎭ information.
              10. 147th   do
              11. 148th   do
              12. War Diary.
              13. War Diary
              14. Retained.
              15. Retained.

Confidential

War Diary

— of —

49th Battn. M.G.C.

From 1.7.18. to 31.7.18.

Vol. 5

Army Form C. 2118.

Sheet 1.

WAR DIARY
or
INTELLIGENCE SUMMARY.
(Erase heading not required.)

Place	Date	Hour	Summary of Events and Information	Remarks and references to Appendices
	1.7.18.		Quiet day on whole front. Enemy registration carried out on YPRES Cloth Hall. Batteries round VLAMERTINGHE area shelled during the day. Casualties Nil.	
	2.7.18.		Two guns of "D" Coy co-operated with the T.M'S in a shoot on MILLKEEP at 12 midnight & 12.20 a.m. Artillery activity quiet except for usual registration on Cloth Hall. Casualties 1 O.R wounded.	
	3.7.18.		Very quiet day. Vicinity of junction of Canal & Warrington Road shelled during the evening. 2,500 rounds fired in harassing fire. Casualties 1. O.R. wounded.	
	4.7.18.		13,000 rounds fired in support of raid. Enemy retaliation very slight. Casualties Nil.	
	5.7.18.		Front line & supports shelled with small calibre shells. 6,000 rounds fired in harassing fire. During night VLAMERTINGHE shelled with shrapnel. Casualties 1. O.R. killed. 1. O.R. wounded (at large).	
	6.7.18.		Usual activity during day. Evening, increasing at night. Heavy concentration of Phosgene into RAILWAY at VLAMERTINGHE at	

WAR DIARY
or
INTELLIGENCE SUMMARY.
(Erase heading not required.)

Army Form C. 2118.
Sheet 2.

Place	Date	Hour	Summary of Events and Information	Remarks and references to Appendices
	6.7.18.		4.9.a.1.7. Reinforcements reported 6 Officers 930 O.R.s	
			"B" Coy relieved "D" Coy in the Left Sector } As per Operation Order No. 53	53
			"C" " " "B" " " Support }	
			"D" " " "C" " " Reserve.	
			Six Officer reinforcements were :- LIEUT. L. R. SPINK. LIEUT. P. CAMERON FORD. 2/LT. M. R. KING. 2/LT. W. A. MARTIN. 2/LT. H. G. ROBERTS. 2/LT. F. SCOTT.	
	7.7.18.		Unusual quietness prevailed. Batteries in vicinity of VLAMERTINGHE shelled with 5.9's & 8". Bath. M.O. proceeded to duty in Front Line. R.E. M.O. took over the medical arrangements of this Unit. Casualties NIL.	
	8.7.18.		Enemy artillery quiet. 3750 rounds were fired in harassing fire on to I.17.b.20.85. and T.18.a.3.7. Casualties NIL.	
	9.7.18.		"C" Coy. shelled out of their Camp near VLAMERTINGHE in the afternoon, but returned later. ECOLE and vicinity shelled in the evening. 3,500 rounds fired in harassing fire on ZONNEBEKE	

Army Form C. 2118.

Sheet 3.

WAR DIARY
or
INTELLIGENCE SUMMARY.
(Erase heading not required.)

Place	Date	Hour	Summary of Events and Information	Remarks and references to Appendices
ROAD	9.7.18.		Casualties 1. O.R. wounded (wheel).	
	10.7.18.		Enemy artillery active in back areas. Casualties NIL.	
	11.7.18.		DRAGOON FARM shelled at 2.30 a.m. Shelling near our guns in I.4.d. KRUISSTRAAT shelled intermittently during the day. 2,500 rounds were fired in harassing fire on 6 targets at I.17.a. 80.55. & I.17.c.72.65. Casualties NIL. 2/Lt. L. MATHAMS and 2/Lt. W.S. COATES rejoined the Battn. from the Base. Casualties NIL.	
	12.7.18.		Vicinity of PINK CHATEAU shelled with 4.2's between 4. and 6. p.m. Usual activity on back areas. 12,000 rounds were fired in harassing fire. Casualties 1. O.R. wounded, & remained at duty.	
	13.7.18.		Usual activity in the back areas. MENIN ROAD & RAMPARTS shelled during the day. Casualties NIL. No harassing fire carried out.	
	14.7.18.		"C" Coy. relieve "A" Coy. in the Right Sector. "D" Coy. relieve	

WAR DIARY
or
INTELLIGENCE SUMMARY.

(Erase heading not required.)

Army Form C. 2118.

Sheet 4.

Place	Date	Hour	Summary of Events and Information	Remarks and references to Appendices
	14.7.18.		"C" Coy. in Support & "A" Coy come out into Reserve, all in accordance with Operation Order No 54. Heavy retaliation S.W. of YPRES during our bombardment in support of attack by the 6th Div. Our M.Guns fired on enemy tracks and approaches to line as a Boche relief was suspected, 6,000 rounds being fired. Casualties NIL.	54.

WAR DIARY
or
INTELLIGENCE SUMMARY.

(Erase heading not required.)

Army Form C. 2118.

Sheet 5

Place	Date	Hour	Summary of Events and Information	Remarks and references to Appendices
	July 15		2000 rounds fired in harassing fire on to J5a 65.31. Casualties 1 O.R. Accidental injury.	
	16		Back areas subjected to more hostile artillery than usual. 2000 rounds fired on ZONNEBEKE ROAD. Casualties - 1 O.R. Wounded (Gas) and 1 O.R. Acc. Injured. The 114th American Machine Gun Battalion becomes attached to the 49th Battalion, M.G.C. "A" and "B" American Companies are attached to the two forward Companies and bring 12 guns each in to the line. "C" and "D" American Companies are attached to our Support and Reserve Companies. All attachments are in accordance with Operation Order No. 55. Casualties - American - 5 O.R's. Wounded (Gas)	00.55

Army Form C. 2118.

WAR DIARY
or
INTELLIGENCE SUMMARY.   Sheet 6.
(Erase heading not required.)

Instructions regarding War Diaries and Intelligence Summaries are contained in F.S. Regs., Part II, and the Staff Manual respectively. Title pages will be prepared in manuscript.

Place	Date	Hour	Summary of Events and Information	Remarks and references to Appendices
	14		Quiet day on whole front. Transport lines and rear headquarters of Companies were shelled between 8pm and 10pm, necessitating the temporary withdrawal of the Transport which returned early next morning. No casualties were incurred.	
	18		Battery areas shelled during the evening. Menin Road and POTIJZE shelled at intervals during the night. No harassing fire was carried out. Casualties Nil. 1 O.R. reinforcement arrived.	
	19		Vicinity of the ECOLE shelled during the night. Heavy bombardment to the South continued throughout the night. 2500 rounds were fired into I.11.a.90.69 during the night. Casualties Nil.	

WAR DIARY
or
INTELLIGENCE SUMMARY.

(Erase heading not required.)

Army Form C. 2118.

Sheet 1

Place	Date	Hour	Summary of Events and Information	Remarks and references to Appendices
	July 20		Enemy Artillery much more active than usual with 8", 5.9" and 4.2". No rounds fired in harassing fire. Casualties, 1 OR Wounded	
	21		Enemy Artillery quiet on the whole front. Casualties Nil.	
	22		"D" Company relieve "B" Company in the left-forward area. "A" Company relieve "D" Company in Support and B Company comes out to Reserve – all in accordance with Operation Order No. 6, of 00.5"1. The enemy fired some gas shells into VLAMERTINGHE during the night. No harassing fire was carried out owing to relief. Casualties Nil.	

WAR DIARY
or
INTELLIGENCE SUMMARY.   Sheet 8
(Erase heading not required.)

Army Form C. 2118.

Place	Date	Hour	Summary of Events and Information	Remarks and references to Appendices
	July 23		Gas was sent over at 12.45 a.m. in the Right Sector. Machine Guns Co-operated to drown the noise of trucks moving up to take up the cylinders to the front line. 8000 rounds were fired. Casualties 1 O.R. Wounded (since died in hospital)	
	24		Considerable activity of enemy bombing planes during the night especially about the Ramparts, one bomb being dropped a few yards away from D Company Headquarters. Considerable hostile shelling of back areas. DEAD END was shelled during the night. 2000 rounds harassing fire. Casualties Nil. 2nd Lieut E.N.A. CLARKE rejoined the Battalion and rejoined "A" Company.	

WAR DIARY
or
INTELLIGENCE SUMMARY.
(Erase heading not required.)

Army Form C. 2118.

Sheet 9

Place	Date	Hour	Summary of Events and Information	Remarks and references to Appendices
	July 25		2500 rounds fired in harassing fire. Vicinity of DEAD END shelled. Casualties 2 O.R. wounded (shell) since died of wounds.	
	26		Hostile Artillery unusually quiet. 2000 rounds fired on to I.11.c.3.9. Casualties 3 O.R. of "B" Coy wounded (shell) and two horses killed. Inter-Company relief of the American M.G. Companies took place in accordance with Operation Order No. 58.	
	24		Sergts OAKDEN, LUFERUM and GARSIDE rejoin the Battalion from the Base Depot. 1000 rounds fired in harassing fire. Casualties Nil.	

Army Form C. 2118.

WAR DIARY
or
INTELLIGENCE SUMMARY.

(Erase heading not required.)

Sheet 10

Instructions regarding War Diaries and Intelligence Summaries are contained in F. S. Regs., Part II. and the Staff Manual respectively. Title pages will be prepared in manuscript.

Place	Date	Hour	Summary of Events and Information	Remarks and references to Appendices
	July 28		Considerable shelling of back areas throughout the day. Enemy artillery not active in the forward area. 4000 rounds were fired by "D" Company in support of a raid by the Left Brigade on T5c, T6.35 and T5a "E.8". Enemy retaliated on the gun positions but no casualties were incurred.	
	29		Enemy Artillery much more active than usual and a few gas shells were fired into YPRES during the night. 3000 rounds fired on to RIFLE FARM and 4400 rounds on T1c and T5a & b. Casualties:- 2nd Lieut W.S. COATES received an accidental injury (fall off horse)	

Army Form C. 2118.

WAR DIARY
or
INTELLIGENCE SUMMARY.

(Erase heading not required.)

Sheet 11

Instructions regarding War Diaries and Intelligence Summaries are contained in F. S. Regs., Part II. and the Staff Manual respectively. Title pages will be prepared in manuscript.

Place	Date	Hour	Summary of Events and Information	Remarks and references to Appendices
	July 30		"A" Company relieve "C" Company in the RIGHT SECTOR; "B" Company relieve "A" Company in Support; and "C" Company come out into Reserve all in accordance with Operation Order No. 59. Casualties NIL.	
	31.		No change. Harassing fire. NIL Casualties. 1 O.R. Wounded. Officer reinforcements:- LIEUT A.C.V. de CANDOLE and 2ND LIEUT J.B. GALE	

SECRET.

Copy No. 13

49th Battalion Machine Gun Corps.
* OPERATION ORDER NO 503 *
——————————oOo——————————

Wednesday. 3.7.18.

1. "B" Company will relieve "D" Company in the LEFT Sector on the night of 6th/7th July 1918.

2. "C" Company will relieve "B" Company in Support on 6th July 1918. Relief to be complete by 12 noon.

3. "D" Company, on completion of relief by "B" Company will be held in reserve in the position now held by "C" Company.

4. Mutual arrangements for relief will be made by O.C. Companies concerned.
O.C.Relieving Companies will visit O.C.Companies to be relieved on the day before relief, and take over all work in hand.

5. NO CONCENTRATION OF TROOPS IN YPRES will be allowed.
Attention is directed to this Office letter S.T. 301/23 dated 7.6.18.
The largest party to be kept together will be one SUB-SECTION.

6. Handing over lists will be forwarded to reach this Office not later than 24 hours after completion of relief.

7. O.C."C" Company will detail a party of 1 Senior N.C.O. and 8 men to remain in his present camp until it has been taken over by "D" Company.

8. Reference 1 & 2 above, after relief by "C" Company, "B" Company will remain in the vicinity of VLAMERTINGHE CHATEAU until moving to relieve "D" Company.

9. Sections of "D" Company will march to Reserve Camp on relief under arrangements to be made by O.C.Company.

10. Completion of reliefs will be wired to this Office using code words as follows:

    "B" Company relieves "D" Company.   =   "LILY"
    "C"   "   "   "B"   "   =   "TULIP"
    "D"   "   "   "C"   "   =   "CROCUS"

11. ACKNOWLEDGE. (A.B.C.and D. Companies only)

Issued at 6·0 pm

Capt. & Adjt.
49th Battn. M/G.C.

Copies to:-

1. O.C."A" Company.   ) For information.
2. O.C."B" Company.
3. O.C."C" Company.
4. O.C."D" Company.
5. Quartermaster.
6. Signalling Officer.
7. Transport Officer.
8. "G" 49th Division.   For
9. 146th Infantry Brigade.   Information.
10. 147th   do
11. 148th   do
12. War Diary.
13.   do
14. Retained.
15.   do

SECRET.

Copy No. 12.

49th Battalion Machine Gun Corps.
* OPERATION ORDER NO 54. *

Friday, 12.7.18.

1. "C" Company will relieve "A" Company in the RIGHT Sector on the night of 14th/15th July 1918.

2. "D" Company will relieve "C" Company in Support on 14th July 1918. Relief to be complete by 12 noon.

3. "A" Company, on completion of relief by "C" Company will be held in Reserve in the Camp now occupied by "D" Company.

4. Mutual arrangements for relief will be made by O.C. Companies concerned.
O.C. Relieving Companies will visit O.C. Companies to be relieved on the day before relief, and take over all work in hand.

5. NO CONCENTRATION OF TROOPS IN YPRES will be allowed. Attention is drawn to this Office letter S.T. 301/23 dated 7.6.18. The largest party to be kept together will be one SUB - SECTION

6. Handing over lists (one copy only required) will be forwarded to reach this Office not later than 24 hours after completion of relief.

7. O.C. "D" Company will detail a party of 1 senior N.C.O. and 8 men to remain in his present Camp until it has been taken over by "A" Company.

8. Reference 1 & 2 above, after relief by "D" Company, "C" Company will remain in the vicinity of VLAMERTINGHE CHATEAU until moving to relieve "A" Company.

9. Sections of "A" Company will march to Reserve Camp on relief under arrangements to be made by O.C. Company.

10. Completion of reliefs will be wired to this Office using code words as under :-

    "C" Company relieves "A" Company,   "DAHLIA"
    "D"   "   "   "C"   "   "FUCHSIA"
    "A"   "   "   "D"   "   "PINK"

11. ACKNOWLEDGE   (A.B.C & D Companies only)

Issued at 3.45 p.m.

Capt. & Adjt.
49th Battn. M.G.C.

-Over-

Copies to :-

1. O.C. "A" Company.
2. O.C. "B" Company.
3. O.C. "C" Company.
4. O.C. "D" Company.
5. Quartermaster.
6. Signalling Officer.
7. Transport Officer.
8. "G" 49th Division.
9. 146th Infantry Brigade.
10. 147th   do
11. 148th   do
12. War Diary.
13.   do
14. Retained.
15.   do

For information.

SECRET.   49th Battalion Machine Gun Corps
                          * OPERATION ORDER NO. 56. *

1.   Operation Order No.55 is cancelled.

2.   The following attachments of American Machine Gun Companies
        of the 114 (American) M.G.Battalion will take place:

3.   "D" (American) Machine Gun Company will take up positions
        in the YELLOW LINE as shown on Map "A" (attached) on 13th
        instant.
        O.C. Reserve (British) M.G.Company ("A" Coy) will be
        responsible for guiding the above Company into the position
        shown on Map "A".
        O.C. American Company will Rendezvous at Reserve (British)
        M.G. Company at Sheet 28, A.29.b.5.8, at 1.0 p.m. 13th instant.
        First American Platoon will arrive at A.29.b.5.8. at 1.0 p.m.
        Remainder American Platoons will follow at 100 yards
        interval.
        "D" (American) M.G.Company Headquarters will also be at
        A.29.b.5.8.
        American Rear Transport will [illegible] be at present
        (TURTLES CAMP)

4.   "C" (American) M.G.Company will take up positions as shown
        on attached Map "B" on 13th instant.
        O.C. Support (British) M.G.Company ("B" Company) will be
        responsible for guiding the above Company into positions.
        O.C. American M.G. Company will Rendezvous at Support
        (British) M.G. Company H.Q. Sheet 28, H.E.b.5.6. at 1.0 p.m.
        First American Platoon will arrive at H.E.b.5.6. at 1.0 p.m.
        Remaining platoons will follow at 100 yards intervals.
        "C" (American) Company Headquarters will also be at H.E.b.5.6.
        American Rear Transport will remain as at present
        (TURTLES CAMP).

5.   One Other Rank (British) will be attached to each American
        Unit. British Companies responsible for detailing.
        American Companies to supply:
        Two Enlisted men (Americans) will be attached to each
        British Gun of the British Companies responsible for
        attaching American Company into positions.
        This amount to 5 & 6 there.

6.   [illegible]

        "D" (American) M.G.Company.

        (a) 2 American Machine Guns [illegible] in
        LEFT Sector as shown on Map [illegible]

        (b) 2 American Machine Guns [illegible] in
        Follows :-

                              Sheet 28.

        1. Gun KAATS   A.[illegible]
        1. Gun BUNKER TRAS.
        1. Gun CHARLIE FARM.
        1. Gun   [illegible]
        1. Gun   [illegible]
        1. Gun   [illegible]
        1. Gun   [illegible]

(c) O.C.LEFT Sector (British) M.G.Company ("B" Company) will be responsible for guiding American Guns into position.

(d) O.C.LEFT Sector M.G.Company will detail Guides to be at DEAD END (I.2.c.15.85.)(Sheet 28) at 9-0 p.m. to conduct American Guns into position.

(e) O.C."B" (American) M.G.Company will arrive at DEAD END at 9-0 p.m. with first American Platoon. Remaining American Platoons will arrive at 5 minute intervals.

7.   RIGHT FORWARD SECTOR.

"A" (American) M.G.Company.

(a)   American Machine Guns will be placed in position in RIGHT SECTOR as shown on attached Map "B".

(b)   American Machine Guns will be placed in position as follows :-

Sheet 28.

2 guns on Island I.7.15.0.
1. Gun   LILLE GATE.
1. Gun   I.14.c.8.8.
1. Gun   PINK CHATEAU I.9.d.4.2.
1. Gun   I.15.a.   1.5.
1. Gun   I.11.d.8.4.
1. Gun   I.14.b.2.0.

(c) O.C.RIGHT SECTOR (British) M.G.Company ("C" Company) will be responsible for guiding American Guns into position.

(d) O.C.RIGHT SECTOR M.G.Company will detail Guides to be at DEAD END (I.3.c.15.65.) (Sheet 28) at 9-30 p.m. to conduct American Guns into position.

(e) O.C."A" (American) M.G.Company will arrive at DEAD END with first American Platoon at 9-30 p.m. Remaining platoons will arrive at 5 minute intervals.

8.   Other Rank (British) will be attached to each American Gun from British Company of the Sector.
Six (6) picked men (American) will be attached to each British Gun in the Company of the Sector.
Guides for these picked men will be at DEAD END as follow:-

LEFT SECTOR   9-25 p.m.

RIGHT SECTOR   9-50 p.m.

O.C.American M.G.Company will ensure that men to be attached to each other Unit leave there time.

9.   Rear Transport Lines of American Companies mentioned in 7 & 8 above will remain at present Camp (WINIFRED CAMP).

10. Each American Gun will take men filled belts in belt Boxes into the line.

Over.

11.   The Signalling Officer will arrange Guides for each Company
        in conjunction with O.C. 114th (American) M.G.Battalion
        subject to... instructions.

12.   SECRECY MUST ON NO ACCOUNT BE LOST SIGHT OF. (This includes
        all maps.)

        The largest number to be kept together at one time will be
        one American Platoon (2 guns & teams) and British Guides.
        This order is to be strictly enforced and all Officers and
        Non - Commissioned Officers are to be made acquainted with
        this.

13.   American personnel will take 24 hours rations and the L.E.
        in addition to the uncooked portion of the days Rations.

14.   Orders for Relief will be issued later to all concerned.

15.   ACKNOWLEDGE. (American M.G.Battalion and British M.G.
        Companies only.)

16.   Headquarters of "C" and American Companies will be at the
        Company Headquarters of British Companies in RIGHT & LEFT
        Sectors respectively.

                                                    Capt. & Adjt.
                                              49th Battn. M.G.C.

Issued at...........

Copies to :-

        1. O.C."A" Company.
        2. O.C."B" Company.
        3. O.C."C" Company.
        4. O.C."D" Company.
        5. Signalling Officer.
        6. 114th (American) M.G.Batt: Hqrs: (3 Copies)
        7. 45th (British Division) "Q".
        8. 59th (American) Divisional Machine Gun Officer.
        9. 146th (British) Infantry Brigade.
       10. 147th   do   do
       11. 148th   do   do
       12. 59th (American) Infantry Brigade.
       13. War Diary.
       14. War Diary.
       15. Retained. (Adjt)
       16. Retained. (File)
       17. Retained. (File)

49th Battalion Machine Gun Corps.
OPERATION ORDERS NO. 37

Thursday, 18.7.18

1. "D" Company will relieve "B" Company in the LEFT SECTOR on the night 22nd/23rd July 1918.

2. "A" Company will relieve "C" Company in Support on the 22nd July 1918. Relief to be complete by 12 noon.

3. "B" Company, on completion of relief by "D" Company will be held in Reserve in the camp now occupied by "A" Company.

4. Mutual arrangements for relief will be made by O.C.Companies concerned.
O.C.Relieving Companies will visit O.C.Companies to be relieved on the day before a relief and take over all work in hand.

5. NO CONCENTRATION OF TROOPS IN TREES will be allowed. Attention is drawn to this office letter S.M. 501/22 dated 7.6.18.
The largest party to be kept together will be one SUB - SECTION.

6. Handing over lists (one copy only required) will be forwarded to reach this office not later than 24 hours after completion of relief.

7. O.C."A" Company will detail a party of 1 senior N.C.O. and 5 men to remain in his present camp until it has been taken over by "B" Company.

8. References 1 & 2 above, after relief by "A" Company, "D" Company will remain in the vicinity of CLAREMONT CHATEAU until moving to relieve "B" Company.

9. Sections of "D" Company will march to Reserve Camp on relief under arrangements to be made by O.C.Company.

10. American personnel attached to American Gun Teams will be relieved and replaced by relieving Company.
American personnel attached to British Gun Teams will remain at the gun position to which they are attached.

11. Completion of reliefs will be wired to this office in code words as under:-

"D" Company relieves "B" Company   "............"
"A"   "   "   "C"   "   "............"
"B"   "   "   "A"   "   "............"

12. ACKNOWLEDGE (A,B,C and D Companies only.)

D.Hudson Jones/
49th Battalion M.G.C.

SECRET.

Copy No. 17.

49th Battalion Machine Gun Corps.
OPERATION ORDER NO. 53.

Harabat. 26.7.18.

1. Inter Company Reliefs of American Machine Gun Companies will be carried out on 27th and night 27th/28th instant in accordance with relief chart issued to all concerned.

2. Orders for relief will be issued by 114th American Machine Gun Battalion for the whole of the relief (to include 117th and 118th Regimental Machine Gun Companies). They should be drawn up on similar lines to Operation Order No. 36. of 49th (British) Bn. M.G.C. of

3. Attachments of British Machine Gunners to American Machine Gun Companies will remain as already laid down.

4. Special attention of O.C. American Companies should be directed to points raised during last relief.

5. Copies of Operation Orders issued by 114th American Machine Gun Battalion should be sent to A.A. & A. Companies 49th Bn. Machine Gun Corps (British) and Headquarters 49th Battn. Machine Gun Corps (British) for information, in addition to those normally issued.

6. O.C. British Companies will assist relief in every possible way.

ACKNOWLEDGE.

Capt. & Adjt.
49th Battn. M.G.C.

Issued at... 12.30 p.m.

Copies to :-

1. O.C. "A" Company.
2. O.C. "B" Company.
3. O.C. "C" Company.
4. O.C. "D" Company.
5. 114th American M.G.Bn.
6. "A" Coy.   "
7. "B" Coy.   "
8. "C" Coy.   "
9. "D" Coy.   "
10. "G" 49th Division. (British)
11. D.A.C.G. 30th American Division.
12. 59th American Brigade.
13. 146th Infantry Brigade. (British)
14. 147th   do   do
15. 148th   do   do
16. War Diary.
17. War Diary. ✓
18. Retained. (Adjt).
19. Retained. (File).
20. Retained. (File).

SECRET   49th Battalion Machine Gun Corps.   Copy No. 13
                         OPERATION ORDER NO. 59.
                      ----------------oOo--------------

                                                        Friday, 26.7.18.

1.   "A" Company will relieve "C" Company in the RIGHT Sector on
      the night 30/31st July 1918.

2.   "B" Company will relieve "A" Company in Support on the 30th
      July 1918. Relief to be complete by 12 noon.

3.   "C" Company, on completion of relief by "A" Company will be
      held in Reserve in the Camp now occupied by "B" Company.

4.   Mutual arrangements for relief will be made by O.C.Companies
      concerned.
      O.C.Relieving Companies will visit O.C.Companies to be relieved
      on the day before relief, and take over all work in hand.

5.   NO CONCENTRATION OF TROOPS IN YPRES will be allowed. Attention
      is drawn to this Office letter S.T. 301/23 dated 7.6.18.
      The largest party to be kept together will be one SUB-SECTION.

6.   Handing over lists (one copy only required) will be forwarded
      to reach this Office not later than 24 hours after completion
      of relief.

7.   O.C."B" Company will detail a party of 1 senior N.C.O. and
      8 men to remain in his present Camp until it has been taken
      over by "C" Company.

8.   Reference 1 & 2 above, after relief by "B" Company, "A" Company
      will remain in the vicinity of VLAMERTINGHE CHATEAU until
      moving to relieve "C" Company.

9.   Sections of "C" Company will march to Reserve Camp on relief
      under arrangements to be made by O.C.Company.

10.   British personnel attached to American Gun Teams will be
      relieved and replaced by relieving Company.

11.   Completion of relief will be wired to this Office using code
      words as under :-

         "A" COMPANY relieves "C" COMPANY.   "ASTON"
         "B"   "   "   "A"   "   "ALNWICK"
         "C"   "   "   "B"   "   "ALLOA"

12.   ACKNOWLEDGE   (A.B.C.&.D. COMPANIES only)

                                                Capt. & Adjt.
                                                49th Battn. M.G.C.

Issued at..................

                                                          -Over-

-2-

Copies to :-

1. O.C. "A" Company.
2. O.C. "B" Company.
3. O.C. "C" Company.
4. O.C. "D" Company.
5. Quartermaster.
6. Signalling Officer.
7. Transport Officer.
8. "G" 49th Division.
9. 146th Infantry Brigade.
10. 147th   do
11. 148th   do
12. 116th M.G.Battalion (American)
13. War Diary.
14. War Diary.
15. Retained.
16. Retained.

For information.

Original

War Diary.

49th Battn. M.G.C.

From 1.8.18. – 31.8.18.

Vol. 6.

49th Battn. M.G.C.

WAR DIARY
or
INTELLIGENCE SUMMARY.

Army Form C. 2118.

Sheet 1.

(Erase heading not required.)

Place	Date	Hour	Summary of Events and Information	Remarks and references to Appendices
	1.8.18.		Vicinity of ECOLE shelled during the evening. 2000 rounds fired in harassing fire. Casualties 1. O.R. wounded ("A" Coy). Lt. J.R. HANDFORD joined Battn. as a reinforcement and 2/Lt. B. THOMPSON rejoined from Base.	
	2.8.18.		Quiet day on whole front. Lt. J.W.D. ACTON joined the Battn. as a reinforcement. Casualties NIL.	
	3.8.18.		Section H.Q. in VLAMERTINGHE demolished. Considerable shelling of rear areas. Casualties 1. O.R. wounded (remained at duty) 4000. rounds fired on to T.5.a.80.69 & T.5.a.58.85.	
	4.8.18.		Area round ZILLEBEKE LAKE shelled during the evening. Activity much quieter on back areas 9500 rounds fired in harassing fire on to T.23.c.15.55. T.23.a.23.54. and on CAVALRY ROAD. This was put down in reply to heavy German harassing M.G. fire. Casualties NIL.	
	5.8.18.		Nothing to report. Casualties NIL.	
	6.8.18.		Vicinity of WARRINGTON ROAD and BARRACKS YPRES shelled during	

WAR DIARY
or
INTELLIGENCE SUMMARY.
(Erase heading not required.)

Army Form C. 2118.

Sheet 2.

Place	Date	Hour	Summary of Events and Information	Remarks and references to Appendices
	6.8.18.		The morning practically no shelling of back areas. Vicinity of VLAMERTINGHE bombed by hostile aeroplanes. 1000 rounds fired on harassing fire on to I.5.c. I.5.a. & T.17.c. Casualties NIL.	
	7.8.18.		"B" Coy relieved "D" Coy in the Left sector. "D" Coy come out into reserve. "C" Coy move from reserve to Support, all in accordance with Operation Order No. 60.	O.O.60.
	8.8.18.		Quiet day. 5,000 rounds fired on harassing fire on to MENIN ROAD and I.23.c. 10.55. Casualties NIL. A/C.S.M. BETHEL. V. joined the Batln. as L and B. Instructor.	
	9.8.18.		Light shelling of the Front line on our right during the day. Hostile artillery quiet on Left sector. 6,500 rounds fired on to I.11.a. and c. I.5.a. T.17.c. 3 Sgts. and 13 O.R. join the Batln. as reinforcements.	
	10.8.18.		2,000 rounds fired on MENIN ROAD. Casualties NIL.	
	11.8.18.		Enemy artillery very quiet throughout the day. 4,500 rounds fired in harassing fire. Casualties NIL.	

Army Form C. 2118.

Sheet 3.

WAR DIARY
or
INTELLIGENCE SUMMARY.
(Erase heading not required.)

Place	Date	Hour	Summary of Events and Information	Remarks and references to Appendices
	12.8.18.		3,000 rounds fired in harassing fire on to I.17.a. I.17.c. and I.23.c. Casualties Nil.	
	13.8.18.		More shelling of back areas than usual. YPRES received attention throughout the day. 1,500 rounds fired on to I.17.c.60.25. and I.22.b.80.40. Casualties Nil. 2/Lt. D.T. JONES appointed 2nd in Command of "B" Coy. and assumed acting rank of Captain.	
	14.8.18.		7,250 rounds fired in harassing fire on to I.11.b. I.5.d. I.5.a. Casualties Nil.	
	15.8.18.		"C" Coy relieve "A" Coy. in the Right sector. "D" Coy relieve "C" Coy. in Support and "B" Coy. come out into reserve. 6000 rounds fired 0.0.61. in harassing fire on to I.5.b.2.0. and I.11.b. 57.90.	
	16.8.18.		Very quiet day in forward area. 6,250 rounds fired in harassing fire on to I.5.a. 80.20. and I.5.6.20.23. Information received that the Batt: will be relieved by the 34th Batt: M.G. Corps. about the 20th August. Vide Warning Order. Casualties Nil.	
	17.8.18.		Enemy artillery more active than usual in the back areas	

Army Form C. 2118.

Sheet 4.

WAR DIARY
or
INTELLIGENCE SUMMARY.
(Erase heading not required.)

Place	Date	Hour	Summary of Events and Information	Remarks and references to Appendices
	17.8.18.		about VLAMERTINGHE CH^T and KRUISSTRAAT. 6,750 rounds were fired on to various targets throughout the night. Casualties Nil.	
	18.8.18.			O.O. 62
	19.8.18.		"B" Coy. 49th Batt^n. M.G.C. is relieved in the Left Forward Sector by a Coy. of the 34th Batt^n. M.G.C. On relief they proceed to "P" Camp. 28/R.15.c.	O.O. 63
			"A" Coy. & "D" Coy. 49th Batt^n. M.G.C. are relieved by two Coys. 34th Bn. M.G.C. in the Support and Reserve Sectors. During the night Aug 20/21 "C" Coy. in the Right Forward Sector are relieved by a Coy. of the 34th Batt^n. M.G.Coys. All 49th Batt^n. M.G.Coys. assemble in "P" Camp with the exception of "A" Coy. who stay at their reserve billets.	
	20.8.18		"A" and "B" Coys. (less transport) move from Reserve & "P" Camp to HERZEELE by march route, & come under the 146th Inf. Bde. Group for purposes of the march down to the rest area. In accordance	

Army Form C. 2118.

WAR DIARY
or
INTELLIGENCE SUMMARY.

(Erase heading not required.)

Sheet 5.

Place	Date	Hour	Summary of Events and Information	Remarks and references to Appendices
	20.8.18.		with O.O. No. 63. H.Q. Transport to RIQUES area by road, staying at LEDERZEELE.	O.O.63.
	21.8.18.		Batln. H.Q. (less transport) move to RIQUES by train from PROVEN. Transport of "A" and "B" Coys. from HERZEELE to LEDERZEELE. "C" and "D" Coys. with transport remain at "P" Camp.	O.O.64. O.O.65.
	22.8.18.		Personnel & Transport of "A" and "B" Coys. arrive PICQUES; Personnel entraining at REXPOEDE and detraining at NORDKERQUE. Transport of "C" and "D" Coys. leave "P" Camp for the WORMHOUDT area. Notification received that the Batln. will move to BONNIQUES area on concentrating in RIQUES area. "C" and "D" Coys. arrive in ZUTKERQUE and come under order of 49th M.G. Bn. Location on 23rd as under:-	
	23.8.18.		Batln. H.Q. and "A" and "B" Coy. RECQUES. "C" and "D" Coy. ZUTKERQUE. Transport of "A" and "B" Coys. arrive RECQUES.	
	24.8.18.		The whole Batln. (less transport of "C" and "D" Coys move from	

Army Form C. 2118.

WAR DIARY
or
INTELLIGENCE SUMMARY.
(Erase heading not required.)

Sheet 6.

Place	Date	Hour	Summary of Events and Information	Remarks and references to Appendices
	24.8.18.		RICQUES area to BONNINGUES in accordance with O.O. No. 66. "C" and "D" Coys. transport rejoin the Batln.	O.O. 66.
	25.8.18.		Command of the Batln. passes to Major W.J.M. SPROULLE during absence on leave of Lt. Col. B.H. BADHAM. Church Parade at BONNINGUES.	
	26.8.18.		Orders received that the Batln. will move to another area. Transport of "C" and "D" Coys. and transport of "A" and "B" Coys. (fighting limbers excepted) move to HELFAUT, staying there for the night. Consequent moves by Brigade Groups.	
	27.8.18.		Battalion in training at BONNINGUES.	
	28.8.18.		Batln. moves to entrain at NORDKERQUE and AUDRUIC as under:- "B" and "D" Coys. with 147th Infy. Bde. from NORDKERQUE. "A" and "C" Coys. with 146th Infy. Bde. from AUDRUIC. "A" and "B" Coys. take their fighting limbers with them.	O.O. 67.
	29.8.18.		"B" and "D" Coys. arrive at WAVRANS near ST. POL. about 2.30 a.m. and proceed to HÉRICOURT. H.Q. "A" and "C" Coys. arrive BRYAS about 5.30 a.m. and proceed to ROELLECOURT and ST. MICHEL.	
	30.8.18.		Day spent in cleaning up kit &c.	

Army Form C. 2118.

Sheet 7.

WAR DIARY
or
INTELLIGENCE SUMMARY.
(Erase heading not required.)

Place	Date	Hour	Summary of Events and Information	Remarks and references to Appendices
	31.8.18.		Orders received at 10.0.a.m. warning all Units to be ready to move at 2 hours notice. At 4.0.p.m. orders were received to move to ST. ELOY area by tactical trains on Sept 1st.	

W H Spindler ?
Commanding 49th Bttn. M.G.C.

SECRET.

49th Battalion Machine Gun Corps.
OPERATION ORDER NO 60.-

Copy No. 13

Saturday 3.8.18.

1. "B" Company will relieve "D" Company in the LEFT Sector on the night 7th/8th August 1918.

2. "C" Company will relieve "B" Company in Support on the 7th August 1918. Relief to be complete by 12 noon.

3. "D" Company, on completion of relief by "B" Company will be held in Reserve in the camp now occupied by "C" Company.

4. Mutual arrangements for relief will be made by O.C. Companies concerned.
O.C. Relieving Companies will visit O.C. Companies to be relieved on the day before relief, and take over all work in hand.

5. NO CONCENTRATION OF TROOPS IN YPRES will be allowed. Attention is drawn to this Office letter S.T. 301/23 dated 7.8.18. The largest party to be kept together will be one SUB-SECTION.

6. Handing over lists (one copy only required) will be forwarded to reach this Office not later than 24 hours after completion of relief.

7. O.C. "C" Company will detail a party of 1 senior N.C.O. and 8 men to remain in his present Camp until it has been taken over by "D" Company.

8. Reference 1 & 2 above, after relief by "C" Company, "B" Company will remain in the vicinity of VLAMERTINGHE CHATEAU until moving to relieve "D" Company.

9. Sections of "D" Company will march to Reserve Camp on relief under arrangements to be made by O.C. Company.

10. British personnel attached to American Gun Teams will be relieved and replaced by relieving Company.

11. Completion of relief will be wired to this Office using code words as under :-

"B" COMPANY relieves "D" COMPANY   "BERWICK"
"C"   "   "   "B"   "   "BELFAST"
"D"   "   "   "C"   "   "BURNLEY"

12. ACKNOWLEDGE. (A.D.C.& B. COMPANIES only)

Issued at... 4-30 pm

D Tudor Jones 2/Lt A/Adjt.
49th Battn. M.G.C.

Copies to :-

1. O.C. "A" Company.
2. O.C. "B" Company.
3. O.C. "C" Company.
4. O.C. "D" Company.
5. Quartermaster.
6. Signalling Officer.
7. Transport Officer.
8. "G" 49th Division.
9. 146th Infantry Brigade.
10. 147th   do
11. 148th   do
12. 114th M.G.Battalion (American)
13. War Diary.
14. War Diary.
15. Retained.
16. Retained.

For Information.

SECRET.

49th Battalion Machine Gun Corps.

OPERATION ORDER NO. 61.

---oOo---

Copy No. 4

Sunday 11.8.18.

1. "C" Company will relieve "A" Company in the RIGHT Sector on the night 15th/16th August 1918.

2. "D" Company will relieve "C" Company in Support on the 15th August 1918. Relief to be complete by 12 noon.

3. "A" Company, on completion of relief by "C" Company will be held in Reserve in the Camp now occupied by "D" Company.

4. Mutual arrangements for relief will be made by O.C.Companies concerned.
O.C. Relieving Companies will visit O.C.Companies to be relieved on the day before relief, and take over all work in hand.

5. NO CONCENTRATION OF TROOPS IN YPRES will be allowed. Attention is drawn to this Office letter S.T. 301/23 dated 7.6.18.
The largest party to be kept together will be one SUB-SECTION.

6. Handing over lists (one copy only required) will be forwarded to reach this Office not later than 24 hours after completion of relief.

7. O.C."D" Company will detail a party of 1 senior N.C.O. and 8 men to remain in his present Camp until it has been taken over by "A" Company.

8. Reference 1 & 2 above, after relief by "D" Company, "C" Company will remain in the vicinity of VLAMERTINGHE CHATEAU until moving to relieve "A" Company.

9. Sections of "A" Company will march to Reserve Camp on relief under arrangements to be made by O.C.Company.

10. Completion of relief will be wired to this Office using code words as under :-

    "C" COMPANY relieves "A" COMPANY   "CHESTER"
    "D"   "   "   "C"   "   "CARLISLE"
    "A"   "   "   "D"   "   "CAMBS"

11. ACKNOWLEDGE (A. B.C. & D COMPANIES only).

Issued at 7.30 p.m.

2/Lt A/Adjt.
49th Battn. M.G.C.

P.T.O.

Copies to :-

1. O.C. "A" Company.
2. O.C. "B" Company.
3. O.C. "C" Company.
4. O.C. "D" Company.
5. Quartermaster.
6. Signalling Officer.
7. Transport Officer.
8. "G" 49th Division.
9. 146th Infantry Brigade.
10. 147th   do
11. 148th   do
12. ~~114th M.G.Battalion. (American)~~
13. War Diary.
14. War Diary.
15. Retained.
16. Retained.

For information.

SECRET.

--- WARNING ORDER ---

Friday 16.8.18.

1. The LEFT Sector Company will be relieved by a Company of another Unit on the night of the 19th/20th instant.

2. If possible arrangements will be made by this Office to relieve the ZILLEBEKE LAKE Gun at the same time as the RIGHT Sector Company.

3. The RIGHT Sector Company will be relieved by a Company of another Unit on the night of 20th/21st instant.

4. The Reserve and Support Companies will be relieved on day of 20th instant.

5. The present arrangements are that all Companies on relief shall proceed to "P" Camp. This will be confirmed.

6. All Kits of Officers not at present in the line will be reduced to a maximum of 50 lbs at once.
Officers in the line will reduce their Kits to as near 50 lbs as practicable.

7. ACKNOWLEDGE.

Capt. & Adjt.
49th Battn. M.G.C.

Copies to :-

    O.C. "A" Company.)
    O.C. "B" Company.) Advanced and Rear.
    O.C. "C" Company.)
    O.C. "D" Company.)
    President Regimental Institute. ✓
    Quartermaster.
    Signalling Officer.
    Transport Officer.
    File.

SECRET.

---WARNING ORDER---

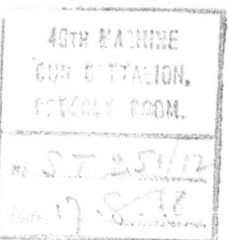

Saturday 17.8.18.

Reference Warning Order issued under this Office S.T. 251/11 dated 16.8.18.

The following are probable dates of leaving this area :-

1. "A" Company and "B" Company will march with 146th Infantry Brigade taking with them 1 Water Cart, 1 Travelling Kitchen and 1 Baggage supply waggon on 22nd instant.

2. "C" Company and "D" Company will march with 147th Infantry Brigade from PROVEN area on 23rd instant with same transport as in 1 above.

3. The Transport enumerated in 1 above is for two Companies and NOT per Company.
The supply waggon is for the purpose of taking Officers Kit; this Kit will be cut down to necessaries for two days.
A small amount of moss kit may be taken by each Company, but the total weight of baggage from each Company must not exceed 15 cwt.

4. The unconsumed portion of the days rations will be carried on the man.

5. O.C. Companies will make mutual arrangements on arriving at "Staging" Camp with regard to using the water cart and Travelling Kitchen.

6. All Officers Kits (except that allowed to be taken by para. 3.) will be handed in to the Camp Commandant at a place to be specified later, and will be sent forward by motor lorry.

7. Rations for consumption on day after arrival at Staging Camp will be waiting at the Staging Camp on arrival of Company.

8. Transport of "A" and "B" Companies will move on 21st, and of "C" and "D" Companies on 22nd instant.

9. Battalion Headquarters will probably move on 21st instant.

10. Definite orders will be issued as early as possible.

M Bates
Capt. & Adjt.
49th Battn. M.G.C.

Copies to :-

    O.C. "A" Company.)
    O.C. "B" Company.) Advanced & Rear.
    O.C. "C" Company.)
    O.C. "D" Company.)
    President Regtl. Institute.
    Transport Officer.
    Quartermaster.
    Signalling Officer.

SECRET.   Copy No... 13

49th Battalion Machine Gun Corps.
-OPERATION ORDER NO.62.-

Saturday. 17.8.18.

1. Battalion Headquarters and Companies will move to RECQUES area according to the attached march tables. On completion of move the Battalion will be concentrated in the RECQUES area.

2. For the move, Companies will accompany Brigade Groupes as follows :-

   146th Infantry Brigade Group.

   "A" COMPANY and "B" COMPANY

   147th Infantry Brigade Group.

   "C" COMPANY and "D" COMPANY.

3. Battalion Headquarters will move with Divisional H.Q. Group.

4. Transport will move by road, except transport which will be detailed in Entraining Instructions to be issued later.

5. The following Officers will be in charge of Transport of the respective Infantry Brigade Groups.

   146th Inf. Brigade Group.   :   Lt. J.R.HANDFORD.
   147th   do   do   :   2/Lt. J.E.GALL.

6. All traffic rules will be observed and correct distances kept on the march. Strict march discipline will be maintained.

7. "A" Company will pass starting point (A.21.a.8.6.) (Railway Crossing) at 4-10 p.m. on 20th instant. "B" Company will follow "A" Company at the correct distance.

8. On arrival at HERZEELE O.C."A" and "B" Companies will report to the Staff Captain 146th Infantry Brigade for billets, and will join the Brigade Group. *An officer will be sent in advance to arrange billets with Staff Capt 146 Infy. Bde gp.*

9. All other necessary orders for marches and entraining will be issued direct to Companies by their respective Brigade Group.

10. NO man will be allowed to fall out without written permission from an Officer. This permission will be granted very sparingly.

11. ACKNOWLEDGE.

                                                    W Bates.
                                                    Capt. & Adjt,
   Issued at. 11.55/am.   49th Battn. M.G.C.

   Copies to :-
            1. O.C. "A" Company.   10. 49th Divn. "G"
            2. O.C. "B" Company.   11. 49th Divn. "Q"
            3. O.C. "C" Company.   12. War Diary.
            4. O.C. "D" Company.   13. War Diary. ✓
            5. Transport Officer.   14. Retained.
            6. Signalling Officer.   15. Retained.
            7. Quartermaster.   16. Retained.
            8. 146th Inf. Brigade.
            9. 147th   do

                                                    P.T.O.

ADMINISTRATIVE INSTRUCTIONS TO ACCOMPANY
OPERATION ORDER No.62.
----------------------oOo--------------------

[Stamp: 49TH MACHINE GUN BATTALION, ORDERLY ROOM. No. ST 351/15 Date 18.8.18]

12

Sunday 18.8.18.

1. "A" and "B" Companies will come under 146th Infantry Brigade Group on reaching HERZEELE 20th instant.
"C" and "D" Companies will come under 147th Brigade Group at midnight 22nd/23rd instant.

2. The following personnel will accompany transport on March Routes and will not be exceeded.

    Per Infantry Brigade Group. :

    1. Officer.
    1st COMPANY.
    1. C.Q.M.S.
    1. Transport Sgt.
    24. Drivers.
    1. O.R. per Vehicle on Company establishment to act as brakesman = 14.
       (composed of 13 limbers G.S, 1 Kitchen.)
    6. Grooms.
    1. A.S.C. Driver with baggage waggon and 1 loader.

    2nd COMPANY.
    1. C.Q.M.S.
    1. Transport Sgt.
    22. Drivers.
    1. O.R. per Vehicle to act as brakesman = 13.
       (composed of 13 limbers.)
    6. Grooms.
    1. Shoeing Smith.
    1. Saddler.
    1. *Driver & brakesman for travelling kitchen*
    ~~146th Brigade Group only 1 A.S.C. Driver with Baggage waggon and 1 loader.~~

    TOTALS : 146th Infantry Brigade Group. 1. Officer. 89 O.Rs.
             147th   do   do   1. Officer. 89 O.Rs.

    ~~The Driver of the Travelling Kitchen belonging to the second Company will travel by train with Horses and Kitchen.~~

3. Kits of Officers of "A" and "B" Companies (146th Infantry Brigade Group) will be carried on limbers.
Kits of Officers of "C" and "D" Companies (less necessaries for two days) will be dumped at a place to be notified later, and will be conveyed to destination by lorry. *LA LOVIE by 6 pm on 20th inst*

4. All returns, including daily detail of casualties, will be suspended from 12 noon 20th instant until 9-0 a.m. 25th instant. Companies will render a consolidated detail of casualties for period 12 noon 20th instant to 12 noon 25th instant by 2-0 p.m. on 25th instant.
Ordinary returns will recommence at 9-0 a.m. 25th instant.
Any returns urgently required will be wired for.

5. 1. Water Cart will accompany "A" Company and also "C" Company. This Water Cart will be carried by train.

10. Transport and personnel from present rear Company Headquarters will join Companies as follows :

    "A" Company in Reserve Camp. As early as possible on 19th instant.
    "B" Company, "C" Company, and "D" Company will proceed to "P" Camp on 19th instant and await arrival of Companies from line.
    P.T.O.

-2-

Headquarters Transport will remain in present Camp.

7. All personnel temporarily employed on Battalion Headquarters (except Officers servants and 2 Canteen personnel) will be returned to Companies on 18th instant by 6-0 p.m. under orders to be issued by Quartermaster and Regimental Sergeant Major. Personnel will resume temporary employ if necessary on 25th instant or as soon after as possible.

8. The following personnel will accompany Battalion H.Q. Transport and will not be exceeded:

    2. Storemen.
    1. Transport Cpl. (L/Sgt).
    5. Grooms.
    12. Drivers (includes 2 A.S.C.).
    4. Brakesmen.
    1. Canteen Representative.

All other Battalion H.Q. personnel except Medical Officer will proceed by train.

9. The Medical Officer will accompany "A" and "B" Companies throughout the move, and will be attached to "B" Company.

10. Limited powers of O.C. Detachment are granted to the Senior Officer of the two Companies in each Brigade Group, and are limited to the award of

    7 days Field Punishment No.1.

    146th Infantry Brigade Group.   :   Major. H.D. HANSON
    147th   do   do   :   Major. H.S. BOXER.

All cases warranting a more severe sentence than the above will be remanded daily and brought before the Commanding Officer on reassembling.

M. Bates.
Capt. & Adjt.
49th Battn. M.G.C.

Issued at 11-30 am

Copies to all recipients of Operation Order No.62 and to Divisional Train and R.S.M.

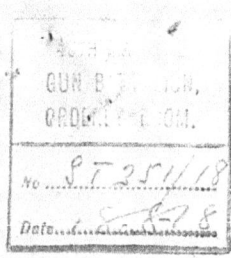

AMENDMENT No.1. TO ADMINISTRATIVE INSTRUCTIONS
TO ACCOMPANY OPERATION ORDER NO.62.

Sunday 18.8.18.

1. Para.2. Delete lines 23 and 24. Only one A.S.C. G.S. Waggon will now proceed with 146th Infantry Brigade Group.

    ADD: under 2nd Company.

      1. Driver and 1 Brakeman for Travelling Kitchen.

    Delete from "The Driver of Second Kitchen" to end of para.

2. Para.3.

    Officers Kit of "C" and "D" Companies will be dumped at Battalion Headquarters LA LOVIE by 6-0 p.m. on 20th instant.

3. Para.8.

    For 11 Drivers read 12 (includes 3 A.S.C.)
    For 3 Brakesmen read 4 Brakesmen.

4. Copies of 49th Division Administrative Instructions Nos. 14 & 15 are attached for A.B.C. and D. Companies.

5. The Battalion Chiropodist will proceed with 146th Infantry Brigade Group and will be attached to "A" Company on 19th instant.
    Regimental Sergeant Major will arrange.

Issued at. 10-45 pm

Capt. & Adjt.
49th Battn. M.G.C.

Copies to all recipients of Administrative Instructions
to accompany Operation Order No.62. Companies Advanced & Rear.

TABLE "A".   146th Infantry Brigade.

Date.	Serial No.	COMPANY.	From.	To	Remarks.
Aug.20th.	1.	"A" Company.	Reserve.	HERZEELE.	On relief by Company of 34th Bn., M.G.C. by Route March.
	2.	"B" Company.	"P" Camp.	HERZEELE.	By Route March.
Aug.22nd.	3.	"A" Company. "B" "	HERZEELE Area	RECQUES Area.	By Train REXPOEDE to NORTKERQUE.
Aug. 23rd.	4.	"A" Company. "B" "	RECQUES Area.	TOURNEHEM Area.	March Route.

TABLE "B"   147th Infantry Brigade.

Aug.23rd.	5.	"C" Company. "D" "	"P" Camp. "P" Camp.	RECQUES Area.	By Train PROVEN to NORTKERQUE.

TABLE "C"   Transport of 146th Infantry Brigade.

Aug.21st.	6.	"A" Company. "B" "	HERZEELE Area.	LEDERZEELE Area.	Route: NORMHOUDT - RUBROUCK.
Aug. 22nd.	7.	"A" " "B" "	LEDERZEELE Area.	RECQUES Area.	Route: WATTEN- BAYENGHEM - and join respective Coys.

P.T.O.

TABLE "D"   Transport 147th Infantry Brigade.

Date	Serial No.	Company.	From	To.	Remarks.
Aug. 22nd.	8.	"C" Company. "D" "	"P" Camp.	WORMHOUDT. "G" Area.	Not to cross WATOU- ROUSBRUGGE Rd. before 9-0 a.m.
Aug.23rd.	9.	"C" " "D" "	WORMHOUDT "G" Area.	LEDERZEELE Area.	Route : ESQUELBECQ - ZEGGERS CAPPEL.
Aug.24th	10.	"C" " "D" "	LEDERZEELE Area.	RECQUES Area.	Route.: WATTEN, BAYENGHEM

TABLE "E"   Battalion Headquarters.

Aug. 21st.	11.	Bn. H.Q.	LA LOVIE	RECQUES.	By Rail.

TABLE "G"   Battalion H.Q Transport.

			Present Billets.		
Aug. 20th.	12.			LEDERZEELE Area.	Route WORMHOUDT.- RUBROUCK- Under an Officer to be detailed by O.C. Div. Signal Company.
Aug. 21st	13.		LEDERZEEL AREA.	RECQUES Area.	Route: WATTEN- BAYENGHEM do.

SECRET.
Copy No. ...

49th Battalion Machine Gun Corps.
-- OPERATION ORDER NO 63 --

Sunday 18.8.18.

1. "B" Coy 49th Bn M.G.C.	"B" Company, 49th Battn. M.G.C. (Left SECTOR) will be relieved on the night of 19th/20th August 1918 by "C" Company 34th Battalion Machine Gun Corps.
2.	On relief, "B" Company 49th Bn. M.G.C. will proceed to "P" Camp (Sheet 28. A.15.c.) "B" Company 49th Bn. M.G.C. will occupy the space vacated by "C" Company 34th Bn. M.G.C.
3. "C" Coy. 49thBn. M.G.C.	The ZILLEBEKE LAKE Gun at I.15.c.12. (RIGHT Forward Sector) will be relieved by one gun of "B" Company 34th Bn. M.G.C. on the night of 19th/20th instant.
4. "D" Coy. 49th Bn. M.G.C.	The Support Guns at I.13.a.2.5. and I.13.a.9.1. will be relieved by two guns of "D" Company 34th Bn. M.G.C. on the night of 19th/20th instant.
5.	The Gun Teams relieved under 3 & 4 above will, on relief proceed to "P" Camp and will be accomodated by "B" Company 49th Bn. M.G.C. until "A" Company and "C" Company 49th Bn. M.G.C. are relieved, when they will rejoin their respective Companies.
6. "D" Coy. 49th Bn. M.G.C.)	"D" Company 49th Bn. M.G.C. (less guns relieved under para.4.) will be relieved in Support on day of 20th instant by "D" Company 34th Bn. M.G.C. Relief to be complete by 12 noon. After relief, "D" Company 49th Bn. M.G.C. will proceed to "P" Camp and will occupy the space vacated by "D" Company 34th Bn. M.G.C.
7. "A" Coy. 49th Bn M.G.C.	"A" Company, 49th Bn. M.G.C. will be relieved in Reserve on day of 20th instant by "A" Company 34th Bn. M.G.C. Relief to be complete by 12 noon. After relief, "A" Company 49th Bn. M.G.C. will remain in present Camp until moving out of the area.
8. "C" Coy. 49th Bn. M.G.C.	"C" Company 49th Bn. M.G.C. less one gun relieved under para.3. will be relieved in the RIGHT Forward Sector on the night of 20/21st instant by "B" Company 34th Bn. M.G.C. THIS RELIEF WILL BE COMPLETE BY 2-0 a.m. On completion of relief "C" Company 49th Bn. M.G.C. will proceed to "P" Camp and will occupy the space vacated by "B" Company 34th Bn. M.G.C.
9 All Coys 49th Bn.M.G.C	O.C.Companies of 49th Bn. M.G.C. will arrange their own guides to "P" Camp and will make arrangements re-occupying the Camp.
10.	Details of relief will be arranged by O.C.Companies concerned. All guns, tripods, belts and belt boxes will be brought out of the line.
11. "C" Coy 49th Bn. M.G.C.	The Lewis Gun complete at LILLE GATE will be brought out by "C" Company.

P.T.O.

12. All Coys. 49th Bn. M.G.C.	All Trench Stores, Battle Stores and Area Stores will be handed over and receipts obtained. Receipts will be forwarded to reach this Office not later than 12 hours after completion of relief.
13.	Anti-gas suits and Reserve Rations will be handed over and <u>separate</u> receipts in duplicate obtained for <u>each</u> and forwarded to Battalion Headquarters.
14. Signals.	Signals and communications will be handed over under arrangements to be made by Battalion Signalling Officers.
15. Work.	All work maps, work in hand and work contemplated will be handed over in detail and receipts for work maps obtained. All Defence Schemes will be handed over and receipts obtained. All A.A. mountings (Lewis and Vickers) will also be handed over and included in receipt obtained for Trench Stores.
16.	Reliefs complete will be wired to this Office using code words as follows :-

    (a) "B" Company 49th Bn. relieved.   "RED"
    (b) ZILLEBEKE Gun relieved.   "LAKE"
    (c) Support guns at I.13.a.2.5. and I.13.a.9.1. relieved - "BROWN"
    (d) "D" Company 49th Bn. relieved.   "BROWN COMPLETE"
    (e) "A" " " " "   "YELLOW"
    (f) "C" " " " "   "BLUE"

17.	The Transport which goes forward to bring out the material of "B" Company 49th Bn. M.G.C. will take forward the guns tripods, etc of "C" Company 34th Bn. M.G.C. to avoid congestion. Guns etc will be picked up at "P" Camp at a time to be arranged between O.C Companies.
18.	O.C.Companies of 34th Bn. M.G.C. will visit O.C.Companies of 49th Bn. M.G.C. on 19th instant to arrange details.
19.	ACKNOWLEDGE.

W Bates
Capt. & Adjt.
Battn. M.G.C.

Issued at.. 7-15 pm

Copies to :-

    1. O.C."A" Company
    2. O.C."B" Company.
    3. O.C."C" Company.
    4. O.C."D" Company.
    5. "G" 49th Division.
    6. 34th Bn. M.G.C.
    7.   do
    8.   do
    9.   do
   10.   do
   11. Quartermaster.
   12. Signalling Officer.
   13. Transport Officer.
   14. War Diary.
   15. War Diary. ✓
   16. File.
   17. File.
   18. File.

SECRET

49th Battn. Machine Gun Corps.
OPERATION ORDER No. 64.

Copy No. 9

Monday 19.8.18.

1. Headquarters Transport will move to new area tomorrow 20.8.18. with Transport of 49th Div. H.Q., H.Q. Divnl Train, H.Q. R.E. and 1/1 Mobile Vet. Section under the command of/J.W.POLLARD A.V.C Capt.

2. Battalion H.Q. Transport will be under the command of 2/Lt. F.SCOTT.

3. Transport will parade on the PROVEN - HOUTKERQUE Rd adjoining Aerodreome at 6-0 a.m. Head of column will be at Chapel E.18.b.4.2. Sheet 27. Transport will move in the following order: 49th Div. H.Q. and M.M.P. 49th Div. Train H.Q. 49th Div. R.E. H.Q. 49th Battn. M.G.C. H.Q. 1/1 Mobile Vet. Section. Route: WORMHOUDT - RUBROUCK.

4. Rations and forage for 21st are being dumped at LEDERZEELE on 20th instant and will be drawn on arrival.

5. S.S. 724 March Discipline will be observed and correct intervals maintained. Steel Helmets will be worn.

6. 2/Lt. F.SCOTT will arrange all further details with regard to time to move from rear Camp.

7. ACKNOWLEDGE.

Capt. & Adjt.
49th Battn. M.G.C.

Issued at.........

Copies to :-

1. Transport Officer.
2. 2/Lt.F.SCOTT.
3. "B" Company.
4. Quartermaster.
5. R.S.M.
6. "Q" 49th Division.
7. "A" do
8. Camp Commandant.
9. War Diary.
10. do
11. File.

SECRET.   40th Battalion Machine Gun Corps.   Copy No...6..
                  OPERATION ORDER NO. 66

                                                     Tuesday 20.8.18.

1. Battalion Headquarters will move to new area tomorrow 21st
    instant by train leaving MEDINGHEM at 6-0 a.m.

2. Headquarters Officers Kits, Orderly Room Kit and Mess Kit
    will be moved by Lorry. Lorry will arrive at Battalion
    Headquarters at 9-0 a.m.
    Cpl. WATERHOUSE (Orderly Room Clerk) and L/Cpl. ALCOCK will
    proceed by this Lorry. Cpl. WATERHOUSE will be responsible for
    seeing all Kit loaded and unloaded and for its safe custody un-
    til handed over in a new area.

3. Personnel at Rear Lines will be marched by the R.S.M. to
    Battalion Headquarters to arrive there at 6-0 a.m. where
    they will be joined by the remainder of Headquarters, and will
    come under the command of Lt. J.E.PATTISON. R.E. The whole
    party will proceed to MEDINGHEM STATION where Lt. PATTISON
    will report to R.T.O. for entrainment.

4. Detraining station will be AUDRUICQ.

5. Dress will be full Marching Order, Steel Helmets will be
    worn.

6. Water Bottles will be filled and rations for mid-day meal
    will be carried.
    R.S.M. and Cpl. WATERHOUSE will issue orders for breakfasts.

7. Strict March Discipline will be maintained and troops will
    be warned regarding the orders to be observed when
    travelling by train.

8. Officers will apply to Capt. T.W.BATES for train accommodation.

9. On detraining the whole party will proceed to RECQUES.

10. The usual Fire and screening of light precautions will
    be taken in the new billets immediately on arrival.

11. ACKNOWLEDGE.

                                                Capt. & Adjt.
                                                40th Battn. Machine Gun
                                                              Corps.
    Issued at... 1.30 pm

    Copies to :-

              1. Quartermaster.
              2. Signalling Officer.
              3. R.S.M.
              4. Cpl. Waterhouse.
              5. War Diary.
              6. War Diary.
              7. File.

Amendment to Operation Order No. 68

20.3.18.

All times will be 1 hour and 30 minutes earlier.

To all recipients of Operation Order No. 68.

[signature]
Capt. & Adjt.
49th Battn. M.G.C.

49TH MACHINE
GUN BATTALION,
ORDERLY ROOM.
ST 351/18

SECRET. 49th Battalion Machine Gun Corps, Copy No. 12.
-OPERATION ORDER No 63.-

Friday 23.8.18.

The Battalion will move to BOMMINGUES tomorrow as follows:-

1. Battalion Headquarters will pass starting point, RED House on right of road running S.W. from Transport Lines and about 700 yards beyond entrance to Transport Lines at 8-30 a.m. "A" Company and "B" Company will follow in this order at the correct intervals.
Major L.J.L. Sproulle M.C. will be in command of the above.

2. "C" and "D" Companies will move from ZUTKERQUE in this order. Head of column to pass starting point, first E in GRASSE PAYALLE (Hazebrouck 5a.) on ZUTKERQUE- RECQUES Road at 9-30 a.m.
Major. H.S. BOXER will be in command of above.

3. On arrival at BOMMINGUES Companies will proceed straight to billets and Transport to Transport Lines.

4. The following Officers will be in charge of Transport :-

   H.Q.   : 2/Lt. F. SCOTT.
   "A" & "B" Coys. Lt. J.R. Handford.
   "C" & "D" Coys. 2/Lt. J.D. GALE.

5. Strict march discipline will be maintained.

6. Steel Helmets will be worn and traffic rules observed.

7. All billets will be provided with a copy of instructions which have been issued from this Office, regarding fires, Latrines, Estaminets etc.

8. ACKNOWLEDGE.

Capt, & Adjt.
Battn. M.G.C.

Issued at 5-20 p.m.

Copies to :-
   1. O.C. "A" Company.
   2. O.C. "B" Company.
   3. O.C. "C" Company.
   4. O.C. "D" Company.
   5. 2/Lt. F. SCOTT.
   6. Lt. HANDFORD.
   7. 2/Lt. J.D. GALE.
   8. Signalling Officer.
   9. Quartermaster.
   10. "G" 49th Division.
   11. "A"   do.
   12. War Diary.
   13.   do
   14. File.

SECRET.

AMENDMENT No1. to Operation Order No.66.

Para.1. line 4.

    for 8-30 a.m. read 6-0 a.m.

Para.2. line 4.

    for 9-30 a.m. read 6-0 a.m.

[signature]

Capt. & Adjt.
49th Battn. M.G.C.

23.8.18.

Copies to all recipients of Operation Order No.66.

SECRET   49th Battalion Machine Gun Corps.   Copy. No. 14
                 - OPERATION ORDER NO. 67 -

                                                            Tuesday 27.8.18.

1. Battalion Headquarters and Companies will move to ST.POL Area by rail as follows :-

     "A" and "C" Companies   -   146th Brigade Group.
     Battalion H.Q. "B" and "D" Companies -   147th Brigade Group.

2. Divisional Administrative Instructions have been issued to Companies. All further orders will be issued by Brigade concerned.

3. Reference para.16 of Divisional Administrative Instructions, the Billetting Officer will arrange billets for Battalion Headquarters of "D" Company as follows :-

Field Officer	1.	Signal Office.	1.
Officers	4.	Officers Mess.	1.
O.Rs.	77	x Guard Room.	1.
x Orderly Room.	1.	Medical Inspection Room	1
Q.M.Stores.	1.		

     x To be near together if possible.

4. Companies will arrange to arrive at entraining station one hour before time of entrainment.

5. Battalion Headquarters (less personnel proceeding to entraining station by lorry) will parade at the Battalion Orderly Room at 5.15 a.m. and will arrive at NORTKERQUE at 8.30 a.m. Lt. J.E. PATTISON will be in command of this party.

6. A lorry will report at the Quartermasters Stores at 5 a.m. to collect any stores and then proceed to the Battalion Orderly Room afterwards calling at billets No. 27, 8, and 9 to collect Mess Kit and Officers Kits. The lorry will arrive at NORTKERQUE by 6.30 a.m. and after unloading will return direct to its unit.

7. 3 men (unfit for marching) of "B" and "D" Companies can be carried on the lorry. They should report at Battalion Orderly Room at 5 a.m.
Men of "A" and "C" Companies certified not fit to march will be carried on limbers of "A" Company under arrangements to be made between O.C. Companies.

8. ACKNOWLEDGE.

                                               Capt. & Adjt.
                                       49th Battn. M.G.C.

Issued at 3.30 p.m.

Copies to :-

1. O.C. "A" Company.	9. "Q" 49th Division.
2. O.C. "B" Company.	10. "A" 49th Division.
3. O.C. "C" Company.	11. 146th Infantry Brigade.
4. O.C. "D" Company.	12. 147th do
5. Quartermaster.	13. War Diary.
6. Signalling Officer.	14. do
7. Medical Officer.	15 Retained.
8. R.S.M.	

Confidential.

Vol 7

Original
WAR DIARY

49th Battn. M.G.C.

From 1.9.18. – 30.9.18.

Vol. 7.

49th Battn. M.G.C.

Army Form C. 2118.

SHEET 1.

WAR DIARY
or
INTELLIGENCE SUMMARY.
(Erase heading not required.)

Place	Date	Hour	Summary of Events and Information	Remarks and references to Appendices
	1.9.18.		Bn. Battalion moves from ROELLECOURT and HERICOURT areas to the AUBIGNY area in accordance with Operation Order No. 68. A. Coy. with 146th Inf. Bde. to MONT ST. ELOY area. B. Coy. with 147th Inf. Bde. to CAMBLAIN AREA and C. Coy. with 148th Inf. Bde. to CHATEAU de la HAIE area. Hdqrs. and D. Coy. move to AUBIGNY. All personnel move by bus and transport by Road.	O.O.68.
	2.9.18.		Locations refer Sept. 1st except for C. Coy. who move to East of ARRAS in accordance with Operation Order No. 70.	O.O.70.
	3.9.18.		Battn. in training. Lt. G. NEY from 55th Battn. joined 49th Battn. 2nd in Command of A. Coy.	
	4.9.18.		Battn. in training. Lt. F.W. KING & 2nd Lt. E.A. MADDISON reported as reinforcements & posted to A. and B. Coys. Lt. A.C.V. de CANDOLE kld in a Bombing raid on BOVINGUES.	
	5.9.18.		Battn. in training. Lt. G.H. SPICH and 2nd Lt. R.C. SCOTT reported as reinforcements & posted to C. and B. Coys.	
	6.9.18.		C. Coy. move from BLAGNY (E. of ARRAS) to GRAND SERVINS.	

49th Bn. M.G.C.　　SHEET 2.　　Army Form C. 2118.

WAR DIARY
or
INTELLIGENCE SUMMARY.
(Erase heading not required.)

Place	Date	Hour	Summary of Events and Information	Remarks and references to Appendices
	7.9.18.		Advanced training. A. Coy. on Tactical scheme with 146th Inf. Bde.	
	8.9.18.		B. Coy. on Tactical scheme with 147th Inf. Bde. Training and Church Parade.	
	9.9.18.		Battn. in training. Lt. Col. B.H. BADHAM returns from leave & assumes Command of the Battn.	
	10.9.18.		Battalion in training.	
	11.9.18.		Orders received that 49th Div. will relieve 51st Div. in the left sector of the XXII Corps front. Orders issued to Coys. &c. regarding relief in Operation Order No. 71.	O.O.71
			A. Coy. move from Le PENDU to Cutting in H.14.a.0.7.	
	12.9.18.		A. Coy. move from Cutting in H.14.a.0.7. to the line in the Right Subsector. C. Coy. move from relieving a Company of the 51st Bn. M.G.C. to the Cutting in H.14.a.0.7. B. & D. Coys. move from GRAND SERVIUS L'ABBEE & AUBIGNY respectively to BRIGADE CAMP A26.6.2.6. Taking over from 2 Coys of the 51st Bn. M.G.C. These 2 Coys. become Battn. reserve.	

49th Battn. M.G.C.   Sheet 3

WAR DIARY or INTELLIGENCE SUMMARY
(Erase heading not required.)   Army Form C. 2118.

Place	Date	Hour	Summary of Events and Information	Remarks and references to Appendices
	13.9.18.		Battn. H.Q. move to Cutting in H.14.a.07. 8 take command of M. Guns in Sector from 51st Battn. M.G.C. at 10 a.m. Casualties 1. O.R. wounded (Gas).	M
	14.9.18.		Casualties NIL.	M
	15.9.18.		Considerable shelling of forward area. Transport & details of Rand. C Coys. move to BRIGADE CAMP. Casualties NIL.	M
	16.9.18.		Rearrangements made to insure 6 guns of A Coy. B the other side of the NARPE in I.22.b. and I.23.a. Lt W.S. COATES transferred to the R.A.F. & attached of A Coy. B Casualties 10 O.R. of the 103rd M.G. Battn. (attached to 49th Battn. M.G.C.) wounded (Gas).	M
	17.9.18.		Some shelling of forward area. Casualties NIL.	M
	18.9.18.		B. & D. Coys. continue advanced training at Brigade Camp. Orders issued for B. Coy. to relieve A. Coy. in Right Sub-sector on night of 20/21st inst. (O.O.72.) and for D. Coy. to relieve C. Coy. in Left sub-sector on night of 21/22nd inst. O.O.73. Relief transpospaned one day as amendments to O.O's 72. and 73. 103rd Bn. to provide transport.	O.O.72. O.O.73. M

Army Form C. 2118.

49th Bn. M.G.C.   Sheet A.

WAR DIARY
or
INTELLIGENCE SUMMARY.
(Erase heading not required.)

Place	Date	Hour	Summary of Events and Information	Remarks and references to Appendices
	18.9.18.		O.O. No. 74 ordered a readjustment of guns in the line on 19/20th inst. thereby relieving "C" Coy. 103rd Battn. from the line. Slight shelling of forward areas. Casualties. Lt. J.W.D. ACTON wounded (remained at duty).	O.O.74
	19.9.18.		Orders received that 49th Division would be relieved by the 51st Division. relief to complete by 10.a.m. 24th inst. The relief of A. Coy. by B. Coy. was cancelled. Quiet on whole front with only slight shelling. Casualties:- NIL.	
	20.9.18.		The relief of D. Coy. by C. Coy. was cancelled. Orders issued (O.O.75.) for relief by 51st Battalion M.G.C. "C" Coy to be relieved night of 22/23rd & to proceed to ARRAS. "A" Coy. to be relieved night of 23/24th & to proceed to "Y" Camp ETRUN. B. Coy. to same unless 147th Inf. Bde. on 23rd & to BLANGY - FEUCHY area. Battn. H.Q. A.C. and D. Coys. to reassemble at "Y" Camp ETRUN on 24th inst. The Command to pass to O.C. 51st Battn. M.G.C. at 10. a.m. 24th inst. Artillery activity on right. Casualties NIL.	O.O.75.

S.

49th Bn. M.G.C.   Sheet 5.   Army Form C. 2118.

WAR DIARY or INTELLIGENCE SUMMARY

Place	Date	Hour	Summary of Events and Information	Remarks and references to Appendices
	21.9.18		A. and C. Coys. A.94 Battn. and B. Coy. 103rd Battn. co-operated in attack to establish posts in SQUARE WOOD & WHACK TRENCH. Barrage put down & 27,000 rounds fired. Relief postponed 24 hours.	AJ
	22.9.18		Scheme as 21/9 not entirely successful & was repeated today. (D.O.76) Fired a couple of barrages. No casualties during firing. Rounds fired 26,000. Casualties: 2/Lt Reynolds out of action.	D.O.75 D.O.76 AJ
	23.9.18		O.R. missing. 50 O.R.'s to O.O.75. i.e. 7.52 B Coy. 51st Bn. M.G.C. co-operated with 23/24 & 67 B & 67 51st Bn. M.G.C. 251st Bn. on night of 24/25.8 B Coy. 51st Bn. M.G.C. Sheet A27 relieved on night of 24/4 Bn. D. Coy 51st Bn. M.G.C. whole enemy attempt to retake SQUARE WOOD and WHACK TRENCH. Out and out entirely repulsed. 23,000 rounds fired. Casualties Nil.	AJ AJ
	24.9.18		Reliefs by C.C.ys. B. Coy 51st Bn. M.G.C. Very quiet day. Casualties Nil.	
	25.9.18		Batn. H.Q. handed over area at 10 a.m. to 51st Bn. M.G.C. N.A.R. Moved by lorry to K. Camp, ETRON. Sheet 51 B 4 2 c 4.7. A.C. and D. Coys billeted up. B. Coy in FEUCHY area 57 H 20 2.	AJ

49th Battn. M.G.C. Sheet 6.

Army Form C. 2118.

WAR DIARY
or
INTELLIGENCE SUMMARY.
(Erase heading not required.)

Instructions regarding War Diaries and Intelligence Summaries are contained in F. S. Regs., Part II. and the Staff Manual respectively. Title pages will be prepared in manuscript.

Place	Date	Hour	Summary of Events and Information	Remarks and references to Appendices
	25.9.18.		Brigade. Casualties NIL.	MS
	26.9.18.		B. Coy. attached to 147th Bde. A.C. & D. Coys. as per Training programme. Casualties NIL.	M
	27.9.18		(do)	MS
	28.9.18		(do)	MS
	29.9.18		(do)	MS
	30.9.18		(do)	MS

Mc Laprayth
Lieut. Colonel.
Commanding 49th Battn. M.G.C.

SECRET   49th Battalion Machine Gun Corps.   Copy No. 18
            - OPERATION ORDER NO. 68.- (68)

Sunday 1.9.18.

1. The Battalion will move to areas as below on 1st September 1918:

    "A" Company with 146th Inf. Brigade Group to MONT ST ELOY Area.
    "B"   "   "   147th   "   "   "   " CAMBLAIN L'ABBE Area.
    "C"   "   "   148th   "   "   "   " CHATEAU de la HAIE Area.
    "D"   "   "   Battalion Headquarters to AUBIGNY.

2. All further orders for the move of "A", "B" and "C" Companies will be issued by Headquarters of their respective Brigades.

3. Transport of Battalion Headquarters and "D" Company will move by March Route head of column passing the starting point, Road Junction on ST POL - SAVY Road ½ mile due South of village of BAILLEUL-aux-CORNAILLES at 8-25 p.m. in the order named.

4. Ten minute halts will be at clock hour MINUS . ten minutes to clock hour.

5. ROUTE :- Main Road ROELLECOURT - AUBIGNY.

6. Dismounted personnel will proceed by Bus under orders to be issued later.

7. 2/Lt GALE will act as Transport Officer to "A" Company, Lt. HANDFORD to "B" Company, and 2/Lt SCOTT to Battalion Headquarters. O.C. "C" and "D" Companies will detail their own Transport Officers.

8. ACKNOWLEDGE.

                                        W Bate
                                        Capt. & Adjt.
                                        49th Batt. M.G.C.

Issued at 10-0 a.m.

Copies To :-
    1. O.C. "A" Company.
    2. O.C. "B" Company.
    3. O.C. "C" Company.
    4. O.C. "D" Company.
    5. Lt. Handford.
    6. 2/Lt. Gale.
    7. 2/Lt. Scott.
    8. Signalling Officer.
    9. Quartermaster.
   10. Medical Officer.
   11. R.S.M.
   12. "Q" 49th Division.
   13. "A" 49th Division.
   14. 146th Infantry Brigade.
   15. 147th   do
   16. 148th   do
   17. War Diary.
   18. War Diary.
   19. File.

SECRET.
49th Battalion Machine Gun Corps,
OPERATION ORDER No. 70.

Copy No. 9

MONDAY, 2.9.18.

1. 148th Infantry Brigade Group will move tonight 2nd/3rd instant to South of the SCARPE River to the General Area DLARGY - PRUGRY - FAUB ST SAUVEUR (inclusive).

2. "C" Company will come under the orders of B.O.C. 148th Infantry Brigade, who will issue all necessary orders for move. O.C. "C" Company will keep in touch with Headquarters 148th Infantry Brigade.

3. 148th Infantry Brigade Group will remain in 1st Army Reserve and under orders of 49th Division.

4. Nucleus will be left out in accordance with S.S. 135 Sec xxx. Packs will be dumped under arrangements of "Q" 49th Division, such arrangements being notified to "C" Company by 148th Infantry Brigade.

5. ACKNOWLEDGE.

W Bates.
Capt. & Adjt,
49th Battn. M.G.C.

Issued at 12.15 pm

Copies to :-
1. O.C. "C" Company.
2. O.C. "A" Company.
3. O.C. "B" Company.
4. O.C. "D" Company.
5. 148th Infantry Brigade.
6. "G" 49th Division.
7. "Q" do
8. War Diary.
9. do ✓
10. File.

) For
) Information.

SECRET.   49th Battalion, Machine Gun Corps.   Copy
                       -OPERATION ORDER No. 71-   No..19..

                                                          Wednesday.11.9.18.

1.   49th Battn. M.G.C., will relieve 51st Battn. M.G.C.
        as follows.

2.   "A" Company, 49th Battn.M.G.C., will move with Company
        Head Quarters and Gun Teams to the CUTTING at H.14.a.7.0.
        on 11th September 1918.
        Transport and 25 percent of the remaining fighting personnel
        will move to G.15.b.2.6. on 11th Septr.1918.
        1 N.C.O. and 4 men will remain in present camp until
        they are relieved by "C" Company, 51st Battn.M.G.C.

3.   "A" Company, 49th Battn.M.G.C. will relieve "C" Company
        51st Battn.M.G.C., in the Right Sub-Sector on the night
        of 12/13th Septr.1918.
        Details of reliefs and guides will be as already arranged.

4.   "C" Company, 49th Battn.M.G.C., will move with Coy.Hd.Qrs.
        and Gun Teams to the CUTTING at H.14.a.7.0 on 12th Septr.
        1918.
        Transport and 25 percent of remaining fighting personnel
        will move to G.15.b.2.6. on 12th Septr.1918.
        "C" Company will not be clear of present camp before
        6.45 p.m. 12th inst.
        1 N.C.O. and 4 men will be left in present camp until
        relieved by "A" Company, 51st Battn.M.G.C.

5.   "C" Company, 49th Battn.M.G.C., will relieve "A" Company
        51st Battn.M.G.C., on the night of 13/14th Septr. in
        the Left Sub-Sector.
        Details of relief and guides will be arranged by O.C.
        Companies concerned.

6.   "D" Company,49th Battn.M.G.C., will relieve "D" Company,
        51st Battn.M.G.C., in BRIGADE CAMP, A.26.b.2.6. on the day
        of 13th Septr.1918.
        "D" Company, 49th Battn.M.G.C., will reach BRIGADE CAMP
        by 9 a.m. on 13th inst.

7.   "B" Company,49th Battn.M.G.C., will relieve "B" Company,
        51st Battn.M.G.C., in BRIGADE CAMP, A.26.b.2.6. on 13th
        Septr.1918.
        "B" Company, 49th Battn.M.G.C., will reach Brigade Camp
        by 8 a.m. on 13th inst.
        1 N.C.O. and 4 men will be left in the present billets
        until relieved by "B" Company, 51st Battn.M.G.C.

8.   No restrictions as to routes are placed on "B" and
        "D" Companies, 49th Battn. M.G.C.

9.   One Officer from 51st Battn. M.G.C. will report at
        49th Battn.M.G.C., Head Quarters, AUBIGNY to take over
        camp and billets at AUBIGNY.

10.   Signalling Officer,49th Battn.M.G.C., will proceed to
        Head Quarters, 51st Battn.M.G.C., at the CUTTING
        H.14.a.7.0. on 13th inst. to take over the 'dug-outs'
        and communications of 51st Battn.M.G.C. and 103rd
        Battn. M.G.C.

                                (1).

(2).

11. 49th Battn.M.G.C., Head Quarters will move to the present Head Quarters 51st Battn.M.G.C., at the CUTTING, H.14.a.7.0. o.4 on 14th instant.
Relief to be complete by 10 a.m.

12. Transport and Q.M.Stores of 49th Battn.M.G.C.,will be at A N.26.b.2.6. and will move on 14th inst. They will be clear of AUBIGNY by a time which will be notified later.

13. Great care must be taken to obviate the possibility of the enemy observing any unusual movement.

14. Usual Distances will be observed and strict march discipline maintained.

15. Water will be taken into the line. The water at present in the line or vicinity must on no account be used.

16. 49th (WR) Division Trench Standing Order 2(a) will be strictly complied with.

17. Rear Coy. Hd.Qrs. of "A" and "C" Companies will open at BRIGADE CAMP A N.26.b.2.6. on 15th inst. when all workshops will open under the Quartermaster.

18. The Medical Officer will make arrangements for the care of sick at A N.26.b.2.6. whilst he is in the line.

19. O.C.Companies will make own arrangements for sending forward an Officer and guides to take over new billets.

20. All moves will be by March Route.

21. ACKNOWLEDGE.

Issued at *10.5.M*.

W Bates
Capt.& Adjt.
49th Battn.M.G.Corps.

Copies to:-

1. O.C."A" Company.
2. O.C."B"   do.
3. O.C."C"   do.
4. O.C."D"   do.
5. O.C. Sigs.
6. Transport Officer.
7. Medical Officer.
8. Quartermaster.
9. R.S.M.
10. 49th Division "G".
11. 49th Division 'Q'.
12. 49th Division 'A'.
13. 51st Battn.M.G.C.
14. 103rd Battn.M.G.C.
15. 146 Inf.Brigade.
16. 147 Inf.Brigade.
17. 148 Inf.Brigade.
18. War Diary.
19.   do.
20. File.

21. File.
22. 49(WR) DIVISIONAL TRAIN

49th Battn.M.G.C. O.O.72/2.

To All Recipients of O.O.No.72.

Operation Order No.72 and Amendment No.1 are cancelled. The relief will not now take place.

M. Tait
Capt. & Adjt.
49th Battn. M.G.C.

20.9.18.

49TH MACHINE
GUN BATTALION,
S.T.351/36
Date: 20.9.18

SECRET.

INSTRUCTIONS REGARDING TRANSPORT TO ACCOMPANY

49th Battalion. M.G.Corps.

- OPERATION ORDERS Nos.72 and 73 -

Wednesday.
18.9.18.

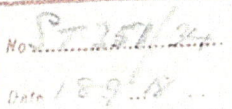

1. Lorries will report at BRIGADE CAMP at 6.45 p.m. on each night and will convey relieving Company to H.16.d.9.4.

2. Lorries will be at H.16.d.9.4. at 11.30 p.m. on each night to bring out the relieved Company.

3. O.C.Coys. to be relieved will ensure that an Officer is at H.16.d.9.4. to supervise embussing. He must report at 11.30 p.m. sharp.

Capt. & Adjt.
49th Battn. M.G.Corps.

Issued at..10.p.m.

TO ALL RECIPIENTS OF OOs 72 -73.

AMENDMENT NO.1 to OPERATION ORDER No. 72.

SECRET.
----

1. Para. 1. Line 2.
            for night 20/21st inst.,
            Read night 21/22nd. inst.

2. Acknowledge.

                                        [signature]
                                        Capt. & Adjutant.,
18.9.18.   49th. Battalion Machine Gun Corps.

Issued at 1.30p.m.

Copies to all recipients of O.O. 72.

49th Battalion, Machine Gun Corps. Copy
-OPERATION ORDER NO.72-   No......

Wednesday 18.9.18.

1. "A" Company, 49th Battalion, M.G.C. will be relieved in the Right Brigade Sector on the night of 20/21st inst. by "B" Company, 49th Battalion, M.G.C.

2. Arrangements for relief will be made mutually by O.C. Coys. concerned.

3. All work in hand, maps, charts etc. will be handed over, also all anti-gas appliances and trench stores. Handing over lists (one copy only) will be forwarded to this office within 24 hours of completion of relief.

4. In the event of guns being moved on the night of relief. O.C. "A" Company will be responsible for placing guns in correct new positions.

5. Transport arrangements will be notified as early as possible.

6. Completion of Relief will be wired to this office using code word "PIP".

7. ACKNOWLEDGE.

W Bates.
Capt.& Adjt.
49th Battn. M.G.Corps.

Issued at 8 a.m.

Distribution:-

1.	O.C."A" Coy. 49th Battn.M.G.Corps.	11.	T.O. 49th Battn.M.G.C.
2.	"B" Coy. do. do.	12.	S.O. do. do.
3.	"C" Coy. do. do.	13.	R.S.M. do. do.
4.	"D" Coy. do. do.	14.	49th Division "G".
5.	"A" Coy. 103 do. do.	15.	146th Inf.Brigade.
6.	"B" Coy. do. do.	16.	147th do. do.
7.	"C" Coy. do. do.	17.	148th do. do.
8.	"D" Coy. do. do.	18.	War Diary.
9.	103 Battn. M.G.Corps.	19.	War Diary.
10.	Lieut.& Q.M. 49th Bn.M.G.Corps.	20.	Retained.

SECRET.

To All Recipients of O.O.No.73.

Operation Order No.73 is cancelled.
Relief named therein will not take place, pending
further instructions from this Office.

                                            Capt.& Adjt.
19.9.18.   49th Battn.M.G.Corps.

AMENDMENT No.1 to OPERATION ORDER No. 73.

S E C R E T.
----

1. Para. 1. Line 3.
          for night 21/22hd September 1918,
          READ night 22/23rd September 1918.

2. Acknowledge.

                                    [signature]

18.9.18.   Capt. & Adjutant.,
                              49th. Battalion MG. Corps.

Issued at 1.30 p.m.

Copies to all recipients of O.O. 73.

SECRET.   49th Battalion, Machine Gun Corps.   Copy
           - OPERATION ORDER NO.73 -   No...18..

                                          Wednesday 18.9.18.

1. "C" Company, 49th Battalion, M.G.C. will be relieved in
    the Left Sub-Sector by "D" Company, 49th Battalion, M.G.C.
    on the night of 21/22nd September 1918.

2. Arrangements for relief will be made mutually between
    O.C. Coys. concerned.

3. All work in hand, maps, charts etc. will be handed
    over also all anti-gas appliances and trench stores.
    Handing over lists (one copy only) will be forwarded
    to this office within 24 hours of completion of
    relief.

4. In the event of guns being moved on the night of relief
    O.C. "C" Company will be responsible for placing guns
    in correct new positions.

5. Transport arrangements will be notified as early as
    possible.

6. Completion of relief will be wired to this office
    using code word "EMMA".

7. ACKNOWLEDGE.

                                    Capt. & Adjt.
    Issued at 8 a.m.   49th Battn. M.G. Corps.

                    Distribution:-

    1. O.C. "A" Company. 49th Bn.M.G.C.   11. O.C. "C" Coy. 103 M.G. Battn.
    2. O.C. "B"   do.   do.   12. O.C. "D" do.   do.
    3. O.C. "C"   do.   do.   13. O.C. 103 M.G. Battn.
    4. O.C. "D"   do.   do.   14. 49th Division "G".
    5. Quarter Master.   do.   15. 146 Inf. Brigade.
    6. T.O.   do.   16. 147 do.   do.
    7. S.O.   do.   17. 148 do.   do.
    8. R.S.M.   do.   18. War Diary.
    9. O.C. "A" Coy. 103 Bn.M.G.C.   19. War Diary.
    10. O.C. "B" do.   do.   20. Retained.

                                    postponed 24 hrs

SECRET.

49th Battalion, Machine Gun Corps.
– OPERATION ORDER NO.74 –

Wednesday,
18.9.18.

1. A Re-adjustment of Guns in this Sector will take place on the night 19/20th September 1918. All moves will be complete by 3 a.m. 20th Septr.1918.

2. The attached map shows new positions to be occupied by guns of Companies and O.C.Companies will make mutual arrangements where interchange of gun position takes place.

3. The above re-adjustment will liberate "C" Company, 103rd Bn.M.G.C., from the line and this Company will withdraw under orders of O.C.Company.
Any gun position being occupied by a relieving gun will not be vacated until the new gun is in position.

4. ACKNOWLEDGE.

W Bates.
Capt.& Adjt.
49th Battn.M.G.Corps.

Issued at 10 p.m.

Copies to:-

No.1,	"A" Coy. 49th Bn.M.G.C.	10. 49th Division "G". x
2.	"B" do. do. X	11. 146th Infantry Brigade. x
3.	"C" do. do.	12. 147th do. do. x
4.	"D" do. do. x	13. 148th do. do. x
5.	"A" Coy. 103 Bn.M.G.C.	14. War Diary.
6.	"B" do. do. x	15. War Diary.
7.	"C" do. do.	16. Retained.
8.	"D" do. do.	
9.	O.C. 103rd M.G.Battn	x – Maps to follow.

SECRET.   49th Battalion, Machine Gun Corps.   Copy
       - OPERATION ORDER No.75 -   No......

                                            Friday.20.9.18.

1. 49th Battalion, M.G.C. will be relieved by 51st Battalion,
    M.G.C. as per attached table.

2. All troops of 51st Battalion, M.G.C. on arrival in the
    Sector will be tactically under 49th Battn.M.G.C. until
    10 a.m. 24th September 1918, at which time command of MG'S IN
    the Left Divisional Sector passes to O.C. 51st (M)
    Bn. MGC.

3. On completion of Relief 49th Bn.M.G.C. will come into
    Army Reserve and will be ready to move at 12 hours
    notice.

4. Regulation Distances laid down in S.S. 724 will be
    observed on the march and strict march discipline
    maintained.

5. All Trench Stores, maps, aeroplane photographs,
    defence schemes, anti-gas appliances etc. will be
    handed over and receipts will be forwarded to this
    office within 24 hours of relief.

6. The Companies of 103rd Battalion,M.G.C. in the line
    will come tactically under 51st Battalion,M.G.C. at
    10 a.m. 24th Septr.1918.

7. Details of Relief will be arranged between O.C.Coys.
    concerned.

8. All guns, tripods and two belt boxes per gun will be
    brought out.

9. Reliefs complete will be wired to this office, using
    following code words:-
        "A" Coy. 49th Bn.M.G.C. relieved   "ACK".
        "B" Coy.   do.   do.   "BEER".
        "C" Coy.   do.   do.   "SIS".
        "D" Coy.   do.   do.   "DON".

10. Battn.Hd.Qrs. will close at the RAILWAY CUTTING at 10
    a.m. 24th Septr.1918 and open at Y Camp at the same hour.

11. ACKNOWLEDGE.

                                    Capt.& Adjt.
    Issued at ....   49th Battalion,M.G.Corps.

                    Copies to:-

    "A","B","C", and "D" Coys.49th Bn.M.G.C.
    "A","B","C", and "D" Coys.103rd. do. do.
    No.9. To T.C. 49th Bn.M.G.C.   No.14. O.C.103 Bn.M.G.C.
       10.   M.O.   do.   15. 49th Division "G".
       11.   S.O.   do.   16. 49th Division "A".
       12.   Q.M.   do.   17. 146 Inf.Brigade.
       13.   R.S.M.   do.   18. 147 Inf.Brigade.
       21.   49th Div.Train.   19. 148 Inf.Brigade.
       22.   O.C.51st Bn.M.G.C.   20. 4th Division "G".
       23.   War Diary.   25. 8th Division "G".
       24.   War Diary.   26. Retained.

                    OVER

TABLE ACCOMPANYING O.O.75.

Date. Septr.	Serial No.	Company.	From.	To.	Relieved by	Route.	Remarks.
22/23.	1.	"C" 49th Bn. M.G.C.	GREENLAND Section.	ARRAS.	"B" Coy. 51st Bn. M.G.C.	Rail.	Billets from Bn. Billeting Officer. Train arrang'm'ts will be notified.
23.	2.	"B" 49th Bn. M.G.C.	BRIGADE CAMP.	BLANGY- FEUCHY Area.	1 Coy. 51st Bn. M.G.C.	---	Under Orders of 147 Infantry Brigade.
23/24.	3.	"D" 49th Bn. M.G.C.	PLOUVAIN Section.	Y Camp. (L.8.b.) ETRUN Area.	"D" Coy. 51st Bn. M.G.C.	Personnel by Rail - Transport by road.	Billets from Bn. Billeting Officer. Train arrangem'ts will be notified.
24.	4.	"C". 49th Bn. M.G.C.	ARRAS.	Y Camp. ETRUN Area.	---	March Route.	To be clear of BAPEAUME Gate at 7 a.m. Route ARRAS - St. POL Main Road. Billets from Bn. Billeting Officer.
24.	5.	"D". 49th Bn. M.G.C.	BRIGADE CAMP.	Y Camp. ETRUN Area.	1 Coy. 51st Bn. M.G.C.	March Route.	To be clear of MADAGASCAR Corner 7 a.m. Route via NEUF - LOUEZ.
24.	6.	Rear Bn. Hd. Qrs. and H.Q. Transport. 49th Bn. M.G.C.	BRIGADE CAMP.	Y Camp. ETRUN Area.	Rear Bn. H.C. and H.C. Transport. 51st Bn. M.G.C.	March Route.	A.R.S - St. POL Main Road. Billets from Bn. Billeting Officer.

SECRET.   ADMINISTRATIVE INSTRUCTIONS No.1 (49th Battn.M.G.C).
to accompany
- OPERATION ORDER No.75 -

1. The following personnel, normally with Battn.Hd.Qrs.
   will proceed with "A" Company, 49th Battn.M.G.C.
       4 Signallers. (1 N.C.O. and 3 men).
       1 Saddler.
       1 Cold Shoer.
       1 Artificer.

2. Billets will be provided for as follows:-
   "A" Company will send their own Billetting Officer
   under arrangements to be made by 147th Inf.Brigade.
   2/Lieut.W.MARSHALL will arrange Billets for Battn.
   Hd.Qrs. and 3 Companies at Y Camp and at ARRAS for
   "C" Company on nights 22/23 and 23/24 Septr.1918.
   Details of numbers will be furnished to 2/Lieut.
   Marshall by the Adjutant.

3. On arrival at Y Camp, O.C.Coy's. will ensure that
   necessary instructions re fires etc. are made known
   to all ranks and that the fire orders are posted in
   each Billet; also that all precautions against fire
   are taken.

4. Reference Serial No.3 of Table Accompanying O.O.75.
   Transport Officer(Lieut.W.W.R.Bone) will make all
   necessary arrangements with O.C."A" Company regarding
   move of Transport of "A" Company after completion of
   Relief. One Officer of "A" Company will move with the
   Transport and will be in charge. The M.Gs and dismounted
   personnel will march to Y Camp under arrangements of
   O.C."A" Company, where they will report to 2/Lieut.
   W.MARSHALL.

5. Transport of "C" Company will move to Billets in
   ARRAS for nights 22/23 and 23/24 under arrangements
   of Battn.Transport Officer, Billetting being done by
   2/Lieut.W.MARSHALL.

                                              Capt.& Adjt.
20.9.18.   49th Battn.M.G.Corps.

Copies to All Recipients of O.O.75.

SECRET.   O.O.75/2.

To O.C. "A" Company.(Adv. & Rear).
   49th Division "G" (for Information).

Reference Table accompanying Amendment No.1 to O.O.75.

1. Six Lorries will be at H.16.c.9.1. at one a.m. on the
    night of 23/24th Septr. 1918 to take your Company
    to ARRAS.
    You will be responsible for embussing your Company.
    An N.C.O. who has been taken round your billets in
    ARRAS will report to your Advanced Company Hd.Qrs.
    by 6 p.m.(This is being arranged by Battalion Hd.Qrs.
    and Rear Company). This N.C.O. will proceed on the
    first Lorry and guide column to destination.

2. On 24th September 1918, your Company will proceed from
    ARRAS to "Y" Camp, ETRUN by March Route ARRAS - St.POL
    Main Road and will be clear of the BAUDEMONT Gate by
    9.30 a.m. On arrival in "Y" Camp, Billets will be
    allotted you by Battalion Billeting Officer(2/Lieut.
    W.MARSHALL).

3. ACKNOWLEDGE.

                                                    [signature]
                                                    Capt.& Adjt.
23.9.18.   49th Battalion, M.G.Corps.
  8.15 a.m.

SECRET.   O.O.75/1.

   49th BATTALION, MACHINE GUN CORPS.
   AMENDMENT No.1 to OPERATION ORDER No.75.
   ─────────────────────────────

1.   Reference paragraphs 2, 3, and 10.
       For 10 a.m. 24th Septr.1918,
       Read 10 a.m. 25th Septr.1918.

2.   The Table accompanying O.O.75 is cancelled and the
     Table on reverse hereof is substituted.

                                                  [signature]
                                                  Capt. & Adjt.
     Issued at   49th Battn. M.G.Corps.
     23. 9.1918.

     Addressed All Recipients of O.O. No.75.
     ─────────────────────────────

              AMENDMENT No.1 to ADMINISTRATIVE INSTRUCTIONS No.1.
                   Issued with Operation Order No.75.
     ─────────────────────────────

     Para 2.
          Delete line 6 and substitute
          "A" Company on nights of 23/24 and 24/25 Sept.1918.

     Para 4 line 1.
          For "Serial No.3 of Table accompanying O.O.75"
          Read "Serial No.5 of Table accompanying Amendment
               No.1 to O.O.75".
          For "O.C. "A" Company" wherever it occurs in this
               para read "O.C. "C" Company".

     Para 5 line 1.
          For "C" Company.
          Read "A" Company.
               line 2.
          For "22/23 and 23/24"
          Read "23/24 and 24/25".

     Add new Para.
     6.   Travelling Kitchen of "A" Company will be
          sent to Billets at ARRAS.

                                                  [signature] Baker
                                                  Capt. & Adjt.
     23. 9.18.   49th Battn. M.G.Corps.

- TABLE ACCOMPANYING O.O.75/1 -

Date. Sept.	Serial Number.	Company.	From.	To.	Relieved by	Route.	Remarks.
23.	1.	"B" 49th Bn.M.G.C.	BRIGADE CAMP.	BLANGY-FEUCHY Area.	1 Coy. 51st Bn. M.G.C.	—	Under orders of 147th Inf.Brigade.
23/24.	2.	"A" 49th Bn.M.G.C. Section.	PLOUVAIN Section.	ARRAS.	"B" Coy. 51st Bn. M.G.C.	Rail.	Billets from Bn. Billeting Officer. Train arrangements will be notified.
24.	3.	"D" 49th Bn. M.G.C.	BRIGADE CAMP.	Y CAMP ETRUN Area.	1 Coy. 51st Bn. M.G.C.	March Route.	To be clear of MADAGASCAR CORNER 9.30 a.m. Route via ANZIN - LOUEZ - ARRAS - St.POL Main Road.
24.	4.	Rear Bn.H.Q. and H.Q. Transport 49th Bn. M.G.C.	BRIGADE CAMP.	Y CAMP ETRUN Area.	Rear Bn.H.Q. and H.Q. Transport 51st Bn. M.G.C.	March Route.	Billets from Bn. Billeting Officer.
24/25.	5.	"C" 49th Bn. M.G.C. Section.	GREENLAND Section.	Y Camp ETRUN Area.	"D" Coy. 51st Bn. M.G.C.	Personnel by Rail - Transport by Road.	Personnel Billets from Bn. Billeting Officer. Train arrangements will be notified.

NOTE:- Orders with regard to move of "A" Company from ARRAS will be issued later.

SECRET. URGENT   Copy No. 7

49th BATTALION, MACHINE GUN CORPS.
- OPERATION ORDER No.76 -

Sunday.
22.9.18.

1. "A" and "C" Companies 49th Battn.M.G.Corps and "A" Coy. 103rd Battalion, M.G.Corps will co-operate with the 148th Infantry Brigade on the night of 22/23rd Septr. 1918, in capturing and consolidating the line of WHINE and WHACK Trenches from C.26.d.75.75. to I.3.a.8.1.

2. Machine Guns will co-operate as laid down in this Office letter S.T.151/52 and S.T.151/54.

3. Zero will be at twelve(12) midnight.

4. The 49th Divisional Artillery "A" Barrage will come down on the line of WHACK TRENCH at Zero, and lift at Zero plus fifteen.
    The "B" Barrage will come down on the ROUVROY-FRESNES line at ZERO.

5. The 8th Division is to capture and consolidate CHEAPSIDE between GAVRELLE SUPPORT and WHINE TRENCH from its junction with CHEAPSIDE down to C.26.d.75.75. with a supporting point at C.26.d.45.60.

6. 8th Division Barrage is to come down at Zero on WHINE TRENCH and lift at Zero plus fifteent.

7. In order to deceive the enemy, the 49th Division Artillery will fire bursts of fire on the line of WHACK TRENCH as follows:-

    Seven p.m. for five minutes.
    Nine-fifteen p.m. for fifteen minutes.
    Eleven p.m. for five minutes.

8. 8th Divisional Artillery is firing similar bursts on WHINE TRENCH.

9. ACKNOWLEDGE.

Issued at 5.30 p.m.

Capt.& Adjt,
49th Battn.M,G.Corps.

Copies to:-
No. 1. "A" Coy.49th Battn.M.G.Corps,
    2. "C" Coy.   do.   do.
    3. "A" Coy. 103rd   do.
    4. 148th Infantry Brigade.
    5. 49th Division "G".
    6. War Diary.
    7. War Diary.
    8. Retained.

TRAINING PROGRAMME. 26.9.18 to 28.9.18 (contd).

Day of Week.	Date.	Company.	7 a.m. - 7.45 a.m.	8.50 a.m. - 9.30 a.m.	9.45 a.m. - 1.15 p.m.	2.15 p.m. - 3.15 p.m.
Saturday.	28.9.18.	"A" and "C".	1. As for 27.9.18. 2. ditto. 3. Sgts. Lecture on Elem.Tactics by Lieut.G.Her. 4. "C" Coy. Lecture by M.O.	P.T. on Battn. Parade Ground under C.S.M.Bethel.	Sub-Sectional Elementary Tactical Exercises.	As for Septr.26th.
"	"	"D".		Close:Order Drill under Adjutant. (S/L Nr. Sgt N(?).)	9 a.m. to 10 a.m. Kit Inspection for men by C.O.(1 Officer per Section will be detailed to be in attendance). 10.30 a.m. to 11.15 a.m. Physical Training for men. 11.15 a.m. to 1.15 p.m. Cleaning Guns etc. 8 a.m. to 1.30 p.m. Tactical Walk for N.C.Os under Section Officers.	

NOTES:- Range work as Ranges available. Company Scouts under 2/Lieut.T.Marshall in Map Reading,Use of Rifle, Use of Ground, Writing Lessages, Clear Verbal Reports.
SIGNALLERS will be under Lieut.J.L.Pattison who will pay particular attention to clear writing. Signallers will attend M.T. Parade daily with Companies.
Correct Procedure in calling up various Officers. Tactical Scheme in conjunction with "D" Company on 27th inst.

CONFERENCE. The Commanding Officer will hold a Conference at 5 p.m. on 25th Septr.1918. Os.C. "A", "C", and "D" Companies will attend. Second-in-Command of Coys. may attend.

GENERAL. The M.O., R.S.M., and Officers who are giving Lectures will notify all concerned of the place they desire to hold their lectures.
Bathing will be arranged to take place in the afternoons when possible.
Football and other Sports will be carried out if possible every afternoon.

MBate
Capt.& Adjt.
49th Battalion,M.G.Corps.

23.9.18.

49th Battalion, Machine Gun Corps -
TRAINING PROGRAMME for "A","C",
and "D" Coys. Septr.26th--Septr.28th.1918.

Day of Week.	Date.	Company.	7 a.m. - 7.45 a.m.	8.50 a.m. - 9.30 a.m.	9.45 a.m. - 1.15 p.m.	2.15 p.m. - 3.15 p.m.
Wednesday.	25.9.18.	A.C.D.	General Cleaning and Checking	P.T. on Battn. Parade Ground under C.S.M.Bethel.		
Thursday.	26.9.18.	"A" and "C".	1. Officers P.T. under C.S.M. Bethel.	Officers at disposal of O.C.Coys. for Conference and discussion.	9.45 a.m. - 1.15 p.m. of Stores. Mechanism and Preliminary Drill under O.C.Companies.	Backward men only. Mechanism under Company Instructors.
			2. Cpls. and L/C under R.S.M. Dress - Drill Order.			
			3. Remainder of Coys. Close Order Drill under Adjt.			
		"D".	As above.	Officers. Staff Ride. O.Rs. (to 9.50) Under R.S.M. Mechanism under N.C.Os.		
Friday.	27.9.18.	"A" and "C".	1. Officers P.T. under C.S.M. Bethel.	P.T. on Battn. Parade Ground under C.S.M. Bethel.	Elementary Work in use of Ground and Cover.	As for 26th inst.
			2. Cpls and L/c under R.S.M. Dress - Drill Order.	Officers at disposal of O.C.Companies for Conference and discussion.		
			3. Sgts. Lecture on maps by Major A.M.R. Lain. I.O.			
			4. "A" Coy. Lecture by I.O. "C" Coy. Close Order Drill under Coy. Sgt. Major.			
		"D".	7.30 a.m. to 1.30 pm. - Tactical Exercises by Sections.			

P.T.O.

--- TRAINING PROGRAMME. ---
------------oOo------------

Monday 30th Sept, 1918.

A.C. & D Companies. - Ranges as details to be issued by 2/Lt. MARSHALL.

Tuesday. 1st Oct. 1918.

8-0 a.m. to 10-0 a.m. - Route March.
Markers report to R.S.M. at 7-45 a.m. Companies march on to markers at 7-50 a.m.
Order of Companies:- C.D.A.
Route will be notified.
DRESS :- Full Marching Order.
10-30 a.m. to 1-0 p.m. under O.C.Companies.
2-0 p.m. to 3-0 p.m. Backward men on mechanism.

Wednesday 2nd Oct. 1918.

7-0 a.m. to 7-45 a.m. A.C. & D Companies.
Officers. : Riding School under Capt. H.C.V.THOMAS.
N.C.O's. : Under Adjutant. DRESS: Drill Order.
C.S.M's and Ptes. : Under R.S.M. Close order drill and Arms drill

8-50 a.m. to 9-30 a.m. A.C. & D Companies.
Other Ranks. : Physical Training under C.S.M.BETHEL.

9-45 a.m. to 1-30 p.m. A.C & D Companies.
Section Tactical Schemes under Section Officers (Fire and
x Movement)

Thursday. 3rd Oct. 1918.

7-0 a.m. to 7-45 a.m. as Wednesday 2.10.18.
8-50 a.m. to 9-30 a.m. as Wednesday 2.10.18.

9-45 a.m. to 1-30 p.m. A.C. & D Companies.
Practice of fire and movement by half Companies.
x

Friday 4th Oct. 1918.

7-0 a.m. to 7-45 a.m. as Wednesday 2.10.18.
8-50 a.m. to 9-30 a.m. as Wednesday 2.10.18.

9-45 a.m. to 1-30 p.m. A.C. & D Companies
Action from Limbers.
x

x 2pm-3pm Backward men. Mechanism etc

M O Bates.
Capt. & Adjt.
49th Battn. M.G.C.

29.9.18.

War Diary
of
10th Bn Machine Gun Corps

OCTOBER
1918

(6392) Wt. W6192/P875 1,500,000 4/18 McA & W Ltd (E 2815) Forms W3091/4. Army Form W.3091

Cover for Documents.

Nature of Enclosures.

Notes, or Letters written.

49th Machine Gun Battn.

WAR DIARY or INTELLIGENCE SUMMARY.

Army Form C. 2118.

Sheet 1.

Place	Date	Hour	Summary of Events and Information	Remarks and references to Appendices
	1.10.18.		Battn in training at "Y" Camp. ETRUN.	
	2.10.18.		(do).	
	3.10.18.		(do)	
	4.10.18.		(do)	
	5.10.18.		(do)	
	6.10.18.		(do)	
	7.10.18.		"D" Coy move to forward area with the 146th Infr. Bde. Group at ARRAS.	
	7.10.18.		H.Q. and A. and C. Coys. move to P. 39. d. with the 148th Infr. Bde.	
	8.10.18.		Group by bus; Transport by road in accordance with O.O. No O.O. 78. B. & D. Coys. remain with 147th & 146th Infr. Bde. Groups.	
	9.10.18.		Battn. H.Q. & A. and C. Coys. move from P. 39. d. to Camp in W. 30. d. B. and D. Coys. move to same vicinity with their Brigade Groups.	
	10.10.18.		Battn. H.Q. move to TILLOY. A and C. Coys to NEUVILLE ST REMY. Capt. T.W. BATES seriously wounded during move. Sergt. McLeod	

29th Batn. M.G.C.   Sheet 2.

WAR DIARY
or
INTELLIGENCE SUMMARY.

Army Form C. 2118.

Place	Date	Hour	Summary of Events and Information	Remarks and references to Appendices
	10.10.18.		wounded, & one O.R. of the Signallers killed. The 146th and 147th Inf. Bdes. with their affiliated M.G. Coys. move up to the line approximately IWUY - PIEUX under orders of the Canadian Corps to attack in conjunction with the 2nd Cdn. Div. on the right and 2nd Canadian Division on the left. Casualties:- 1 Officer wounded (Capt. T.W. BATES) 1. O.R. killed. 3. O.R. wounded. LIEUT. A.C. SKINNER joined the Battn. as a reinforcement.	
	11.10.18.		Attack of 146th & 147th Bdes. commenced well, but the enemy counter-attacked with 6 tanks, forcing us back to the high ground immediately in front of the starting off positions. Casualties:- 6. O.R. killed. 1 Officer & 53. O.R. wounded. 6 O.R. wounded (gas) & 1. O.R. missing.	
	12.10.18.		It was intended to attack again at 12.30. with the Railway running from AUESNES LE SEC to VILLERS EN C AUCHIES as the final objective. Early in the morning however, the enemy withdrew & was closely followed up by the 146th & 147th Inf. Bdes. to the	

49th M.G. Batt. Sheet 3.

Army Form C. 2118.

WAR DIARY
or
INTELLIGENCE SUMMARY.

(Erase heading not required.)

Place	Date	Hour	Summary of Events and Information	Remarks and references to Appendices
	12.10.18.		Line of the river SELLE. During the night our patrols attempted to cross the SELLE, but found the ground on the opposite side occupied.	
	13.10.18.		An attack was launched by the 147th and 148th Inf. Bdes. supported by A.B. and D. Coys. M.G.C. with the object of gaining the high ground on the E of the SELLE river. Overhead Fire was provided by our Machine guns in accordance with O.O. No. 79. Very little headway was made owing to the enemy holding SHULZUIR and HASPRES very strongly with Machine guns. Enemy tanks also were in action about HASPRES. During the night 8 guns of C. Coy. relieved B. Coy. in the 147th Bde. sector. B. Coy. came out into reserve in accordance with O.O. No. 80. Casualties :- 1. Officer Killed (2/Lt L. MATTHANS) 2. O.R. Killed. 28. O.R. wounded. 1. O.R. missing.	O.O.79. O.O.80.
	14.10.18.		Disposition as for Oct 13th. Considerable shelling of forward area on the right. Casualties :- 1. O.R. Killed.	

49th Battn. M.G.C. Sheet 4.

Army Form C. 2118.

WAR DIARY
or
INTELLIGENCE SUMMARY.
(Erase heading not required.)

Place	Date	Hour	Summary of Events and Information	Remarks and references to Appendices
	15.10.18.		Dispositions as under:—	
			A. Coy. Line; Left sub-sector.	
			C. " Line; Right sub-sector.	
			D. " Support.	
			B. " Reserve.	
			There was heavy shelling of the forward area on the right with H.E. 8 guns during the night. The remaining 8 guns of C. Coy. were sent forward, thus making C. Coy. 16 guns in the line.	
	16.10.18.		Dispositions in the line as for the 15th. A reinforcement of 1 Officer (Lt A.C. SHINNER) & 40. O.R. arrived for the Battn. Casualties:— 1. O.R. wounded. 6. O.R. wounded (gas).	
	17.10.18.		Information received that the 4th Battn. M.G.C. will relieve 49th Battn. M.G.C. on the 17/18th and 18/19. B. Coy. move from NAVES to ESCADOEUVRES and C. Coy. 49th Battn. M.G.C. are relieved by D. Coy. 4th Battn. M.G.C. in the right sector. On relief C. Coy. come out to NAVES, all in accordance with	

49th Batt. M.G.C.　　　　　Sheet 5.　　　Army Form C. 2118.

WAR DIARY
or
INTELLIGENCE SUMMARY.
(Erase heading not required.)

Place	Date	Hour	Summary of Events and Information	Remarks and references to Appendices
	17.10.18.		O.O. N°81. 39 O.R. joined the Batt. as reinforcements.	O.O. 81.
	18.10.18		"B" Coy. move from NAVES to ESCADOEUVRES. "D" Coy are relieved in support by 4th Batt. M.G.C. "A" Coy are relieved in the left sector by 4th Batt. M.G.C. "B" and "D" Coys move to ESCADOEUVRES, all in accordance with O.O. 81. Capt. A. Oswell reported to Batt. as Adjutant. Lt. H.C.W. PILE, 2/Lt A.W. NICHOLSON and 26 O.R. reported as reinforcement.	
	19.10.18.		Day spent in cleaning up etc. "D" Coy move from ESCADOEUVRES with 146th Inf. Bde. Group to RAMILLES. Thence to IWUY.	
	Oct 20.		Batt. in training at ESCADOEUVRES.	
	21.10.18.		"D" Coy rejoin the Batt. from IWUY. Batt. in training.	
	22.10.18.		" " "	
	23.10.18		" " "	
	24.10.18		" " "	

49th Batt. M.G.C.   Sheet 6.   Army Form C. 2118.

WAR DIARY
or
INTELLIGENCE SUMMARY.
(Erase heading not required.)

Place	Date	Hour	Summary of Events and Information	Remarks and references to Appendices
	25.10.18.		Batn. in training. 2/Lt. C.T. LOTT and 2/Lt W.E. WILTON and 65 O.R. joined the Batn. from the Base as reinforcements.	
	26.10.18.		Batn. in training at ESCADOEUVRES.	
	27.10.18.		Batn. completes move from ESCADOEUVRES to NEUVILLE SUR L'ESCAUT in accordance with O.O. No 83.	
	28.10.18.		Rear Batn. H.Q. move from NEUVILLE SUR L'ESCAUT & establish rear H.Q. at THONVILLE near DENAIN. "A" Coy. move to HAULCHIN. "B","C" and "D" Coys. move to line of Reserve, and take over from 51st Battn. M.G.C. with their advd. H.Q. in THIANT & rear H.Q. in THONVILLE. Batn. advd. H.Q. remain at NEUVILLE SUR L'ESCAUT, all in accordance with O.O. No. 84. "C" and "D" Coys 102nd = 0.0.84. Batn. M.G.C. attached to the 49th Division. Casualties: 1 wounded (gas), 1 missing.	
	29.10.18.		Dispositions in the FARMET Sector as follows:- Right Sector "D" Coy. Left Sector "C" Coy. Support "B" Coy.	

49 Bttn. M.G.C.

Sheet 7.

Army Form C. 2118.

WAR DIARY
or
INTELLIGENCE SUMMARY.

(Erase heading not required.)

Place	Date	Hour	Summary of Events and Information	Remarks and references to Appendices
	29.10.18.		Reserve "A" Coy. Am. Battn. H.Q. move to AVESNES LE SEC. All disposition in the line & arrangements for Cattack on 90th Contained in O.O. N° 84.	O.O.84
	30.10.18.		Casualties 1 Killed 3 wounded (O.rs). O.O. N° 84 and S.I. 351/57. Postponement of attack 24 hours. Dispositions remain the same. Heavy hostile shelling of FAMARS & MONT HUOY. Casualties. 2 killed: 4 wounded (O.rs).	
	31.10.18.		Further postponement of attack to the morning of Nov. 1st. "B" Coy. move up to their Barrage positions in K.8.b.8. near FAMARS. Casualties 1 wounded (O.rs).	

W M Smyth
Major
Lt. Col. Commanding 49 Bn. M.G.C.

49th Battalion Machine Gun Corps.   Copy No. 15
– OPERATION ORDER No. 78 –

Tuesday 8.10.18.

1. Battalion Headquarters Personnel and Transport will move to new area as follows with 148th Infantry Brigade Group. today.

2. TRANSPORT.

   (a) Starting Point and time.   Starting Point will be at Cross Roads 51.c/ L.2.c.3.5. Head of Column to pass starting point at 15.00 hrs.

   (b) Order of March :

   148th Infantry Brigade Headquarters.
   1/4th Bn. K.O.Y.L.I.
   1/4th Y & L Regt.
   1/5th Y & L Regt.
   458th Field Coy.
   H.Q. 49th Bn. M.G.C.
   "A" Company   do
   "C" Company   do
   1/3rd (W.R.) Field Ambulance.

   (c) Route.   Sheet 51.c./L.2.c.3.5. – ARRAS-CAMBRAI Rd to Sheet 51.b./P.35.c.1.2.
   Guides will meet transport at P.26.d.1.2.
   Location will be approximately P.34.d.

   (d) Column will be under command of Brigade Transport Officer (Lt. J.R. HARRIS).

   (e) Transport will be parked in Battalion area on arrival at destination where they will be split up over the area.

3. PERSONNEL.

   (a) Personnel will proceed by bus. The Head of Bus Column will be on the ETRUN – HARBARCQ Road at 51.c./K.6.c.5.6. facing east.

   (b) Order of embussing will be :

   (1) Brigade H.Q. and T.M.B. H.Q.
   (2) H.Q. 49th Bn. M.G.C.
   (3) "A" Company   do
   (4) "C"   do   do
   etc   etc.

   (c) The Adjutant will be in charge of the embussing. Men will be told off into parties of 25 on arrival at embussing point.

   (d) Troops will be formed up on the SOUTH side of the road and clear of it by 16.45 hrs.

   (e) Battalion H.Q. will be paraded at 15.40. hrs. March off 15.45 hrs.

4. PACKS & BLANKETS.

   Each man will carry own pack and blanket.

Capt. & Adjt.
49th Bn. M.G.C.

Issued at 1200.

-2-

1. O.C."A" Company.
2. O.C."B" Company.
3. O.C."C" Company.
4. O.C."D" Company.
5. R.S.M.
6. Quartermaster.
7. Transport Officer.
8. Signalling Officer.
9. Medical Officer.
10. 146th Infantry Brigade.
11. 147th   do
12. 148th   do
13. "G" 49th Division.
14. "A"   do
15. War Diary. ✓
16. War Diary.
17. File.

SECRET. 49th Battalion Machine Gun Corps.   Copy No....7.
OPERATION ORDER No. 79.

Saturday 12.10.18.

1. Machine Guns will assist the attack of the Division on the high ground EAST of the SELLE River on the morning of the 13th Oct. 1918, the objective being the line P.28.d.5.7. - P.22. central to P.8 central - P.2.b.0.7.

2. "A" Company will have
1 Section about O.23.b. to neutralise fire from NORTH of HASPRES.
1 Section about P.19.c. to neutralise fire from the EAST of HASPRES.
1 Section about P25.b. to fire on high ground in P.14.d. and P.15.c.
1 Section will be used as a section of opportunity in the 148th Brigade Area.

On the objective being taken, the Section at O.23.b. will advance to cover the objective.

"B" Company will have
Two Sections situated about P.25.d. and P.31.b. to barrage the sunken roads in squares P.21. - P.27. and P.28.
One section will advance to cover the objective when gained.

"D" Company will have
One Section in P.25.b. to neutralise fire from SAULZOIR.

3. "C" Company will be in readiness to move as ordered.
"C" Company will form an A.A. dump at O.29.c.4.2.

4. On completion of the operation "D" Company will rejoin the 148th Brigade Group.

5. Advanced Battalion Headquarters will be at U.13.d.19. at 0830.

6. ZERO hour 0900.

7. ACKNOWLEDGE.

Major.
49th Bn. M.G.C.

Issued at.....

Copies to :-

1. O.C. "A" Company.
2. O.C. "B" Company.
3. O.C. "C" Company.
4. O.C. "D" Company.
5. 49th Division "G".
6. War Diary.
7. War Diary.
8. File.

O.C. "C" Company (Rear)   SECRET   Office
O.C. "C" Company (Advanced) for information.
"G" 49th Division.
146th Infantry Brigade.

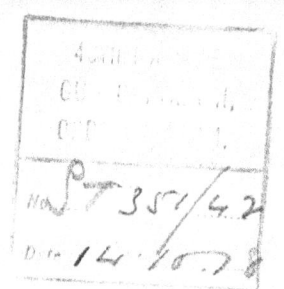

        The 2 Sections of "C" Company, 49th Battalion Machine Gun Corps at present in Reserve, will, on receipt of this order proceed to Advanced Company Headquarters at the Cross Roads in U.13.d. They will there come under the command of Capt. HESKETH (O.C. "C" Company)

        They will be used in the Right Brigade Sector and will take up positions in accordance with arrangements made by Major W.J.M. OPENSHAW D.M.G. with the G.O.C. 146th Infantry Brigade.

                                B.H. Badham
                                        Lt.-Colonel.
                     Commanding 49th Bn. Machine Gun Corps.

14.10.18.

SECRET.　　　　　　49th Battalion Machine Gun Corps.　　　Copy No....
　　　　　　　　　　OPERATION ORDER No. 80.

　　　　　　　　　　　　　　　　　　　　　　Sunday 13.10.18.

1. 8 guns of "C" Company under Capt. HESKETH will relieve "B" Company in the 147th Infantry Brigade Sector tonight 13th/14th October 1918.
The remaining 8 guns of "C" Company will remain in their present location, and will be held in Reserve.

2. All details of relief will be arranged mutually between O.C. Companies concerned.

3. On completion of relief "B" Company will occupy accomodation vacated by "C" Company in the railway cutting in T.17.c. Headquarters of "B" Company will be at T.22.b.7.3.

4. Reliefs to be reported to Headquarters using code word "IRON".

5. ACKNOWLEDGE.

　　　　　　　　　　　　　　　　　　　　[signature]
　　　　　　　　　　　　　　　　　　　　　　　　Major.
　　　　　　　　　　　　　　　　　　　　49th Bn. M.G.C.

Issued at......

Copies to :-

1. O.C. "B" Company.
2. O.C. "C" Company.
3. O.C. "A" Company.
4. O.C. "D" Company.
5. 146th Inf. Brigade.
6. 147th　do
7. 148th　do
8. "G" 49th Division.
9. Transport Officer.
10. Quartermaster.
11. Signalling Officer.
12. War Diary.
13. War Diary.
14. File.

SECRET. 49th Battalion Machine Gun Corps. Copy No. 15
-- OPERATION ORDER NO. 81. --

Ref. Map. 51.A. Thursday 17.10.18

1. The 49th Battalion Machine Gun Corps will be relieved by the 4th Battalion Machine Gun Corps on the 17th and 18th October 1918, and will take over billets and accomodation vacated by the 4th Bn Machine Gun Corps at ESCAUDOEUVRES.

2. "C" Company 49th Bn. M.G.C. will be relieved by "D" Company 4th Bn M.G.C. in the RIGHT Sector on the night of 17th/18th October 1918 under arrangements to be made mutually by O.C. Companies concerned. On relief, "C" Company 49th Bn. M.G.C. will be accomodated in billets vacated by "B" Company 49th Bn. M.G.C. at NAVES.

3. "B" Company 49th Bn. M.G.C. will move from their present billets in NAVES to billets vacated by "D" Company 4th Bn. M.G.C. at ESCAUDOEUVRES. To arrive ESCAUDOEUVRES by 1700 hrs Oct 17th.1918.

4. "A" Company 49th Bn. M.G.C. will be relieved by "B" Company 4th Bn. M.G.C. in the LEFT Sector on the night 18th/19th Oct. 1918 under arrangements to be made mutually by O.C. Companies concerned. On relief "A" Company 49th Bn. M.G.C. will proceed direct to ESCAUDOEUVRES and take over billets vacated by "B" Company 4th Bn. M.G.Corps.

5. "D" Company 49th Bn. M.G.C. will be relieved in U.1.d. by "A" Company 4th Bn. M.G.C. under arrangements to be made mutually by O.C. Companies concerned. Relief to be complete by 1430 hrs. 18th Oct. 1918 at which hour "D" Company will move off.
On relief "D" Company will take over billets vacated by "A" Company 4th Bn. M.G.C. at ESCAUDOEUVRES.

6. "C" Company 49th Bn. M.G.C. will be relieved by "C" Company 4th Bn M.G.C. in NAVES. "C" Company 49th Bn. M.G.C. to move off at 1430 hrs 18th October 1918, and take over billets vacated by "C" Company 4th Bn. M.G.Corps at ESCAUDOEUVRES.

7.
49th Battalion Headquarters will close at NAVES at 1000 hrs on the 19th instant at which hour command of Machine Guns in the sector will pass to O.C. 4th Battalion Machine Gun Corps.
49th Battalion Headquarters will open at ESCAUDOEUVRES at the same hour.

8. Arrangements for relief of Signal Sections to be made mutually by Signal Officers concerned.

9. Completion of reliefs will be reported to Battalion Headquarters using code words as under :-

"C" Company, 49th Bn. Machine Gun Corps. - "ZINC"
"A"   "   "   "   "   "   - "COPPER"
"D"   "   "   "   "   "   - "LEAD"

10. Companies will make their own arrangements as regards billeting parties. These parties should be at ESCAUDOEUVRES at least 3 hours before arrival of Companies.

11. Tracks will be used wherever possible and main roads only used where absolutely necessary. Every effort will be made to avoid interfering with traffic on the main roads.

P.T.O.

-2-

12.   (a) No movement in larger bodies than sections.
       (b) Regulation distances to be strictly observed by Transport on the march.

13.   ACKNOWLEDGE 4th Battalion Machine Gun Corps and M.G. Companies 49th Battalion Machine Gun Corps only.

Issued at......1315hrs   Major,
                                                  49th Battn. M.G.C

Copies to :-

    1. O.C. "A" Company.
    2. O.C. "B" Company.
    3. O.C. "C" Company.
    4. O.C. "D" Company.
    5. Headquarters, 4th Bn. M.G.C.   (2)
    6. 146th Infantry Brigade.)
    7. 147th   do   )
    8. 148th   do   )
    9. Signalling Officer.   )
  10. Transport Officer.   )   For
  11. Quartermaster.   )
  12. "G" 49th Division.   )   Information.
  13. "A" 49th Division.   )
  14. 49th Div. Train.   )
  15. War Diary. ✓   )
  16. War Diary.   )
  17. File.   )

MARCH TABLE

Date.	Serial No.	Unit.	From.	Relieved by.	To	REMARKS.
Oct. 17th/18.	1.	"C" Coy. 49th Bn. MGC.	RIGHT Sector.	"D" Coy 4th.Bn.MGC.	NAVES.	Billets vacated by "B" Company 49th MGC.
17th.	2.	"B" Coy. 49th Bn. M.G.C	NAVES.	—	ESCAUDOEUVRES.	To take over Billets vacated by "D" Company 4th Bn. M.G.C. to arrive ESCAUDOEUVRES by 1700 hrs.
18th/19th.	3.	"A" Coy. 49th Bn. M.G.C.	LEFT Sector.	"B" Coy. 4th Bn. M.G.C.	ESCAUDOEUVRES.	To take over billets vacated by "B" Company 4th Bn. M.G.C.
18th.	4.	"D" Coy. 49th Bn. M.G.C.	U.l.d.	"A" Coy. 4th Bn. M.G.C.	ESCAUDOEUVRES.	Relief to be complete by 1430 hrs. To take over billets vacated by "A" Company 4th Bn. M.G.C.
18th.	5.	"C" Coy. 49th Bn. M.G.C.	NAVES.	"C" Coy. 4th Bn. M.G.C.	ESCAUDOEUVRES.	To move off at 1430 hrs. and take over billets vacated by "C" Company 4th. Bn. M.G.C.
19th.	6.	Signal Section.	NAVES.	4th Bn. MGC Signals.	ESCAUDOEUVRES.	Under orders of Signalling Officers.
19th.	7.	H.Q. 49th Bn M.G.C.	NAVES.	H.Q. 4th Bn M.G.C.	ESCAUDOEUVRES	Close at NAVES 1000 hrs. and open ESCAUDOEUVRES at same hour. Orders for move to be issued later.

49th Battalion Machine Gun Corps.   Copy No. 17
-- OPERATION ORDER NO. 83 --

Saturday 26.10.18.

1. 49th Battalion Machine Gun Corps will move from their present billets to NEUVILLE SUR L'ESCAUT tomorrow 27th October 1918.

2. Order of march: Signallers, "A" Company, "B" Company, "C" Company "D" Company, Headquarters. DRESS: Fighting Order. Packs to be carried on limbers.
Transport will march in rear of their respective Companies.

3. Head of Column will pass Div. Headquarters (T.19.d.9.2.) at 0900 hrs and will proceed by the following route:
ESCAUDOEUVRES - IWUY - PAVE de VALENCIENNES (N.3.)-Second class road through I.25.A - NEUVILLE-SUR-ESCAUT.

4. Strict march discipline will be observed during the march, and the usual distances maintained between Companies and transport.

5. All transport will lead on behind its respective Company from the Transport Lines, and no vehicle will be on the road prior to moving off.
Companies prior to moving off will not be formed up in the roadway.

6. One Officer and 4 O.Rs per Company, C.S.M.BETHEL. and 4 O.Rs from Headquarters will meet Major W.J.M.SPROULLE M.C. at the church in NEUVILLE -SUR-L'ESCAUT at 1000 hrs. 27th instant to arrange for billets in the new area.

7. All blankets will be deposited at the Quartermasters Stores by 0700 hrs 27th instant, rolled up and labelled in bundles of 10.

8. Instructions regarding move of Quartermasters Stores have been issued to Quartermaster.

9. The Signalling Officer will arrange to synchronise all Company watches prior to moving off.

10. ACKNOWLEDGE.(A.B.C. & D Companies only.)

Issued at 2200 hrs.

W/M. Sproulle
Major.
49th Bn. M.G.C.

Copies to :-
1. O.C."A" Company.
2. O.C."B" Company.
3. O.C."C" Company.
4. O.C."D" Company.
5. Signalling Officer.
6. Transport Officer.
7. Quartermaster.
8. Medical Officer.
9. "G" 49th Division.
10. "A"   do
11. "Q"   do
12. 49th Div. Train.
13. A.D.M.S. 49th Divn.
14. 146th Infantry Brigade.
15. 147th   do
16. 148th   do
17. War Diary. ✓
18. War Diary.
19. File.

SECRET.

49th Battalion Machine Gun Corps.
OPERATION ORDER No. 84.

Copy No. 18.

Reference Map: Sheet 51.A.   Monday 28.10.18.

1. (a) On the night 28th/29th October 1918, 49th Division will relieve the Right Brigade of the 51st Division and portion of the Left Brigade of the 4th Division.

    (b) <u>Boundaries</u>:   As marked on Map A. (issued to all concerned).

2. The 49th Bn. M.G.C. will take over from the 51st Bn. M.G.C. on the night 28th/29th. Guns will be in position by 2359 hrs. On 29th inst At 0100 hrs. the guns of the 51st Bn. M.G.C. will withdraw.

3. Companies will be disposed as follows:
    <u>"A" COMPANY</u>. will move to HAULCHIN, take over from Company of 51st Bn. M.G.C. there and be Company in Reserve.

    <u>"B" COMPANY</u>. will move to TRITH ST LEGER taking over from Company of 51st Bn. M.G.C. there - for protection of Divisional LEFT Flank.

    "D" and "C" Companies will operate respectively in the RIGHT and LEFT Brigade Sectors taking over from the Companies of the 51st Bn. M.G.C. under arrangements made at Commanding Officer's conference this morning.
    The Company of the 102nd Bn. M.G.C. will remain in the line.

4. Group Commanders will be :

    RIGHT Group : Capt. H.C.V.THOMAS.
    LEFT Group : Capt. H.R.HESKETH.

5. Companies will move independently, but will not pass EAST of line THIANT - LE GRAND BOIS before dark. There will be no movement EAST of THIANT in parties larger than a section.
    O.C.Companies will arrange to be rear of this line by dusk.
    A hot meal will be arranged before moving.
    There is no restriction as to route.

6. Rear Headquarters and rear echelon of "B", "C", and "D" Companies will move independently to THONVILLE this afternoon.
    Rear Headquarters will form up in grounds of Battalion Headquarters at 1400 hrs.

7. Battalion Headquarters (C.O. Adjutant, Signalling Officer and Orderly Room Staff) will move to AVESNES LE SEC and take over from Headquarter 51st Bn. M.G.C.
    They will move off from Battalion H.Q. at 1430 hrs.

8. O.C.Companies will make their personal reconnaisance this morning.

9. Expendable belts will be filled and placed on the Western edge of FAMARS, if possible in a cellar, under arrangements to be made between Major. W.J.N.SPROULLE.M.C. and the 2nds-in-command of Companies. Reserve of water will be kept at the same place.

10. The Signalling Officer has been given instructions with regard to communication. He will inform Companies direct of his arrangements.

11. Blankets of "B", "C", and "D" Companies will be dumped at Quartermasters Stores properly labelled, and packed in bundles of 10 by 1300 hrs.
    "A" Company will retain theirs.

P.T.O.

12. ACKNOWLEDGE. (A.B.C.& D Companies only)

Issued at 1145 hrs.

A. Divell
Capt. & Adjt.
49th Bn. M.G.C.

Copies to:-

1. O.C. "A" Company.
2. O.C. "B" Company.
3. O.C. "C" Company.
4. O.C. "D" Company.
5. Quartermaster.
6. Signalling Officer.
7. Transport Officer. (3).
8. "G" Division.
9. "A" 49th Division.
10. "Q" 49th Division.
11. 51st Bn. M.G.C.
12. 146th Infantry Brigade.
13. 147th do
14. 148th do
15. A.D.M.S. 49th Division.
16. War Diary.
17. War Diary.
18. File.

SECRET.

Amendment to 49th Bn. M.G.C. Operation Order No. 84.

Reference Map: Sheet 51.A.

Para.3.
For   TRITH ST LEGER, read THIANT.

Para.7.
For 1430 hrs. on the 28th instant.

Read 0830 hrs. on the 29th instant.

28.10.18.

Capt. & Adjt.
49th Bn. M.G.C.

SECRET.　　　　　49th Battalion Machine Gun Corps.　　　Copy No. 9
　　　　　　　　　-- OPERATION ORDER NO. 86 --
　　　　　　　　-------------oOo-------------

Reference Map: Sheet. 51.A.　　　　　　　　　　　Tuesday. 29.10.18.

1.　On the 31st October. 1918 the 49th Division in conjunction with the
　　4th Canadian Division on the LEFT and the 4th British Division
　　on the RIGHT will attack the enemy with the object of gaining the
　　line of the　　PRESAU - VALENCIENNES Road.

2.　The attack will be made by the 147th Infantry Brigade on the RIGHT
　　and the 146th Infantry Brigade on the LEFT.　　148th Infantry
　　Brigade in reserve.　Boundaries as shown on attached map "A"
　　(issued to Company Commanders).

3.　The 49th Bn. M.G.C. and "D" and "C" Companies of the 102nd Bn M.G.C.
　　will support the attack as follows:

(a)　"B" Company, 49th Bn. M.G.C. and "C" Company, 102nd Bn. M.G.C. from
　　　positions in K.8.d., K.9.c. and K.15, will barrage the line K.4.a.5.0
　　　K.10.a.8.8. - K.11.c.5.5., from ZERO to ZERO plus thirty.
　　　They will then lift to the line of the sunken road AULNOY - PRESAU;
　　　and will cease fire at ZERO plus seventy.

(b)　"D" Company and "C" Company, 49th Bn. M.G.C. will advance in conjuncti
　　　with the right and left Brigades respectively. A half of each
　　　Company will follow the leading Battalion in each sector at an
　　　approximate distance of eight hundred yards from the front line.
　　　As soon as the high ground in K.11. and K.4. has been secured, they
　　　will push on and consolidate the line of this ridge.
　　　One section of "C" Company will be especially detailed to watch the
　　　valley of the RHONELLE between AULNOY and MARLY.
　　　These guns will NOT leave this line.

(c)　On the final objective being gained, the other half of each of "D" and "C"
　　　Companies will take up positions on the approximate line K.6.c.0.0.-
　　　E.29. central - E.23.c.0.0. to cover the final objective.
　　　One section of "C" Company being especially detailed to guard the left
　　　flank, and to watch the exits from MARLY.
　　　All guns will keep a special lookout for tanks.

(d)　The barrage guns of "B" Company, 49th Bn. M.G.C., and of "C" Company,
　　　102nd Bn. M.G.C. on completion of their tasks will remain in their
　　　positions and come into Divisional Reserve.
　　　"A" Company, 49th Bn. M.G.C. (eight guns) will remain in Divisional
　　　Reserve at HAULCHIN.
　　　"D" "A" Company, 102nd Bn. M.G.C. will remain in Divisional Reserve
　　　at HAULCHIN.

4.　The rate of fire for the barrage guns will be one belt per gun
　　per three minutes.

5.　The Battalion Signalling Officer has notified arrangements for
　　communication directly to those concerned.

6.　The Battalion Signalling Officer will arrange for synchronisation
　　of watches at 1600 hrs on the 30th Oct. 1918, and at four hours
　　before ZERO.

7.　ZERO hour will be notified later,

8.　ACKNOWLEDGE.

　　　　　　　　　　　　　　　　　　　　　　　A.O.Swell
　　　　　　　　　　　　　　　　　　　　　　　Capt. & Adjt.
　　Issued at.... *2000 hrs.*　　　　　　　　49th Bn. M.G.C.

　　　　　　　　　　　　　　　　　　　　　　　　　　　　P.T.O.

Copies to :-

1. O.C."A" Company.
2. O.C."B" Company.
3. O.C."C" Company.
4. O.C."D" Company.
5. Signalling Officer.
6. 102nd Bn. M.G.C.
7. "D" Company, 102nd Bn. M.G.C.
8. "C" Company, 102nd Bn. M.G.C.
9. War Diary.
10. War Diary.
11. File.
12. 49th Bn. M.G.C. (Rear)

SECRET.

ADDENDUM NO. 1. to 49th Bn. M.G.C.
OPERATION ORDER NO. 85.

Thursday. 31.10.18.

For the operations of November 1st the Forward Battalion Report Centre will be at THIANT. (J.15.c.2.5.)

"D" Company 49th Bn. M.G.C. advanced Company Headquarters will move to MAING (J.24.a.6.2.)

"C" Company 49th Bn. M.G.C. Forward Report Centre will move to the Headquarters of the 146th Infantry Brigade (J.17.d.5.6.).

The Company. H.Q. of "C" Company 102nd Bn. M.G.C. and "B" Company 49th Bn. M.G.C. will remain as at present.

ACKNOWLEDGE. (Companies of 49th Bn. M.G.C. and 102nd Bn. M.G.C. concerned).

Issued at 1045 hr.

Llewelly
Capt. & Adjt.
49th Bn. M.G.C.

To all recipients of Operation Order No. 85.

SECRET.   ADDENDUM NO.2. to 49th Battalion
Machine Gun Corps OPERATION ORDER NO.86.
------------------oOo------------------

Reference Map: Sheet 51.A.   Thursday 31.10.18.

1. When the final objective of the 1st day's operations has been
    taken, the situation will be exploited towards the objective given
    for the second day's operations with the following objects
    in view:

    (a) Ascertaining whether the enemy resistance has ceased or
    has become so weak that it can be overcome without artillery support
    other than that of forward sections.

    (b) (If enemy resistance has ceased or has become so weak that
    it can be overcome without artillery support other than that of
    forward sections). capturing enemy artillery batteries in
    E.24. - E.30. - F.25. - and L.1.a.

    (c) (If enemy resistance has ceased or has become so weak that
    it can be overcome without artillery support other than that of
    forward sections). capturing and occupying the following line:
    In case of LEFT Brigade. - The VALENCIENNES - SAULTAIN railway from
    E.23.a.5.2. to E.24.d.5.5.

    In case of the RIGHT Brigade. - The LA VILLETTE - SAULTAIN - PRESAU
    Road from E.24.d.5.5. to L.1.b.2.2.

    Unless further orders are issued to the contrary this will be regarded
    as the limit of exploitation.

2. Similar exploitation will be carried on on Right and Left flanks
    by the 4th British Division and 4th Canadian Division respectively.

3. The troops allotted to the Right Brigade for exploitation purposes
    are:

        1. Squadron Australian Light Horse.
        1. Platoon. N.Z. Cyclists.
        1. Section "A" Company. 49th Bn. M.G.C.

4. Exploitation will be carried out x in 2 stages as follows:

    First Stage. - As soon as the protective barrage ceases at
    ZERO plus 190 minutes patrols assisted in the case of the Right Brigade
    by one Section "A" Company, 49th Bn. M.G.C. will be pushed out
    to ascertain the state of the enemy resistance. They will
    overcome any enemy resistance which they are strong enough to
    deal with and prevent the enemy removing any enemy guns left on
    the ground.

    Second Stage. - As soon as the patrols report that the enemy
    resistance is weak or non-existent - sufficient Infantry will be pushed
    out to occupy as an outpost line, the line limiting exploitation.

5. The second stage will NOT be undertaken before ZERO plus 6 hours.

6. S.O.S. - After the formation of the protective barrage in front
    of the final objective the artillery will reply to an S.O.S. signal
    whenever received, but the barrage will fall on the line of the

                                                            P.T.O.

protector (vide Barrage Tracing "C" already issued).

In event of exploitation being possible, troops in advance of the final objective will be kept 400 yards clear of the barrage line, and if the S.O.S. is brought down behind them they will remain out until the situation is quiet.

7. The Section of "A" Company, 49th Bn. M.G.C. detailed to assist the exploitation by the squadron of Australian Light Horse will be in position at K.10. central by ZERO plus 2 hours moving under the Sub-Section Officer in accordance with orders already issued to O.C. "A" Company.

8. The Section Officer will be with the O.C. Squadron Australian Light Horse at ZERO hour. The location of this Officer will be obtained from 147th Infantry Brigade Headquarters.

9. These guns will remain in support until ordered to withdraw.

10. Personnel will be as lightly equipped as possible.

11. ACKNOWLEDGE (Companies of 49th Bn. M.G.C. only).

Issued at..........

Capt. & Adjt.
49th Bn. M.G.C.

Copies to all recipients of Operation Order No. 86.
and "G" 49th Division.
    147th Inf. Brigade.

SECRET.

NOTES ON THE RHONELLE RIVER.

To accompany 49th Bn. M.G.C. Operation Order No. 86.

(a)   It is possible that the RHONELLE will offer a more serious obstacle than as formerly thought.
    It has a muddy bottom, and the water being dammed up is reported in places to be about four feet deep.   C.R.E. will arrange to provide 30 ft. lengths of rope as required by Infantry Brigades to assist the troops in fording the river if necessary.

(b)   ~~The last sentence is amended to read as follows~~:
    "Trestle bridges will be constructed about K.10.c.4.2. and K.9.b.9.5. if the situation permits, commencing at ZERO plus one hundred and sixty.
    "The completion of either bridge will be notified by the code message "ACROSS A" or ACROSS B", respectively.

C.H.A. Clarke 2/Lt
for Capt. & Adjt.
49th Bn. M.G.C.

30.10.18.

Copies to all recipients of Operation Order No. 86.

SECRET.   49th Battalion Machine Gun Corps.   Copy No. 19
           --OPERATION ORDER NO. 87.--

Reference Map: Sheet 51.A.   Thursday. 31.10.18.

1. "C" Company 49th Bn. M.G.C. will be relieved by a Company of the
    Canadian M.G.Corps on the night of 1st/2nd November 1918.

2. Details of relief will be arranged directly between O.C."C" Company
    and O.C.Company Canadian M.G.C. at 11th Canadian Brigade Headquarters
    THIANT.

3. On relief "C" Company, 49th Bn. M.G.C. will proceed to billets
    near MAING.

4. On the night of the 1st/2nd November 1918, half Company of "B"
    Company, 49th Bn. M.G.C. and half Company of "C" Company, 102nd.
    Bn. M.G.C. will move up to positions for the close defence of the
    line gained on the 1st Novr. 1918. These half Companies will
    assist the attack of the 148th Infantry Brigade on the 3rd Nov. 1918.

    The objective on the 3rd being the main line of resistance -
    these guns will be pushed well forward to defend it.

5. The remaining half Companies will withdraw to billets in THIANT.

6. "D" Company, 49th Bn. M.G.C. will remain in the position reached
    on the 1st November 1918.
                       will be
7. The group Commander, Major. H.D.HANSON. This Officer will report
    to Headquarters 148th Infantry Brigade on the evening of the 2nd
    November 1918.

8. On the night of the 3rd/4th November 1918   (a) "A" Company,
    49th Bn. M.G.C. will relieve half Company of "B" Company 49th Bn. M.G.C
    and half Company of "C" Company, 102nd Bn. M.G.C.
    (b) "C" Company, 49th Bn. M.G.C. will relieve "D" Company, 49th
    Bn. M.G.C. in Support.

9. On relief "B" Company, 49th Bn. M.G.C. will occupy the billets
    vacated by "A" Company 49th Bn. M.G.C. at HAULCHIN. : " D" Company,
    49th Bn. M.G.C. will occupy the billets vacated by "C" Company
    49th Bn. M.G.C. near MAING. Location of billets for half Company of
    "C" Company 102nd Bn. M.G.C. will be notified later.

10. Details of relief will be arranged direct between O.C.Companies
    concerned.

11. Completion of reliefs and moves will be notified to 49th Bn
    Headquarters by code as follows :

    Para. (1).   June.   12. On the night 3rd/4th. Divnl.Reserv
      "   (4).   will   will consist of:
      "   (5).   follow   "B" & "D" Coys, 49th Bn. M.G.C.
      "   (8).   May.   "C" & "D" Coys, 102nd Bn.M.G.C.

13. ACKNOWLEDGE. (Companies 49th Bn. M.G.C. and   O.C.Welly
    102nd Bn. M.G.C. only)   Capt. & Adjt.
    Issued at 2140   49th Bn. M.G.C.
                                                             P.T.O.
    Copies to :-
        1. O.C."A" Company.   13. "G" 49th Division.
        2. O.C."B" Company.   14. 146th Infantry Brigade.
        3. O.C."C" Company.   15. 147th   do
        4. O.C."D" Company.   16. 148th   do
        5. Quartermaster.   17. 11th Canadian Bde H.Q.
        6. Signalling Officer.   18. War Diary.
        7. Transport Officer.   19. War Diary. ✓
        8. Medical Officer.   20. File.
        9. 102nd Bn. M.G.C.
       10. "C" Company, 102nd M.G.C.
       11. "A" 49th Division.
       12. "Q" 49th Division.

Cancelled

SECRET

O.C. "A" Company.
O.C. "B" Company.
O.C. "C" Company.
O.C. "D" Company.

49TH MACHINE
GUN BATTALION.
ORDERLY ROOM.
No. S.7.357/5
Date 28-10-18

OUTLINE OF MACHINE GUN CO-OPERATION IN ATTACK ON THE 30th October, 1918.

On the night of the 29th/30th "B" Company will move up 16 guns to K.8.d. and K.9.c.

At ZERO Hr. They will barrage a line corresponding to the Artillery barrage line C. They will then lift to the Eastern approaches to AULNOY and sunken roads in K.4.

A Company of the 102nd Bn. M.G.C. will move to positions in K.15., and barrage a line corresponding to barrage line C.

They will then lift to the sunken roads between B.M. 69.7 and B.M. 86.5.

A half Company of "D" Company will be prepared to follow the Infantry in the attack at an approximate distance of 800 yards.

On the high ground in K.11. being obtained they will push on and consolidate this line.

"C" Company will be prepared to do the same thing and consolidate the high ground in K.4.- one section especially being detailed to watch the exits of AULNOY.

These guns will not move forward from this line.

On the final objective being obtained 8 other guns of each of these two Companies will take up positions to cover the final objective.

One section of "C" Company will be detailed to guard the left flank.

The barrage guns of "B" Company and of the 102nd M.G.Company will remain in their positions.

Exact times for barrage will be issued as soon as possible.

Capt. & Adjt.
49th Bn. M.G.C.

28.10.18.

Confidential

Original

49 Bn M.G Corps Vol 9

WAR DIARY

From 1.11.18 – 30.11.18.

Vol. 9.

49th Battn. M.G.C.

Army Form C. 2118.

Sheet 1.

WAR DIARY
or
INTELLIGENCE SUMMARY.
(Erase heading not required.)

Instructions regarding War Diaries and Intelligence Summaries are contained in F.S. Regs., Part II. and the Staff Manual respectively. Title pages will be prepared in manuscript.

Place	Date	Hour	Summary of Events and Information	Remarks and references to Appendices
	1.11.18		The 49th Division in conjunction with the Canadian Corps on the left and 4th British Division on the right attack at 05.15 hours under a heavy barrage. All objectives gained 9th line firmly established on Road running from E.30.a.2.1. to K.6.d.2.0. C and D Coys consolidated the line gained 9 a barrage was put up by B. Coy. and C. Coy. 102nd M.G.Batn. A. Coy. (less one section) remained in reserve at HAULCHIN. In the evening A. Coy. (less one section) take up positions about the final objective as a jumping off position for the attack which is to take place on the morning of the 2nd by the 149th Inf. Bde. B. Coy. come out to THIANT and C. Coy. come out to HAULCHIN. O.R's:- 3 killed, 25 wounded, 9 wounded gas.	O.O. 88.
	2.11.18		C and D Coys. 102nd Batn. M.G.C. are withdrawn to DOUCHY. Orders received that the Battn. would be relieved by the 56th Batn. M.G.C. B. Coy. sent forward from Reserve in THIANT to high ground about FAMARS. Battn. rear H.Q. and C. Coy. move to BASSEVILLE. D. Coy. relieved in forward area and move to THONVILLE. Casualties:- O.R's:- 8 wounded, 6 wounded gas. 2/Lt W.F. WILTON wounded.	
	3.11.18		Battn. advanced H.Q. move from AVESNES LE SEC to BASSEVILLE.	

49th Battn. M.G.C. Sheet 2. Army Form C. 2118.

WAR DIARY or INTELLIGENCE SUMMARY.

(Erase heading not required.)

Instructions regarding War Diaries and Intelligence Summaries are contained in F. S. Regs., Part II. and the Staff Manual respectively. Title pages will be prepared in manuscript.

Place	Date	Hour	Summary of Events and Information	Remarks and references to Appendices
	3.11.18.		D. Coy. move from THONVILLE to BASSEVILLE. A. Coy. relieved in the forward area by the 56th Battn. M.G.C. and move to HAULCHIN for the night. B. Coy. move to BASSEVILLE.	W/Wel
	4.11.18.		A. Coy. move to BASSEVILLE. Whole Battn. is now assembled there.	W/Wel
	5.11.18.		Lt. G. ROBINSON and 2/Lt A.B. PENDER joined the Battn as reinforcements. The whole Battn. move by Bus (Transport by March route) in accordance with O.O. 91. and are billeted in AUBY.	W/Wel O.O.91.
	6.11.18.		Battn. in training at AUBY.	W/Wel
	7.11.18		(do)	W/Wel
	8.11.18		(do)	W/Wel
	9.11.18		(do)	W/Wel
	10.11.18		(do) 2/Lt. D.C. STEVENSON. 2/Lt V. LYLE & 30 O.R. joined the Battn. as reinforcements.	W/Wel
	11.11.18.		Armistice with Germany 11. a.m.	W/Wel
	12.11.18.		Battn in training at AUBY.	W/Wel
	13.11.18.		(do)	W/Wel

49th M.G. Battn.   Sheet 3.

Army Form C. 2118.

WAR DIARY
or
INTELLIGENCE SUMMARY.
(Erase heading not required.)

Instructions regarding War Diaries and Intelligence Summaries are contained in F. S. Regs., Part II. and the Staff Manual respectively. Title pages will be prepared in manuscript.

Place	Date	Hour	Summary of Events and Information	Remarks and references to Appendices
	14.11.18.		Battn. in training at AUBY. Educational Scheme commenced	
	15.11.18.		2/Lt. A.B. PENDER.	
	16.11.18.		Battn. in training. Lt. A.O. REES rejoined the Battn.	
			(do)	
	17.11.18.		Church Parade. 2 O.R's reinforcements arrived.	
	18.11.18.		Battn. in training. 1 O.R. " "	
	19.11.18.		(do)	
	20.11.18.		(do)	
	21.11.18.		(do)	
	22.11.18.		(do) 16. O.R's reinforcements arrived.	
	23.11.18.		(do)	
	24.11.18.		Church Parade.	
	25.11.18.		Battn. in training.	
	26.11.18.		(do) 11. O.R's joined the Battn.	
	27.11.18.		(do)	
	28.11.18.		(do)	

49th Battn. M.G.C.

Sheet A.

Army Form C. 2118.

WAR DIARY
or
INTELLIGENCE SUMMARY.
(*Erase heading not required.*)

Instructions regarding War Diaries and Intelligence Summaries are contained in F. S. Regs., Part II. and the Staff Manual respectively. Title pages will be prepared in manuscript.

Place	Date	Hour	Summary of Events and Information	Remarks and references to Appendices
	29.11.18.		Battn. in training. 12 O.R.'s joined the Battn.	
	30.11.18.		Battn. in training.	

R McSmith
Lieut. Col. Commanding 49th Bn. M.G.C.
Major for

"A" Form
MESSAGES AND SIGNALS.

Army Form C. 2121
(in pads of 100.)

To: C.in C.

TO: 49 Div

Sender's Number	Day of Month	In reply to Number	AAA
OR454	4		

Herewith War Diary for month of November. Please acknowledge.

49TH MACHINE GUN BATTALION, ORDERLY ROOM.
No. ST. 302/81.
Date 4-12-18

From: 49 Bn M.G.C.

SECRET.   49th Battalion Machine Gun Corps.   Copy No....
           OPERATION ORDER No. 88.

Ref Map. 51.A.   Friday 1..11.18.

1.   The 49th Bn. M.G.C. Operation Order No. 87 is cancelled.

2.   On the afternoon of the 1st Nove "A" Company 49th Bn. M.G.C.
     less one section will move from HAULCHIN to MAING leaving
     their present billets at 1400 hrs preparatory to taking
     over the Forward Area.

3.   This Company will work in close support of the 148th Infantry
     Brigade and will take up positions on or near the main line
     of resistance.

4.   Officers will make their reconnaissance of the Forward Area
     this afternoon.

5.   Guns will be in position by 2300 hrs.

6.   O.C."A" Company, 49th Bn. M.G.C. will be prepared to assist
     the attack of the 148th Infantry Brigade on the 2nd. He will
     report to the B.G.C. 148th Infantry Brigade this afternoon
     and remain with him during the operations.

7.   "D" Company, 49th Bn. M.G.C. will remain in their present
     position.
     On the attack of the 148th Infantry Brigade being successful
     the half Company in K.11.b. & 5.c. will move to positions in
     E.30.c. & K.6.d.
     Any loss of guns by "D" Company, 49th Bn. M.G.C. will be made
     good by "D" Company 102nd Bn. M.G.C.

8.   "C" Company, 49th Bn. M.G.C. will be relieved on the night
     1st/2nd by a Company of the Canadian M.G.C. as stated in
     Operation Order No 87.
     On relief, Company will move to HAULCHIN to billets vacated
     by "A" Company, 49th Bn. M.G.C.

9.   "B" Company 49th Bn. M.G.C. will withdraw at 2000 hrs on the
     1st Novr. 1918. to billets at THIANT.

10. "C" Company 102nd Bn. M.G.C. will be withdrawn at 23.59 hrs
     on the 1st Novr. to billets in DOUCHY.
     Four limbers of "D" Company 49th Bn. M.G.C. will assist their
     withdrawal.
     Arrangements to be made this afternoon between Company
     Officers concerned. There will be no movement East of MAING
     in parties larger than a section.
     On withdrawal of "B" Company, "A" Company 49th Bn. M.G.C. will
     take over expendable belts from "B" Company 49th Bn. M.G.C.

11. Ammunition dump and reserve water supply will be formed near
     K.5.b.1.6.

12. Completion of relief will be reported to Battalion Headquarters
     by code word "BEATRICE".

13. ACKNOWLEDGE (Companies of 49th Bn. M.G.C. and Companies 102nd
     Bn. M.G.C. only)

                                        (sd) A.OSWELL. Capt. & Adjt.
        Copies to :   49th Bn. M.G.C.
              O.C. "A", "B", "C", & "D" Companies.
              "G" 49th Division.
              War Dairy.
              War Diary.
              File.

SECRET. 49th Battalion Machine Gun Corps.
OPERATION ORDER NO. 89.

Ref. Map. 51.A.   Friday. 1.11.18.

1. For the operations of the 2nd Novr. Machine Guns will be disposed
    as follows:

    (a) "A" Company, 49th Bn. M.G.C. will be in the Forward
    Area of the 148th Infantry Brigade.
    When the Infantry after preliminary reconnaissance or
    artillery barrage reach the objective of Novr. 1st (vide map
    "A" already issued) they will push their guns well forward
    in support of the Infantry.
    " A" Company will be in positions at 0300 hrs on the 2nd Novr.

    (b) "C" Company, 49th Bn. M.G.C. now the Left Brigade Sector
    will withdraw to billets in HAULCHIN at 0300 hrs.

    (c) "D" Company, 49th Bn. M.G.C. will remain in their
    present positions.

    (d) "B" Company, 49th Bn. M.G.C. will be in MAING at
    1000 hrs on tthe 2nd.

    (e) "C" Company, 102nd. Bn M.G.C will pass through
    "D" Company 49th Bn. M.G.C. taking up positions about
    K.5. central and K.11.b.
    They will be prepared to move forward at any hour for the
    close protection of the objective of the 1st Novr. O.C."C"Coy.
    102nd Bn.M.G.C. will report to B.G.C. 147th Inf. Bde.
    (f) "D" Company, 102nd will occupy the area about AULNOY
    and K.5.a. in support of the 148th Infantry Brigade.
    O.C."D" Company 102nd Bn. M.G.C. will report to D.M.G.C.
    49th Bn. M.G.C. at once for detailed orders.

2. ACKNOWLEDGE.

                                        (sd)B.H.BADHAM. Lt.-Colonel.
Copies to: Commanding 49th Bn, M.G.C.
O.C."A" "B" "C" & "D" Coys.
"G" 49th Divn.
War Diary.
War Diary.
File.

SECRET.
Copy. No..........

ADDENDUM No.1. to 49th Bn. Machine Gun Corps.
OPERATION ORDER No. 01.

Ref Map. Sheet. 51.A.   Wednesday. 6.11.18.
      VALENCIENNES.

1. The 49th Bn. M.G.C. will embus today at O.1.a.0.7. on the main DOUCHAIN - DOUCHY Road as part of the 146th Infantry Brigade Group.

2. The Battalion will parade at the BARRACKS at 1425 hrs and move off at 1430 hrs.

3. Order of March : D.C.B.A. H.Q.

4. DRESS: Full Marching Order - Waterproofs sheets will be worn.

5. The Battalion will march in file, and form up at the embussing point immediately in rear of 49th Divisional H.Q, head of column facing S.W.

6. 2/Lt.G.N.A.CLARKE will report to the Staff Captain, 146th Infantry Brigade at O.1.a.O.7. at 1500 hrs, and hand in embussing strength.

7. Debussing point - AUBY.

8. ACKNOWLEDGE. (Companies of 49th Bn. M.G.C. only)

1130 hrs.
                                   (sd) A.COWELL. Capt. & Adjt.
                                              49th Bn. M.G.C.

Copies to :

   1. O.C."A" Company.
   2. O.C."B" Company.
   3. O.C."C" Company.
   4. O.C."D" Company.
   5. Signalling Officer.
   6. 146th Infantry Brigade.
   7. War Diary.
   8. War Diary.
   9. File.

SECRET.   49th Battalion Machine Gun Corps.   Copy No......
                              --- ORDER NO.91 ---

Ref. Map. VALENCIENNES. 1/100,000.   Monday 4.11.18.

1.   The 49th Battalion Machine Gun Corps will move tomorrow 5th instant
     to the vicinity of DOUAI. Personnel by bus, Transport by Route
     March under the 146th Infantry Brigade Transport Officer.
2.   All transport will move off from Transport Lines at 0535 hrs,
     and be clear of the Canal BOUCHAIN by 0600 hrs.
     ROUTE :   Main road through BOUCHAIN and DOUAI.
     DRESS :   Fighting Order.

3.   Order of march :   H.Q, A, B, C, & D Companies.

4.   The usual march intervals and the strictest march discipline will
     be maintained.

5.   Personnel will embuss at 1600 hrs.   DRESS : Full Marching Order,-
     blankets carried on man.

6.   A lorry will report at Battalion Headquarters at 1100 hrs. to
     convey surplus stores.
     Advance billeting party consisting of Major W.J.M.SPROULLE.M.C.
     1. Officer per Company and C.S.M. BETHEL will travel on this lorry.
     1. Small box per Company Mess may be taken on the lorry.

7.   Further orders will be issued re embussing of personnel.

8.   ACKNOWLEDGE.

                                                    [signature]
                                                    Capt. & Adjt.
Issued at....   49th Bn. M.G.C.

     Copies to :-

                 1. O.C. "A" Company.
                 2. O.C. "B" Company.
                 3. O.C. "C" Company.
                 4. O.C. "D" Company.
                 5. Quartermaster.
                 6. Signalling Officer.
                 7. Transport Officer.   (3)
                 8. Medical Officer.
                 9. "A" 49th Division.
                10. "Q" 49th Division.
                11. "G" 49th Division.
                12. 146th Infantry Brigade.
                13. 147th   do.
                14. 148th   do.
                15.   49th Div. Train.
                16. A.D.M.S. 49th Division.
                17. War Diary.
                18. War Diary.
                19. File.

Nr 10

Mon Grand f
la Bonne tempe.
Décembre 1918

Army Form C. 2118.

49th Bn
M. Corps.

WAR DIARY
or
INTELLIGENCE SUMMARY.
(Erase heading not required.)

Instructions regarding War Diaries and Intelligence Summaries are contained in F. S. Regs., Part II. and the Staff Manual respectively. Title pages will be prepared in manuscript.

Place	Date	Hour	Summary of Events and Information	Remarks and references to Appendices
AUBY	Dec 1/18		Battalion Training	K/W
"	2		Do	K/W
"	3		Do	K/W
"	4		Battalion moves from AUBY to HENIN-LIETARD in accordance with oo92	K/W
HENIN/LIETARD	5		Cleaning up new Area.	K/W
"	6		Do	K/W
"	7		Battalion Training	K/W
"	8		Do	K/W
"	9		Do	K/W
"	10		Do	K/W
"	11		First batch of 14 miners are despatched to England	K/W
"	12		Battalion Training	K/W
"	13		Battalion Training	K/W
"	14		Battalion in Training	K/W
"	15		Church Parade	K/W
"	16		Battalion on Divisional Ceremonial Parade	K/W

Army Form C. 2118.

WAR DIARY
or
INTELLIGENCE SUMMARY.

(Erase heading not required.)

Place	Date	Hour	Summary of Events and Information	Remarks and references to Appendices
HENIN-LIETARD	Dec 18		Battalion Training	
"	19		Do.	
"	20		Do.	
"	21		Salving Gun Ammunition	
"	22		Battalion Training	
"	23		Church Parades	
"	24		Battalion Training	
"	25		Do.	
"	26		Holiday	
"	27		Holiday	
"	28		1 Off and 33 O.R. reinforcements from Base Depot.	
"	29		Battalion Training	
"	30		Do.	
"	31		Church Parade	
"			Salvage work.	
"			Do.	

Army Form C. 2118.

WAR DIARY
or
INTELLIGENCE SUMMARY.
(Erase heading not required.)

4/9 Bn
M.G. Corps

Place	Date	Hour	Summary of Events and Information	Remarks and references to Appendices
HENIN LIETARD	1st Jany 1919		Salvage work.	
"	2		4 ORs to Concentration Camp for transfer to England to demobilize	
"	3		Battalion Training	
"	4		Do	
"	5		Do	
"	6		Church Parades.	
"	7		Battalion Training	
"	8		Do	
"	9		Do	
"	10		Do	
"	11		Do	
"	12		11 ORs. to Concentration Camp for transfer to England to demobilize	
"	13		Church Parades (20 ORs to Concentration Camp for transfer to England to demobilize	
"	14		Battalion Training	
"			Do	

Army Form C. 2118.

WAR DIARY
or
INTELLIGENCE SUMMARY.
(Erase heading not required.)

Instructions regarding War Diaries and Intelligence Summaries are contained in F. S. Regs, Part II. and the Staff Manual respectively. Title pages will be prepared in manuscript.

Place	Date	Hour	Summary of Events and Information	Remarks and references to Appendices
HENIN (IETARI)	15th Jany 1919		Battalion Training	WMc
"	16		Lt A.H. Skinner and 9 ORs To Concentration Camp for transfer to England to demobilize	WMc
"	17		Battalion Training	WMc
"	18		Battalion Training	WMc
"			Battalion Training	WMc
"			5 ORs To Concentration Camp for transfer to England to demobilize	WMc
"	19		Church parade. (6 ORs) " " " " " "	WMc
"	20		Battalion Training	WMc
"			(18 ORs) " " " " " "	WMc
"	21		Battalion Training	WMc
"			2nd Lt W.J. Wilton and 16 ORs " " " " " "	WMc
"	22		Battalion Training	WMc
"			Battalion photographed on parade	WMc
"			11 ORs to Concentration Camp for transfer to England to demobilize	WMc
"	23		Battalion Training	WMc
"	24		Battalion Training	WMc

Army Form C. 2118.

WAR DIARY
or
INTELLIGENCE SUMMARY.
(Erase heading not required.)

Instructions regarding War Diaries and Intelligence
Summaries are contained in F. S. Regs., Part II.
and the Staff Manual respectively. Title pages
will be prepared in manuscript.

Place	Date	Hour	Summary of Events and Information	Remarks and references to Appendices
HENIN LIETARD	25 Jany 1919		Divine Service	
"	26		4 ORs. to Concentration Camp for transfer to England to demobilize	
"			Battalion Training	
"	27		1st R.G. Robinson and 5 ORs " " " " "	
"	28		Battalion Training 9 ORs " " " " "	
"			Battalion Training 5 ORs " " " " "	
"	29		Battalion Training 15 ORs " " " " "	
"	30		Battalion Training	
"	31		Battalion Training	

49th Bn. M.G.C.   Vol 12

Army Form C. 2118.

WAR DIARY
or
INTELLIGENCE SUMMARY.
(Erase heading not required.)

Place	Date	Hour	Summary of Events and Information	Remarks and references to Appendices
HENIN LIETARD	1.2.19 to 28.2.19		Demobilization carried on during the month. Following despatched for dispersal. 6. 2.19 Lt A. Batt. 7. 2.19 Major H.S. Boxer. 9. 2.19 Lt J.R. Dawson. 13. 2.19 2/Lt H. Eckett. Major W.J. Hall. 14. 2.19 2/Lt B. Thompson. 160 Other Ranks	

Lieut. Colonel
Commanding 49th Bn. M.G.C.

49th Bn.M.G.C.

WAR DIARY
or
INTELLIGENCE SUMMARY.
(Erase heading not required.)

Army Form C. 2118.

Instructions regarding War Diaries and Intelligence Summaries are contained in F. S. Regs., Part II. and the Staff Manual respectively. Title pages will be prepared in manuscript.

Place	Date	Hour	Summary of Events and Information	Remarks and References to Appendices
HÉNIN LIETARD	1st March 1919		Battalion Training	
"	2		Lt C.V. Hancock, 2nd Lt D.C. Stephenson, 2nd Lt E.A. Maddison and 90 O.Rs proceeded to join the 6th Bn M.G.C.	
"	3		Church Parade	
"	3		Battalion Training	
DOUAI	4		Battalion moved to Billets in Douai in accordance with operation order No 93	Order No 93
"	5		Cleaning of Billets	
"	6		Boxing and bagging of Stores	
"	7		Battalion Training	
"			12 O.Rs proceeded to Concentration Camp for Demobilization	
"	8		Battalion Training	
"	9		Church Parade	
"	10		Battalion Training. Notification received that the Battalion will be reduced to Cadre "A"	Do
"	11		Do	
"	12		Do	
"	13		Do	
"	14		Do	Do

WAR DIARY
or
INTELLIGENCE SUMMARY.
(Erase heading not required.)

Army Form C. 2118.

Place	Date	Hour	Summary of Events and Information	Remarks and references to Appendices
Douai	15 March 1919		Battalion Training	
"	16		Church Parade	
"	17		Battalion Training	
"	18		Cleaning & packing of saddlery also Cleaning of limber	
"	19		Battalion Training	
"	20		Do	
"	21		Do	
"	22		Do	
"	23		Church Parade	
"	24		Battalion Training	
"	25		Do	
"	26		Do (Major J.M. Sproule M.C. proceeded to join the 33rd Bn MGC to assume duties of 2nd i/c	
"	27		Do (2nd Lt L.G. Nathan, 2nd Lt A.B. Ponder, 2nd Lt M.A. Clarke, 2nd Lt W. Lyle proceeded to 5th Bn MGC	
"	"		Capt A.O. Rees and 2nd Lt E.W. Brown proceeded to 6th Bn MGC.	
"	28		Battalion Training	
"	29		Do.	

Army Form C. 2118.

WAR DIARY
or
INTELLIGENCE SUMMARY.
(Erase heading not required.)

Instructions regarding War Diaries and Intelligence Summaries are contained in F. S. Regs., Part II. and the Staff Manual respectively. Title pages will be prepared in manuscript.

Place	Date	Hour	Summary of Events and Information	Remarks and references to Appendices
Douai	30th March 1919		Church Parade.	
	31		Cadre "A" Parade for instruction in the lashing of Vehicles	

O. Smith Captain
L⁹ ⁄ᵗ Parks M.T.

49 Bn M.G. Corps

Army Form C. 2118.

WAR DIARY
or
INTELLIGENCE SUMMARY.
(Erase heading not required.)

Instructions regarding War Diaries and Intelligence Summaries are contained in F. S. Regs., Part II. and the Staff Manual respectively. Title pages will be prepared in manuscript.

Place	Date	Hour	Summary of Events and Information	Remarks and references to Appendices
Douai	April 1/1919		Battalion Training	
"	2		Route march.	
"	3		Battalion Training	
"	4		" "	
"	5		Cleaning of Saddlery.	
"	"		Route march under Major H.D. Hanson M.C.	
"	"		Cleaning of Saddlery.	
"	6		Battalion Training	
"	"		Lt. F.T.G. Bone & 2nd Lt. H.G. Roberts proceeded to join the 6th Bn. M.G.C.	
"	"		2nd Lt. C.T. Pott " " " 5th Bn. M.G.C.	
"	7		Battalion Training (2nd Lt. A.T.M. Galeloni proceeded to join 6th Bn. M.G.C.	
"	8		Route march under Capt. W. Marshall M.C.	
"	9		Scrubbing and Cleaning of equipment.	
"	"		Major H. Hanson M.C. Capt. Pugh 2 offrs. & Becky and 19 O.Rs proceeded to	
"	"		Concentration Camp for Demobilization	

Army Form C. 2118.

WAR DIARY
or
INTELLIGENCE SUMMARY.
(Erase heading not required.)

Instructions regarding War Diaries and Intelligence Summaries are contained in F. S. Regs., Part II. and the Staff Manual respectively. Title pages will be prepared in manuscript.

Place	Date	Hour	Summary of Events and Information	Remarks and references to Appendices
Douai	10th April 1919		Battalion Training	
"	11		" "	
"	12		" (30 o'rs proceeded to join 42nd Bn M.G.C.	
"	13		" (100 " " " 34th " "	
"	14		Kit and Equipment Inspection	
"	15		Cleaning and handing in of S.A.A.	
"	16		Battalion Training	
"	17		Lt F Scott posted to 6th Bn M.G.C.	
"	18		Battalion Training	
"			Cpt Marshall &c, Lt T H Carlile proceeded to U.K. for demobilization	
"	18		Church Parade.	
"			Lt G.H. Saich proceeded to U.K. for demobilization	
"	19		Cleaning and repairing of limbers	
"	20		Church parade.	OWJ
"	21		Cleaning of limbers and saddlery	

Army Form C. 2118.

WAR DIARY
or
INTELLIGENCE SUMMARY.
(Erase heading not required.)

Instructions regarding War Diaries and Intelligence Summaries are contained in F. S. Regs., Part II. and the Staff Manual respectively. Title pages will be prepared in manuscript.

Place	Date	Hour	Summary of Events and Information	Remarks and references to Appendices
Dover	21st April 1919		Capt. H.C.V. Thomas, Lt James, 2nd Lt D.T. William's proceeded to Concentration Camp for demobilization.	
"	22		Route march	
"	23		Battalion training	
"	24		Route march	
"	25		Packing of limbers	
"	26		" " "	
"	27		Church Parade	
"	28		Packing of limbers	
"	29		" " "	
"	30		Route march.	a.a.
			Battalion strength on April 30th:— Officers 7. Other ranks 134.	

Oswell Capt.
49th Bn M.G.C.

Pioneers
49th Division.

3rd M O N M O U T H S

N O V E M B E R

1 9 1 5

Army Form C. 2118

WAR DIARY
or
INTELLIGENCE SUMMARY

(Erase heading not required.)

Instructions regarding War Diaries and Intelligence Summaries are contained in F. S. Regs., Part II. and the Staff Manual respectively. Title Pages will be prepared in manuscript.

Place	Date NOVEMBER	Hour	Summary of Events and Information	Remarks and references to Appendices
ELVERDINGHE	1st		Battalion employed on usual day and night working parties on drainage at Canal Bank. Lieut-R.J. O'Connor joined the Battalion for duty, from the Base.	
	2nd		The detachment (2 Companies) at Canal Bank Dugouts were relieved. Relief completed at 4.30. Battalion employed on usual day and night working parties.	
	3rd		Battalion employed as working parties. 3609. Pte White D.Coy, was wounded (self inflicted) (G.S.) in foot.	
	4th		Battalion employed as working parties. Capt. O.W.D. Steel (R.A.M.C.) re-attached to Battalion, vice Capt. N.J. Watt.	
	5th		Battalion employed as working parties. 1186. Sgt Aubrey. D.Co. was wounded. (G.S.) in thigh. 2/Lt C.M. Stafford was detailed for special duty at Divisional Headquarters, as Officer i/c Shelters	
	7th		Battalion employed as working parties.	
	8th		Enemy shelled ELVERDINGHE heavily in the morning and again at 2.30 p.m. Battalion employed as working parties. Capt. W.P. Abbott & Capt. A.H. Newman proceeded on special duty, on the Divisional drainage scheme.	
	9th		Battalion employed as working parties.	
	10th		Battalion employed as working parties. 2558 Pte Gray.T. B.Co. fatally wounded (G.S.) head. 2621 Pte Dembleton. D.Co. wounded (G.S.) arm & leg.	

Place	Date	Hour	Summary of Events and Information	Remarks and references to Appendices
ELVERDINGHE	NOVEMBER			
	11th		Battalion employed on usual day and night working parties.	
	12th		Battalion employed as working parties.	
	13th		Battalion found usual working parties.	
	14th		The detachment (2 Coys) at Canal Bank Dugouts were relieved. Relief completed 5.7 p.m.	
	15th		Battalion found the usual working parties.	
	16th		Usual working parties. 3427 Pt Winter. A seriously wounded (G.S.) in stomach.	
	17th		Mr. R. Toley. I. Coy. slightly wounded (G.S.) in calf of leg.	
	18th		Usual working parties. Leg found. 2602 Pt. Jones R. A Coy. wounded (G.S.) buttock.	
	19th		Usual working parties. Well found. Leg found. 2668 Pt Wydoke B Co. wounded (G.S.) night thigh	
	20th		Battalion employed as working parties. 2668 Pt Wydoke B Co. wounded (G.S.) night thigh Relief completed about 7 p.m.	
	21st		The J (a Coy) at Canal Bank Dugouts relieved. Relief completed about 7 p.m. 2114 Pt Cowdroy B Co. wounded (shell) thigh.	
	22nd		Usual working parties. Wire found. Four South Wales Miners of introductions called at the Chateau while on tour of inspection. 10411 Pt Wolham L. B.Co. wounded (G.S.) thigh. 1792 Pt Cooper. B Co. wounded (G.S.) left leg. 2367 Pt Crowder T. wounded (shell) in arm.	

Army Form C. 2118

WAR DIARY
or
INTELLIGENCE SUMMARY
(Erase heading not required.)

Instructions regarding War Diaries and Intelligence Summaries are contained in F.S. Regs., Part II. and the Staff Manual respectively. Title Pages will be prepared in manuscript.

Place	Date NOVEMBER	Hour	Summary of Events and Information	Remarks and references to Appendices
ELVERDINGHE	22nd		Battalion found usual day & night working parties.	
	23rd		Usual working parties were found. Three Officers were attached to the Battalion for instruction in Trench warfare.	
	24th		Usual working parties were found. 280 Coy. sent Major Stewart R.E. fatally wounded (G.S.) head	
	25th		Battalion employed as working parties. 2566 Pte Nicklin D.Co. wounded (G.S.) right forearm.	
	26th		The attachment (2 Coys) at Canal Bank Dugouts were relieved. Usual working parties.	
	27th		Usual working parties, day & night.	
	28th		Battalion found usual working parties.	
	29th		Battalion employed as working parties. 1852 Pte Gough J. B.Co. wounded (G.S.) cheek & neck.	
	30th		Usual working parties. The sick wastage for month of November was 69 admitted, 32 discharged from Hospital	

1875 Wt. W593/826 1,000,000 4/15 J.B.C. & A. A.D.S.S./Forms/C. 2118.

Pioneers
49th Div.

3rd MONMOUTHS

DECEMBER

1 9 1 5

Army Form C. 2118

WAR DIARY
or
INTELLIGENCE SUMMARY
(Erase heading not required.)

Instructions regarding War Diaries and Intelligence Summaries are contained in F. S. Regs., Part II. and the Staff Manual respectively. Title Pages will be prepared in manuscript.

Place	Date DECEMBER	Hour	Summary of Events and Information	Remarks and references to Appendices
Elverdinghe	1st		Usual working parties were found for drainage work on the Canal Bank. Day & night.	
	2nd		The Battalion found usual working parties for drainage.	
	3rd		Usual working parties were found.	
	4th		Battalion found usual working parties, day & night.	
	5th		Usual working parties were found.	
	6th		Battalion found usual working parties. 3596 Pte Brown. R. wounded (GS) left thigh.	
	7th		Usual working parties were found, for drainage work.	
	8th		The Canal detachment (2 Coys) were relieved by 2 Coys from Elverdinghe. Relief completed by 7.30 p.m. Usual working parties found.	
	9th		Only day parties were found, owing to heavy rain, & usual day & night state of land. 2490 Pte Thomas. S. fatally wounded (GS) Head. 3296 Pte Owrid, wounded (GS) thigh.	
	10th		Battalion found usual day & night working parties.	
	11th		Usual working parties were found.	
	12th		Battalion found usual working parties. 2265. Cpl. Clifton. C. wounded (GS) thigh.	
	13th		Usual day & night working parties were found. 2307 Pte Pritchard. H.E. wounded (shell) hand and left leg. 2/Lt Radcliffe seriously wounded (GS) both thighs.	
	14th		Canal bank detachment were relieved by 2 Coys from Elverdinghe was found.	

Army Form C. 2118

WAR DIARY
or
INTELLIGENCE SUMMARY
(Erase heading not required.)

Instructions regarding War Diaries and Intelligence Summaries are contained in F. S. Regs., Part II. and the Staff Manual respectively. Title Pages will be prepared in manuscript.

Place	Date	Hour	Summary of Events and Information	Remarks and references to Appendices
	DECEMBER			
	19th continued		3557. Pt. Goldingham. 16606. Pt. Robb. 1433. Pt. Holland. 2116 Cornacher. 2789. Pt. Thompson 1457. Pt. Furry, were all gassed.	
Canal Bank	20.		Enemy bombarded heavily all day. The following message received from 148th Brigade. "The Corps Commander wishes all ranks to be informed of his appreciation of the steadness displayed by them during the Boo attack yesterday, aaa. It is possible owing to the steadness and discipline displayed that a more serious attack was avoidable." The Blurdinghe detachment (2 Coys) returned to Blurdinghe at 9 pm without casualty.	
Blurdinghe	21st		A few shells fell in Chateau grounds. The Canal Bank detachment (2 Coys) was relieved by 2 Coys from Blurdinghe at 11 pm. 2278 Serg. Pritchard. 16040. Pt. Murphy. 3568 Pt. Smith, were wounded by shrapnel.	
	22nd		A party of SD men were found for drainage work, and 2 parties of officers & 30 men.	
	23rd		Each working party for the 148th Brigade.	
	24th		Same working parties as previous day, were found.	
	25th		Working parties as previous 2 days, were found.	
	26th		No working parties were found.	
	27th		Working parties were found for divisional dranage on Canal Bank, and a party of 60 men working on front line trenches for 148th Brigade. 114th Division was relieved by the 7th R.B., 14th Division, at 5.45 pm. Canal Bank detachment were relieved by	

Army Form C. 2118

WAR DIARY
or
INTELLIGENCE SUMMARY
(Erase heading not required.)

Instructions regarding War Diaries and Intelligence Summaries are contained in F. S. Regs, Part II. and the Staff Manual respectively. Title Pages will be prepared in manuscript.

Place	Date DECEMBER	Hour	Summary of Events and Information	Remarks and references to Appendices
Elverdinghe	15th		Battalion found usual day & night working parties for drainage on Canal bank.	
	16th		Usual day and night working parties found.	
	17th		Usual working parties were found.	
	18th		Battalion found usual working parties.	
	19th		About 6.30 a.m. message received that enemy was making gas attack. The Elverdinghe detachment had orders to move to Canal Bank. At 8.30 a.m. the Battalion was in position; the Canal Bank detachment manning the Reserve Fire Trenches, the Elverdinghe detachment at Canal Bank dug-outs; one Machine Gun and from in emplacement on ELVERDINGHE – BOESINGHE road, and another at MILL MOUND in Elverdinghe. Enemy contended heavily all day and night. During the morning 8–17" shells fell in the grounds of Elverdinghe Chateau, where the Q.M. branch had been left. The following message was received from 49th Division:—

"The Divisional Commander is very pleased with the behaviour of all ranks, and the promptitude with which all necessary steps were taken this morning."

2022 Pte. Loyd and 1683 Pte. Rees JB were killed by shell.
2444 Pte. Marks. R and 1315 Pte. Clark. S. died of Gas poisoning.
2012 Pte. Saunders. S. was wounded and gassed.
1195 Cpl. Rumsey. A. 2066 Pte. Childs. 2527 Pte. Millard. 1868 Sergt. Hookham. 2286 Sergt. Jones. W.H.
1108. Sergt. Morris, were all wounded.
2121. Cpl. Williams. 1425 Cpl. Green. 121 Pte. Coleman. 1881 Pte. Gibson. 2163. Pte. Meredith.
2157. Pte. Ryan. R. 1043 Pte. Rogers. 1565 Pte. Walton. W. 1570. Pte. Brown. 2521 Pte. Brown.
1781. Pte. Wilton F. 2443. Pte. Davies. 2400 Cpl. Hinton. 1840. Pte. Evan. 2547 Pte. Davies. 1721 Pte. Warner.
2581 Pte. Lawrence. 361.6 Pte. Davies Wm. 2340 Pte. Brown. 2296 Pte. Hughes. 2595 Pte. Williams. | |

Army Form C. 2118

WAR DIARY
or
INTELLIGENCE SUMMARY
(Erase heading not required.)

Instructions regarding War Diaries and Intelligence Summaries are contained in F. S. Regs., Part II. and the Staff Manual respectively. Title Pages will be prepared in manuscript.

Place	Date	Hour	Summary of Events and Information	Remarks and references to Appendices
Elverdinghe	28th DECEMBER		Several showers up of Camp. Enemy sent over some gas shells about 6.30 p.m. Battalion moved by march route to Camp B.10, situated in Sq A 8 sheet 28. Four 17 shells fell in the company lines at Elverdinghe before marching off, and 69 casualties were sustained. 2088 Pte Dalton. 2913 Sjt Plummer. 1810 Pte Sgt Lee Barre. 1567 L/Cpl. O'Rourke. 1308 Cpl Meacham. 1053 L/Cpl Jones. 3253. Cpl Skeus. 121. Pte Coleman. 1855. Pte Price. W.H. 1702 Pte Gallagher. 2582 L/Cpl Baker T.J. 2110 L/Cpl Styford. 3365. Pte Morgan. 3618 Pte Driver. 2007 Pte Williams. 2336 Pte Williams. S. 3398. Pte Walker. 2202. Sergt Dixon. 1990. Sergt Small. 1987 Pte Pugh. 3135. Pte Brown. 3070 Pte Fay. 1711 Pte Hughes. 3162 Pte Lloyd. 3569 Pte Moore. 2926. Pte Neal. 3457. Pte Parfitt. 1818 Pte Lowe. 3077. Pte Rogers 1170. Pte Thomas. 3284 Pte Griffiths. 3000 Pte Bryant. The above were all killed. 3285. Cpl Williams. 3285 Pte Budd. 3456 Pte Blackmore. 2439 Pte Lyne. 1540. Pte O'Brien. 1319 Pte Rowell. 1790 Pte Chinn. 3591 Pte Williams. 3460. Pte Pugh. 556. Pte Smith. 1657. Pte Taylor. 2066 Pte Childs. 3110. Pte Evans. 164. L/M Pont (slight) 3381. Pte North (slight) 3911 L/Cpl Yarrell (killed) 2598. Pte Burns 1289 Pte Coates. 1196. Pte Jones 2050 Pte Edwards. 3378 Pte Stroud. 2900. Pte Griffiths. 2304. Pte Mason. 1286 Pte Sutton. 1726. Pte Taylor. 2442 Pte Tucker. 1966. Cpl Gardener (slight) 1897. Pte Neave (slight) 3613. Pte Ward. 2108. Pte Morgan. Nearly all wounded.	

Army Form C. 2118

WAR DIARY
or
INTELLIGENCE SUMMARY

(Erase heading not required.)

Instructions regarding War Diaries and Intelligence
Summaries are contained in F. S. Regs., Part II.
and the Staff Manual respectively. Title Pages
will be prepared in manuscript.

Place	Date December	Hour	Summary of Events and Information	Remarks and references to Appendices
Elverdinghe	29th		Continued 1896 Pt Davies B.Coy. 2503 Pt Morgan B.Coy. 1969 L/Cpl Harris C.Coy. 2858 Pt Roy C.Coy. 2189 Pt Morgan C.Coy. These 5 Men were missing. Day spent in re-equiping men, who had their equipment destroyed by shell fire.	
Camp H. 28.A.8.	30th		Battalion moved by march route, via Crombeke, and Proven to Watou, taking over billets of 11th Liverpools.	
	31st			

Wakely Lt Col
Commanding 1st Mon: R
approved 11th Jan 16
U

#9

H.Q. 2nd troops.

3rd Monmouth Regt.
Jan 1916
Vol IX
Aug 1916

WAR DIARY or INTELLIGENCE SUMMARY

Army Form C. 2118

(Erase heading not required.)

Instructions regarding War Diaries and Intelligence Summaries are contained in F.S. Regs., Part II. and the Staff Manual respectively. Title Pages will be prepared in manuscript.

Place	Date	Hour	Summary of Events and Information	Remarks and references to Appendices
RIETVELD	1916 JANUARY 1st			
	2nd		The Battalion marched by road route, via Winnizelle, and St Temple to billets in the vicinity of RIETVELD.	
	3rd		Day spent in general cleaning up. Battalion rested.	
	4th		Battalion rested. 2/Lieut. J.A. Finlay now Gazetted Lieutenant d/22/11/15.	
	5th		Battalion rested in billets.	
	6th		Battalion rested in billets.	
	7th		Battalion rested in billets.	
	8th		Company Training and Adjutants parade from 11am to 12 o'clock.	
	9th		Commanding Officers parade from 11am to 12 o'clock.	
	10th		Battalion had Church parade.	
	11th		Company training carried on.	
	12th		Company training carried on. Company training carried on. Three gallantry cards were received from the Divisional Commander for the information of N.C.O.'s for gallant conduct on 19th Dec 1915, during hostile Gas attack. 1425 L/Cpl Stoton. 13.17 Pt Powell J. 1343 Pte. J.J. Moore. The Cards were presented by Capt Off Moore on the Battalion parade governed by the C.O. A draft of 15 other ranks joined the Battalion from the base.	
	13th		Company training carried on. Extract from London Gazett d/11/11/16. H.A. Williams to Brig. Gen. of Infantry.	
	14th			

C.A. Whifford

WAR DIARY
or
INTELLIGENCE SUMMARY

(Erase heading not required.)

Army Form C. 2118

Instructions regarding War Diaries and Intelligence Summaries are contained in F.S. Regs., Part II. and the Staff Manual respectively. Title Pages will be prepared in manuscript.

Place	Date	Hour	Summary of Events and Information	Remarks and references to Appendices
REITVELD	1916 JANUARY 15th		Company training carried on. The undermentioned Officers joined the Battⁿ for duty. 2/Lieut. T.J.J. Lloyd. A.M. Watkins. C.S. Stokes. E.S.L. Jenkins.	
	16th		Battalion Church parade. Extract from Gazette dated 14/1/16. Awarded the Military Cross. Capt. Dugan William Lyon. Died. Awarded the D.C.M. 135 Serjt Major G. Gardner. 1920. Serjt. B. Jenkins. 2172 Serj. F. J.W. Aitchelley. 2440 Pte. Skidmore.	
	17th		Company training carried on.	
	18th		Company training carried on.	
	19th		Company training carried on.	
	20th		Company training carried on.	
	21st		Training carried on. 2/Lieut W.T. Raymont proceeded to 2nd Corps Headquarters. 2/Lieut Lieut Stafford for a week.	
	22nd		Battalion route march.	
	23rd		Battalion Church parade 1425 2/Cpl Moor. 9.1343 Pte J.J. Moore were awarded D.C.M. 2/Lieut Moore proceeded to VIth Corps Headquarters and were presented with the ribbon by General Sir H.C.D. Plumer. Commanding the 2nd Army.	
	24th		Company training carried on.	
	25th		Company training carried on.	
	26th		Company training carried on.	
	27th		Training carried on.	

Army Form C. 2118

WAR DIARY
or
INTELLIGENCE SUMMARY
(Erase heading not required.)

Instructions regarding War Diaries and Intelligence Summaries are contained in F.S. Regs., Part II. and the Staff Manual respectively. Title Pages will be prepared in manuscript.

Place	Date	Hour	Summary of Events and Information	Remarks and references to Appendices
REITVELD	1916 JANUARY 28th		Company training carried on; and Route March.	
	29th		Church parade.	
	30th		Company training carried on.	
	31st		Company training carried on. A special Divisional Routine order was received, on the address made by General Sir H.C.O. Plumer, G.C.M.G. K.C.B. Commander of the 2nd Army, at his presentation of decorations on 30th Jany 1916, to General Monrevel and representatives of the 49th Division, when he expressed his appreciation of the work which the 49th Division had carried out their duties during the time they had been attached to the 2nd Army; and wished the Division Good-bye, and this may best of luck.	

WAR DIARY
or
INTELLIGENCE SUMMARY

(Erase heading not required.)

Army Form C. 2118

Instructions regarding War Diaries and Intelligence Summaries are contained in F. S. Regs., Part II. and the Staff Manual respectively. Title Pages will be prepared in manuscript.

Place	Date FEBRUARY	Hour	Summary of Events and Information	Remarks and references to Appendices
REITVELD	1st		The Battalion were exercised in Company route marches.	
	2nd		General cleaning up preparatory to move.	
	3rd		Battalion paraded at 10 p.m. in REITVELD, and moved by march route to ESQUELBECQ railway station, entrained & entrained.	
	4th		Battalion detrained at AMIENS and proceeded by march through AILLY to SAISSEVAL.	
SAISSEVAL	5th		Battalion rested.	
	6th		Church parade.	
	7th		Physical Exercise & Battalion drill.	
	8th		Battalion drill and Physical Exercise.	
	9th		Lecture by Company Commanders.	
	10th		Battalion carried out an Inspection.	
	11th		Physical Exercise and Company Drill.	
	12th		Battalion moved by march route to AILLY-SUR-SOMME.	
AILLY-SUR-SOMME	13th		Battalion moved by march march, via ST SAUVEUR & VILLERS, to MOLLIENS-AU-BOIS.	
MOLLIENS-AU-BOIS	14th		Battalion moved by march route, via BEAUCOURT, WARLOY & SENLIS to BOUZINCOURT.	
BOUZINCOURT	15th		Battalion rested in billets.	
	16th		Physical Exercise, inspection of rifles and Company Drill.	
	17th		Battalion commenced the special work allotted by the C.R.E. to men.	

Army Form C. 2118

WAR DIARY
or
INTELLIGENCE SUMMARY
(Erase heading not required.)

Instructions regarding War Diaries and Intelligence Summaries are contained in F. S. Regs, Part II. and the Staff Manual respectively. Title Pages will be prepared in manuscript.

Place	Date MARCH	Hour	Summary of Events and Information	Remarks and references to Appendices
BOUZINCOURT	1st		Battalion continued doing special work allotted by C.R.E. 149th Division. Making new road called Northumberland Avenue, and constructing a Trench railway	
	2nd		Work carried on as usual	
	3rd		Work carried on as usual	
	4th 5th		Work carried on as usual. Owing to Division having been relieved, no more work was done on the front allotted	
	6th		Tasks. Day spent in collecting tools, and returning them to stores. Companies placed at disposal of Company Commanders. Extract from London Gazette. 2nd Lieut to be Lieutenant (March 2nd) Thomas J. L. Lloyd.	
	7th		Companies at the disposal of their Company Commanders.	
	8th		2 Companies (B & D) moved by march route via HEDAUVILLE to FORCEVILLE	
FORCEVILLE	9th		Companies at the disposal of their Company Commanders	
	10th		Companies commenced on the allotted tasks of road repairing. B Coy moved back to MARTINSART, and carried on with the construction of Trench railway, under CRE 36th Dis.	
	11th		1 platoon of D Co. moved to HEDAUVILLE. Lieut T. J. L. Lloyd to Hospital	
	12th		Work carried on. Transport moved from SENLIS to FORCEVILLE.	

Army Form C. 2118

WAR DIARY
or
INTELLIGENCE SUMMARY
(Erase heading not required.)

Instructions regarding War Diaries and Intelligence Summaries are contained in F. S. Regs., Part II. and the Staff Manual respectively. Title Pages will be prepared in manuscript.

Place	Date	Hour	Summary of Events and Information	Remarks and references to Appendices
BOULINCOURT	FEBRUARY 17th		(continued) A.C. on road repair. B.C. instructing on Trench railway. (& D.) Coy. making a new road called Northumberland Avenue.	
	18th		2 Platoons of F. Co. moved to CONTAY as a wood cutting detachment; remainder of Battalion carried on work as previous day.	
	19th		Work carried on as previous day.	
	20th		2 Platoons of D. Co. taken off the Northumberland Avenue Work at work at road repairing. The remainder carried on as previous day.	
	21st		Work carried on as previous day.	
	22nd		Work carried on as previous day.	
	23rd		B. Co. struck off work for purposes of interior economy; remainder as previous day.	
	24th		C. Co. struck off work for purposes of interior economy; remainder worked as usual.	
	25th		Work carried on as usual.	
	26th		Work carried on as usual.	
	27th		Work carried on as usual.	
	28th		Work carried on as usual.	
	29th		Work carried on as usual. Major London 2nd Lieut Fry 2 I.C. CROIX de GUERRE. 135 O.R. Major E.A. Barnes 3rd Monm. Regt. During the month 38 admitted to hospital, and 21 discharged from hospital.	

Army Form C. 2118.

WAR DIARY
INTELLIGENCE SUMMARY

(Erase heading not required.)

Instructions regarding War Diaries and Intelligence Summaries are contained in F. S. Regs., Part II. and the Staff Manual respectively. Title Pages will be prepared in manuscript.

Place	Date	Hour	Summary of Events and Information	Remarks and references to Appendices
FORCEVILLE	1/4/16.		"C" Coy were struck off work for purposes of interior economy. Remainder of Battalion carried on work as usual.	
	2/4/16.		Work carried on as usual.	
	3/4/16.		Work carried on as usual.	
	4/4/16.		Work carried on as usual.	
	5/4/16.		Work carried on as usual. Capt. S. J. D. Gattie proceeded to Headquarters 49th Division for attachment. "A" Coy struck off work for purpose of interior economy. Lieutenant & Quartermaster A. A. Ing took over duties of Adjutant.	
	6/4/16.		Work carried on as usual.	
	7/4/16.		"B" & "D" Coys struck off work for purpose of interior economy. A valedictory message was received from C.R.E. 48th Division through the C.E.X. Corps and endorsed by the G.O.C. 49th Division upon the good work done by Captain T.D. Whitehead commanding "C" Company who were employed on roads in the neighbourhood of BUS-LES-ARTOIS from 8th March to 31st March 1916.	
	8/4/16.		Work carried on as usual.	
	9/4/16.		Work carried on as usual. "E" Coy struck off work for purposes of interior economy.	
	10/4/16.		Work carried on as usual. Lieut. M. H. Nefton proceeded on leave.	
	11/4/16.		Work carried on as usual. A draft of 40 other ranks joined Battalion from England.	
	12/4/16.		Work carried on as usual.	

2449 Wt. W14957/M90 750,000 1/16 J.B.C. & A. Forms/C.2118/12.

Army Form C. 2118

WAR DIARY
INTELLIGENCE SUMMARY
(Erase heading not required.)

Instructions regarding War Diaries and Intelligence Summaries are contained in F.S. Regs., Part II. and the Staff Manual respectively. Title Pages will be prepared in manuscript.

Place	Date MARCH	Hour	Summary of Events and Information	Remarks and references to Appendices
FORCEVILLE	13.		Work carried on.	
	14.		Work carried on. Capt. R.D. Gattie relinquishes the appointment of Adjutant.	
	15.		Work on road repairing carried on as usual.	
	16.			
	17.			
	18.			
	19.		Work carried on as usual.	
	20.			
	21.		Work carried on as usual. Lieut M Vaughan-Lloyd, proceeded to H.Q. R.F.C. for duty with that corps	
	22.			
	23.			
	24.			
	25.		Work as usual done as usual.	
	26.			
	27.			
	28.			
	29.			
	30.			
	31.		"C" Coy. moved to FORCEVILLE from BUS-LES-ARTOIS.	

WAR DIARY
INTELLIGENCE SUMMARY

(Erase heading not required.)

Army Form C. 2118

Instructions regarding War Diaries and Intelligence Summaries are contained in F. S. Regs., Part II. and the Staff Manual respectively. Title Pages will be prepared in manuscript.

Place	Date	Hour	Summary of Events and Information	Remarks and references to Appendices
FORCEVILLE	13/4/16		Work carried on as usual.	
	14/4/16		Work carried on as usual. "B" & "D" Coys struck off work for purposes of interior economy.	
	15/4/16		Work carried on as usual. "A" Coy struck off work for purpose of interior economy.	
	16/4/16		Work carried on as usual. "C" Coy struck off work for purpose of interior economy.	
	17/4/16		Work carried on as usual. Lieut. M.H. Lipton returned from leave.	
	18/4/16		Work carried on as usual.	
	19/4/16		Work carried on as usual.	
	20/4/16		Work carried on as usual.	
	21/4/16		Work carried on as usual. "B" Coy struck off work for purposes of interior economy. 2/Lieut. E.C.L. Stokes proceeded on special leave to England.	
	22/4/16		Work carried on as usual. "A" Coy struck off work for purposes of interior economy.	
	23/4/16		Work carried on as usual.	
	24/4/16		Work carried on as usual. "D" Coy struck off work for purpose of interior economy	
	25/4/16		Work carried on as usual. "C" Coy struck off work for purpose of interior economy.	
	26/4/16		Work carried on as usual.	
	27/4/16		Work carried on as usual. Gallantry Card received from G.O.C. 49th Division for 2372 Pte. R.S. Stevens "B" Coy for conspicuous gallantry when under heavy shell fire on 15/4/16 in dressing the wounded.	
	28/4/16		Work carried on as usual. Major W.A. Kerr proceeded on leave to England.	
	29/4/16		"B" Coy struck off work for purposes of interior economy. Capt. D. Whitehead admitted to Hospital	
	30/4/16		Work carried on as usual. "A" Coy struck off work for purposes of interior economy. Sq admitted to Hospital & 46 discharged from Hospital during current month.	

Army Form C. 2118.

1/3 Monmouth Rgt 49
Pioneers
Vol 13

WAR DIARY
or
INTELLIGENCE SUMMARY

(Erase heading not required.)

Instructions regarding War Diaries and Intelligence Summaries are contained in F. S. Regs., Part II. and the Staff Manual respectively. Title Pages will be prepared in manuscript.

Place	Date	Hour	Summary of Events and Information	Remarks and references to Appendices
FORCEVILLE	MAY 1st		Battalion Employed on road repairing, &c, under instructions of C.E. & Corps.	
	2nd		Work carried on as usual. Half of D.Co. moved to WARLOY, to commence work on a new Ammunition dump, to be constructed there.	
	3rd		Work carried on as usual.	
	4th		Work carried on as usual.	
	5th		Work carried on as usual.	
	6th		Work carried on as usual.	
	7th		A short memorial service was held in the Evening, in memory of those who fell in action, during the engagement in the Ypres salient in May last.	
	8th			
	9th		Work carried on as usual.	
	10th		Work carried on as usual. B. Co. moved to FORCEVILLE.	
	11 & 12		Work carried on as usual. 2nd Lieuts. W.R. Nokes, J. Brand, H. Parry joined the Battalion for duty from England	
	13th		Work carried on as usual. A draft of 143. O.R. joined the Battalion from England	
	14th 15th 16th 17th 18th 19th		Work carried on as usual. The remaining half of D.Co. moved to WARLOY, to complete the Ammunition dump.	

Army Form C. 2118.

WAR DIARY
or
INTELLIGENCE SUMMARY
(Erase heading not required.)

Instructions regarding War Diaries and Intelligence Summaries are contained in F. S. Regs., Part II and the Staff Manual respectively. Title Pages will be prepared in manuscript.

Place	Date	Hour	Summary of Events and Information	Remarks and references to Appendices
FORCEVILLE	MAY 20		Work carried on as usual.	
	21		Extract London Gazette, of 24/5/16. Reg.t Q.M.Sgt. Walter M. Porter, to be Quarter Master	
	22		and Hon. Lieut. May 24th, 1916.	
	23		Copy of letter rec.d. The Divisional Commander wishes you to convey to Capt. H.E.	
	24		Hodges, 13th Monmouth Reg.t, his appreciation of the plucky conduct displayed by him during the recent fire at FORCEVILLE on 27th April 16.	
	25		Work carried on as usual.	
	26			
	27		Work carried on as usual.	
	28		Extract H.Q. Orders: Robert's orders 4/d 27th May 1916. Lieut C.M. Stafford, 9th	
	29		13.t Monmouth Reg.t, is appointed Camp Commandant, Div.l Headquarters.	
	30		Work carried on as usual.	
	31		Work carried on as usual. Half of D.Co. moved from WARLOY to VARENNES to commence work on a new Ammunition dump, to be constructed there.	

49th Divisional Pioneers

PIONEERS

1/3rd BATTALION

MONMOUTHSHIRE REGIMENT

JUNE 1916

A.G.
3rd Echelon Base

L.B. 795.

Herewith Battalion War Diary on Army Forms C2118 from 1st to 30th June inclusive.

5/7/16.

[signature]
Lieut-Colonel,
Comdg 1/3rd Monmouth Regt

Army Form C.2118

11th Monmouth Regt

WAR DIARY
or
INTELLIGENCE SUMMARY

(Erase heading not required.)

Instructions regarding War Diaries and Intelligence Summaries are contained in F. S. Regs., Part II. and the Staff Manual respectively. Title Pages will be prepared in manuscript.

Place	Date	Hour	Summary of Events and Information	Remarks and references to Appendices
FORCEVILLE	JUNE 1st		Work carried on as usual, under instructions of C.E. X Corps.	
	2nd		2 Companys (B+C) at FORCEVILLE. 1 Company (A) at SENLIS. 1 Company (D) at WARLOY.	
	3rd		Work carried on as usual. His Majesty's Birthday Honours Gazette dated June 3rd..16. The following awards were made. Capt K.F.D Gattie "Military Cross" 13114 1/Cpl Andrews, and 1317 P.g. Powell "Military Medal".	
	4th			
	5th			
	6th		Work carried on as Usual	
	7th			
	8th			
	9th			
	10th		Work carried on as usual. 2 Platoons (D.Co) moved to MARTINSART	
	11th			
	12th		Work carried on as usual.	
	13th			
	14th			
	15th			
	16th		2/Lieut G.H Lock joined for duty from England. Lieut F.J.K Lloyd proceeded to Headquarters of Royal Flying Corps for duty as an observer, in that Corps.	Return attd.
	17th		Work carried on as usual. 2 platoons moved back from MARTINSART to WARLOY.	

WAR DIARY
or
INTELLIGENCE SUMMARY

(Erase heading not required.)

Army Form C. 2118.

Place	Date JUNE	Hour	Summary of Events and Information	Remarks and references to Appendices
FORCEVILLE	18th		Work carried on as usual. The following names appeared in Sir Douglas Haig's despatches, dated 30th April 1916. Major Watson. Captain J.M. Jones. Lieut-Adjt. A.A. Foy. 1122 C.S.M. Howells A. 1975. C.S.M. Johnson. T. 2026 Sergt Hall.	
	19th		Work carried on as usual. A party of 2 O.R. with Lieut O'Connor moved to ENGLEBELMER: remainder of D.Co. moved to MARTINSART. The whole Coy. engaged in making dug-outs and observation posts.	
	20th		Work carried on as usual. The road from FORCEVILLE to ENGLEBELMER made by B Coy completed, and named "MONMOUTH ROAD".	
	21st 22nd 23rd			
	24th 25th		Work carried on as usual.	
			All companies moved to FORCEVILLE.	
RUBEMPRE	26th		Battalion moved by march route to RUBEMPRE, where it rejoined the 49th Division.	
	27th		Battalion rested.	
			Battalion moved by march route to Contay.	
CONTAY	28th		Battalion moved by march route to HARPONVILLE.	

Army Form C. 2118.

WAR DIARY
or
INTELLIGENCE SUMMARY

(Erase heading not required.)

Instructions regarding War Diaries and Intelligence Summaries are contained in F. S. Regs., Part II. and the Staff Manual respectively. Title Pages will be prepared in manuscript.

Place	Date	Hour	Summary of Events and Information	Remarks and references to Appendices
HARPONVILLE	JUNE 29th		Battalion rested.	
			The following is a copy of a letter received from H.Q. 4th Division.	
			"The Divisional Commander directs me to inform you that he is very pleased with all that he has heard and seen of the work carried out by the Battalion under your Command during the past four months. He has no hesitation in saying that the success of the coming operations that he confidently anticipates will be due in no small measure to the skill, devotion, and unsparing labour of the Pioneer Battalion of the 4th Division."	
	30.		Battalion paraded at 10.30 p.m. and moved by march route via VARENNES and HEDAUVILLE to BOUZINCOURT.	
			During the month 34 O.R. were admitted to Hospital, and 34 O.R. discharged from Hospital.	

Battalion HQ.

Pioneers.
49th Div.

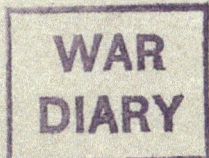

1/3rd BATTN. THE MONMOUTHSHIRE REGIMENT.

J U L Y

1 9 1 6

Army Form C. 2118

Warwick Regt 49
Kft 15

WAR DIARY of 6 R.W.
3rd Echelon Base

OAG

Diary on Army Form C2118
from 1st to 30th July 1916.
(inclusive)

N. Fry
Lieut Col
for 9th Bn Warwickshire Regt
3/5/16.

Instructions regarding War Diaries and Intelligence Summaries are contained in F. S. Regs., Part II. and the Staff Manual respectively. Title Pages will be prepared in manuscript.

Place	Date	Hour	Battalion...	Remarks and references to Appendices
BOUZINCOURT	JULY 1st		Battalion at ...	Started for work under 7. Brigade.
	2nd		Battalion d...	of Trenches held by 10th Bn of line to (obliterated position) d and arm.
	3rd		Batt'n dis... lae	
	4th		party of	...micador trench dug on ...
				...the British front to ...ince. The trench ...y north which it was
	5th		2/Lieut Roy	WOOD for work on ...ed for work under ...148th Brigade.
	6th		Remarks	...ted in back (S.W.) ...A Coy. wounded.

Army Form C. 2118

Monmouth Bn
K.W. 15

Instructions regarding War Diaries and Intelligence Summaries are contained in F.S. Regs., Part II. and the Staff Manual respectively. Title Pages will be prepared in manuscript.

INTELLIGENCE SUMMARY
(Erase heading not required.)

Place	Date	Hour	Summary of Events and Information	Remarks and references to Appendices
BOUZINCOURT	JULY 1st		Battalion arrived at BOUZINCOURT, about 2 a.m. B, C & D Coys detailed for work under C.R.E. of 36th Division, in sector of Trenches held by the 107th Brigade.	
	2nd		Battalion detailed for work under C.R.E. 49th Division in sector of Trenches held by 49th Div — A Battn. detailed to dig communication Trenches from old British front line to Captured position.	
	3rd		Casualties 935. 2/Lt Parsons H. C. Coy. shellwound head and arm. 2622. Pt. Root L. Coy. shell wound in back. 3358. Pt Shaw B. Coy. missing.	
	4th		4 party of 1 Officer and 30 O.R. detailed to complete communication trench dug on previous night. The following message received from B.H.Q. 49th Division. "The work of digging communication Trenches from the British front to Captured German position was of great importance. This Divisional Commander is very pleased with the rapidity with which it was done by the 3rd Monmouthshire Regt."	
	5th		2/Lieut Raymont and 50 O.R. of B. Coy. proceeded to AVELUY WOOD to work on LANCASHIRE DUMP under C.R.E. C. Coy detailed for work under 148th Brigade.	
	6th		Remainder of B. Co. less 25. O.R. proceeded to AVELUY WOOD. A Coy detailed for work under 147. Brigade. Casualties 2/Lieut C.C.L. Wheeler severely wounded in back (S.W.) 3170 Pt W.G. Edwards A.Co. Killed. 3209 Pt Brook H. A.Coy. wounded.	

WAR DIARY or INTELLIGENCE SUMMARY

Army Form C. 2118

Place	Date	Hour	Summary of Events and Information	Remarks and references to Appendices
BOUZINCOURT	July 6.		Casualties continued:- 2771 Pt Edwards J. A.Coy. 3191 Pt Griffiths G.R. A.Coy. 3527 Pt Lloyd H. A.Coy. 3164 Pt Williams H. A.Coy. 3155 Pt Jenkins B. A.Coy. 3481 Pt Higgs T. B.Coy. 1224 Col.Serjt H. D.Coy. 2927 Pt Lloyd J. H.Coy. 3005 Pt Evans R.B. C.Coy. were wounded by shellfire. 2255 Pt Kentish W. H.Coy. 1344 Pt Price R. A.Coy. 2719 Pt Oakley J. H.Coy. 3381 Pt Powell R.J. 2144 Pt Terry H. B.Coy. 1300 Pt Krebs W.H. H.Coy. 3552 Pt Andrews L.S. B.Coy. 1635 Pt Daniel J. D.Co. 2540 Pt Price D.Co. were slightly wounded but remained on duty. 2690 Sergt Ford J. 2175 Cpl Froyd D. 3103 Pt Mutter D. 3129 Pt Jones L.O. 1370 Pt Shield A. all of A Co were missing. 2657 Pt Cook J. H.Coy. 3619 Pt Hurley J.R. 2798 Pt Buell T. Pt Travis S. A.Coy. 3508 Pt Brewer C.Coy. were admitted to hospital suffering from shell shock.	
	7.		Battalion received under instructions from C.R.E. for 148th Brigade. 3085 Pt Powell B.Coy. was wounded by shrapnel in shoulder.	
	8.		Battalion received under instructions from C.R.E. for 146 & 147 Brigades. 2/Lieut C.A.R. Drake reported as having died 7/7/16.	
	9.		Battalion received under instructions from C.R.E. 2886 Pt Turle A. D.Coy. Kill'd. 3502 L/Cpl Fisher A.B. C.Coy. wounded in Arm. 2209 Serjt McCarthy 3122 Pt Haven W.H. 3106 Pt Davis C. 2569 Pt Watts F. were slightly wounded but remained on duty.	

Army Form C. 2118

WAR DIARY
or
INTELLIGENCE SUMMARY
(Erase heading not required.)

Instructions regarding War Diaries and Intelligence Summaries are contained in F.S. Regs., Part II. and the Staff Manual respectively. Title Pages will be prepared in manuscript.

Place	Date JULY	Hour	Summary of Events and Information	Remarks and references to Appendices
BOUZINCOURT	10th		Battalion Head Quarters and Transport moved by route march to HEDAUVILLE.	
HEDAUVILLE	11th		Battalion worked under instructions of C.R.E. for 146th & 147th Brigade. A draft of 114 O.R. B's 1st & 2nd Batts joined from Base. 2103 Pt Murdoch E. Killed. 1496 Pt Arnett W. B.E. wounded in knee.	
	12th		Battalion carried on with their work. 2870 Pt Bennett B.E. 1721 Pt Warmer W. 2741 Pt Moody att L: D C's were severely wounded.	
	13th		Companies carried on with their work, under instructions of C.R.E. 2127 Corp Harris W. "B Coy" shell wounded in left hand. A draft of 33 O.R. B's 1st & 2nd Batts joined from Base.	
	14th		Companies carried on with their work. 2865 Pt Ruskelp "B Coy" 3435 Pt Hodge V. 1774 Pt T. Williams D Co. 2678 Pt Strong for "A Co." were all wounded.	
	15th		Under orders from C.R.E. "C Co" was withdrawn from 147th Brigade to HEDAUVILLE.	
	16th		Companies carried on with their work. 3405 Pt Carpenter D. and 2262 Pt Reynolds E. Killed. 2847 Cpl Hitchen E. 2863 Cpl Howe G. 3722 Pt Crooks T. J. 3543 Pt Parr W. 1892 Pt Mitchell W. 2843 Pt Buttrell T. 2572 Pt Gallimore. 1817 Pt Baker F. 1570 L/Cpl Warren Jos 2 Pt Whitfield. 2151 Pt Wilbd D. 3057 Pt Bellington E. were all wounded by shell. 2190 Pt Berry J. 3604 Pt Maunders A. 3116 Pt Lytsey S. 3074 Pt Dummey. 3058 Pt Bellington Y., were all admitted to 57 hospital suffering from shell shock.	

1875 Wt: W593/826 1,000,000 4/15 J.B.C. & A. A.D.S.S./Forms/C. 2118.

WAR DIARY or INTELLIGENCE SUMMARY

Army Form C. 2118

Place	Date	Hour	Summary of Events and Information	Remarks and references to Appendices
HEDAUVILLE.	JULY 17th		Companies carried on with their work, under instructions of C.R.E. 1156 Sgt. T. Davies S.A. 1530 Sgt. Buck, S. 28 & Sgt. Baynham W.S. 2507 L/Cpl. Pd. H. Co. 2876 Pt. K. Smyth B.Co. were wounded (shell).	
	18th		"C" Coy relieved "A" Co in forward Area. "A" Co returned to HEDAUVILLE.	
	19th		Companies carried on with their work as usual.	
	20.		The C.O. presented La Baillie cards to 1122 C.L.M. Howell C.Q. 2623 Pt. Baker S.A. 2679 Pt. Burrey T. 1510 Pt. Pickford, for gallant conduct in the field on July 3rd. "A" Coy moved to MARTINSART (WOOD), to construct a track for horse traffic from Crucifix Corner to X.1.6.4.1 (sheet 57D S.E.)	
	21st		Companies carried on with their work as usual.	
	22nd 23rd		Half of D. Co. moved back to HEDAUVILLE. Remainder of Batt. worked as usual. 2/Lieut. N.F.C. Story proceeded to Machine Gun Corps. for duty with same.	
	24th		Companies carried on with their work as usual. 3570 Pt. T. Willis "C" Coy was wounded (shell) right thigh.	
	25th		Half of D. Co. at HEDAUVILLE, moved back to MARTINSART. Remainder of Batt. worked as usual	
	26th		Battalion carried on with its work under instructions of C.R.E.	

Army Form C. 2118

WAR DIARY
or
INTELLIGENCE SUMMARY
(Erase heading not required.)

Instructions regarding War Diaries and Intelligence Summaries are contained in F. S. Regs., Part II. and the Staff Manual respectively. Title Pages will be prepared in manuscript.

Place	Date	Hour	Summary of Events and Information	Remarks and references to Appendices
HEDAUVILLE	JULY 26th		The following was published as a special Divisional Routine Order. "On their temporarily leaving his command, the G.O.C. Xth Corps wishes to record to the G.O.C. and all ranks of the 49th Division, his appreciation of their gallant and devoted conduct during the recent operations, more especially in the LEIPZIG REDOUBT. He feels sure that they will continue to give a good account of themselves."	
	27th		Companies carried on with their work as usual. 26.5. 2/Lt Redmond wounded (shrapnel) in back. 2188. Pte J. Lacey "C" Coy wounded (shell) in elbow. 3562. Pte A. 107 "C" Coy wounded (shell) right thigh. 787. L/Cpl Flanaghan "B" Co (shell) in arm, but returned to duty. 1290 L/Cpl B. Smith wounded (shell) left shoulder.	
	28th		Work carried on as usual.	
	29th		Companies carried on with their work as usual.	
	30th			
	31st		Companies carried on with work as usual, under instructions of C.R.E.	

1875 Wt. W593/826 1,000,000 4/15 J.B.C. & A. A.D.S.S./Forms/C. 2118.

D.A.G.
3rd Echelon.
　　Base.

L.B.958.

Herewith Battalion War Diary on Army Form C 2118 for August ~~& September~~.

No. H. I.B.D.
10-10-16.

W. Lister 2/Lieut.
Officer i/c Base Details
13th Monmouthshire Regt.

WAR DIARY or INTELLIGENCE SUMMARY

Army Form C. 2118.

From 49 Div HQ GHQ
AUG. 8

13th Bn Monmouthshire Regt.

Place	Date	Hour	Summary of Events and Information	Remarks and references to Appendices
HEDAUVILLE	1/8/16		Work carried on with.	
Do.	2/8/16		Half of "D" Coy at HEDAUVILLE returned to MARTINSART in the evening.	
"	3/8/16		Work carried on with.	
"	4/8/16		" " " "	
			3663 Pte W.E. Jones wounded (shell) left thigh. 2844 " " " wounded (shell) right arm.	
"	5/8/16		Work carried on with. Orders received to the effect that the Battalion would be broken up in consequence of the difficulty of reinforcing the 3 Monmouthshire Battalions. Work carried on with.	
"	6/8/16		"B" Company relieved by 19th Lancashire Fusiliers, and returned to FORCEVILLE where Battalion Headquarters had moved to.	
"	7/8/16		"C" & "D" Coys relieved by 19th Lancashire Fusiliers and returned to FORCEVILLE. Battalion paraded at 4-10 p.m and was inspected by Maj-Gen. E.M Percival M.O.C H.Q- (49th) Division, who delivered a farewell speech to the Battalion. The following is a copy of Divisional Routine Order 2041 dated 7th inst:—	
FORCEVILLE	8/8/16	20111	Departure of 1/3rd Battalion the Monmouthshire Regiment. "The Divisional Commander cannot allow the 1/3rd Battalion Monmouthshire "Regiment to leave the Division without placing on record his appreciation "of their services and the regret at parting which they have known is "felt by the whole Division. "Since this fine unit became the Divisional Pioneer Battalion on 3rd Sept 1915 "it has constantly done good work under very trying conditions. It is impossible "to speak too highly of the value of this work and its help towards our	

WAR DIARY or INTELLIGENCE SUMMARY

Army Form C. 2118.

(Erase heading not required.)

Place	Date	Hour	Summary of Events and Information	Remarks and references to Appendices
FORCEVILLE	8/8/16		Final victory, the 49th (West Riding) Division. The Divisional Commander thanks on behalf of the 49th (West Riding) Division. His Officers and men went abroad to 1st Brigade. His Officers, Non-commissioned Officers and men for their loyalty and devotion and in bidding them farewell wishes all ranks of the 1/3rd Monmouths "Good Luck" wherever they may be.	
"	9/8/16.		Battalion paraded at 10.0 a.m. and moved by march route to ACHEUX Station where it entrained for HESDIN, arriving at the latter place about 7.30 p.m. Battalion then proceeded by march route to CAPELLE, a village about 4 miles South of HESDIN, where it was billeted.	
CAPELLE	10/8/16 11/9/16. 12/8/16		Days at disposal of Company Commanders.	
	13/8/16		Church Parade for all denominations. Battalion paraded after Church Parade and the Commanding Officer made a farewell speech on account of a draft of 200 Other Ranks proceeding to join the 1/2nd Battalion Monmouthshire Regt on record duty. The following is an extract from Battalion Routine Orders:— "It having been decided that the Battalion be disintegrated 2. Farewell Order. for the purpose of supplying drafts to the 1/1st & 1/2nd Battalions of the Monmouthshire Regiment to Lieut Col W. S. Bridge avails this opportunity, just before the process commences to place on record how deeply he deplores the separation of the Battalion and himself after being in command of the same for nearly 15 months. He wishes to express his heartfelt thanks for and his appreciation of the help, good will, and soldier-like behaviour that he has at all times received from, and never found wanting in, any rank of the battalion during the period he has had the honour to command it. He wishes all ranks the "best of luck" and a safe return to England eventually where it will ever be his most earnest hope to meet them again one day. He feels confident that wherever	

Army Form C. 2118.

WAR DIARY

INTELLIGENCE SUMMARY

(Erase heading not required.)

Place	Date	Hour	Summary of Events and Information	Remarks and references to Appendices
CAPELLE	13/8/16		they may be posted, such men will continue to do their duty in the same willing spirit in which they have hitherto done it."	
"	14/8/16		Battalion (less draft of 200) were employed on filling-in trenches on South East side of HESDIN—MOBRIEZ Road. Draft of 200 Other Ranks paraded at 4.30 p.m. marched to HESDIN railway station, and entrained there to join 1/2nd Batt. Monmouthshire Regiment.	
"	15/8/16 16/8/16 17/8/16		Battalion carried on with filling-in of trenches.	
	18/8/16		Battalion carried on with filling in of trenches. Lieut A.G.J.A. Goddard rejoined Battalion for duty from England. The following Officers from Reserve Battalion joined for duty:— Capt. N.G.N.H. Lewis, relinquished the Temporary Rank of Captain. Capt. W.G.D. Bonway; relinquished Temp. Rank of Capt & Lieut. Lieut. J.A. Watson; relinquished Temp. Rank of Lieut.	
	19/8/16		'A' & 'B' Coys bathed in swimming pond at HESDIN. 'C' & 'D' " carried on with the filling in of trenches. Lieut G.A.H. Davies (Reserve Battalion) joined Batt for duty; relinquished Temp. Grade of Lieut. Church parade for all denominations.	
"	20/8/16. 21/8/16. 22/8/16.		'C' & 'D' Coys bathed in swimming pond at HESDIN. Orders received that the Battalion less 50 who would proceed to the Base to form a nucleus on which the Battalion may be eventually reformed, would proceed to join the 9th Entrenching Battalion (2nd Army) on the 24th inst.	

Army Form C. 2118.

WAR DIARY
INTELLIGENCE SUMMARY

(Erase heading not required.)

Instructions regarding War Diaries and Intelligence Summaries are contained in F. S. Regs., Part II. and the Staff Manual respectively. Title Pages will be prepared in manuscript.

Place	Date	Hour	Summary of Events and Information	Remarks and references to Appendices
CAPELLE	23/8/16		Battalion rested. Extract London Gazette of 22nd August 1916. "MONMOUTH REGT. Lieut A.A. Tny to be Captain and remain Adjutant dated 22nd July 1916.	
"	24/8/16		The Battalion, less 50 Other Ranks for Base and 38 Transport, moved to HESDIN where they entrained for STEENWERCK to proceed to join No. 9 Entrenching Battalion. 2528 Other Ranks was the actual that entrained.	
"	25/8/16		2/Lieut W.E. Jenkins and 2/Lieut A.M. Watkins proceeded on short leave to U.K. Orders received so as to reporting of Officers.	
"	26/8/16		The following Officers proceeded to join the Units stated against their names:— Major W.A. Lewis, to 1/1st Battn of Monmouthshire Regt. 46th Division. Capt H.A. Hodges / 2/Lieut E.J. O'Connor / 2/Lieut C.J. Wood } to 11th Battn South Lancs Regt. 30th Division. / 2/Lieut M.W. Gorman / 2/Lieut E.F. Boulton / Lieut J.A. Finlay / 2/Lieut W.G.R. Conway } 22nd Durham Light Infantry, 8th Division. Lieut H.B. Williams / " E.N. Stafford / 2/Lieut J.C.J. Reynolds / " W. Collings } to 12th Battn K.O.Y.L.I. 31st Division.	
"	27/8/16		The following Officers proceeded to join the Units stated against their names:— Capt A.G. Newman / Lieut B.F. Jones / 2/Lieut H. Parry } to 20th Battn King's Royal Rifle Corps. 3rd Division.	

Army Form C. 2118.

WAR DIARY
or
INTELLIGENCE SUMMARY
(Erase heading not required.)

Instructions regarding War Diaries and Intelligence Summaries are contained in F. S. Regs., Part II. and the Staff Manual respectively. Title Pages will be prepared in manuscript.

Place	Date	Hour	Summary of Events and Information	Remarks and references to Appendices
CAPELLE.	27/8/16.		Capt. W. P. Abbott. Lieut N.E.N.H. Lewis " A.M.A.J. Goddard. } to 8th Battn Royal Sussex Regt. 18th Division. 2/Lt. I.C. Watson. " G.A.H. Davis. Lieut M.H. Lifton. " J.J. Branford. } to 18th Battn Middlesex Regt. 33rd Division. " J.O. Carpenter 2/Lieut D.B. Evans 2/Lieut W.P. Jenkins } to 21st Battn West Yorks Regt. 4th Division. " G.H. Funk 2/Lieut T.G. Davies - to 19th Battn Middlesex Regt. 2/Lieut V.G. Knapp (3rd Welsh Regt attached) proceeded on special leave to U.K. and to join 19th Battn. Welsh Regt, 38th Division on return to France. 2/Lieut A.M. Watkins to join 8th Batt Royal Sussex Regt on return from leave. 2/Lieut W.E. Jenkins to join 19th Batt Middlesex Regt on return from leave The nucleus of 50 other ranks under 2/Lieut W.L. Lister proceeded to No. 4 Infantry Base Depot ROUEN. All transport, under Lieut W. Bridge, was taken to ABBEVILLE and handed in at the Advanced Horse Transport Depot, there. The 39 Transport men entrained at ABBEVILLE and proceeded to join No 9 Entrenching Battalion. Lieut-Col W.F. Bridge, Capt & Adjt A.Q. Fry, Capt J.M. Jones, 2/Lieut W.E. Rayment and Lieut & Qr.M. W.J. Porter moved into HESDIN. The medical officer (Capt A.W.D. Steel) proceeded to join the 65th Field Ambulance 21st Division.	

Army Form C.

WAR DIARY
or
INTELLIGENCE SUMMARY
(Erase heading not required.)

1/3rd Bn Monmouthshire Regiment

Instructions regarding War Diaries and Intelligence Summaries are contained in F. S. Regs., Part II. and the Staff Manual respectively. Title Pages will be prepared in manuscript.

Place	Date	Hour	Summary of Events and Information	Remarks and references to Appendices
ROUEN.	1/9/16 to 9/9/16		Lieut W Bridge to be attached for 1 month to 1st Pontoon Park. R.E. Nucleus at Base found guards, fatigues etc.	
HESDIN.	10/9/16		Captain J. Morton Jones proceeded to H.Q. Gen II Corps for attachment to Royal Engineers of that Corps.	
ROUEN	11/9/16 to 16/9/16		Nucleus at Base found guards, fatigues etc.	
HESDIN.	17/9/16		Captain & Adjutant A.A. Fry, proceeded to Command No 19 Prisoners of War Company, Fourth Army.	
HESDIN.	18/9/16.		2/Lieut W.B. Raymont proceeded to join 5th Battn South Wales Borderers.	
ROUEN	19/9/16		Nucleus at Base found guards fatigues etc.	
HESDIN.	20/9/16		Lieut-Col W.S. Bridge proceeded to Hd Qrs Second Army for attachment to Staff.	
ROUEN.	21/9/16 to 30/9/16		Nucleus at Base found fatigues etc.	

W. Sieber 2/Lieut.
Officer i/c Nucleus at Base.
1/3rd Bn Monmouthshire Regiment.

Army Form C. 2118.

WAR DIARY
or
INTELLIGENCE SUMMARY

(Erase heading not required.)

Instructions regarding War Diaries and Intelligence Summaries are contained in F. S. Regs., Part II. and the Staff Manual respectively. Title Pages will be prepared in manuscript.

Place	Date	Hour	Summary of Events and Information	Remarks and references to Appendices
HESDIN.	28/8/16		Nothing to record.	
"	29/8/16		Lieut. & B.M. W.M. Porter proceeded to join 1st Battalion Monmouthshire Regiment. N.6. Division, The Nucleus of 50 Other Ranks arrived at No 4 Infantry Base Depot ROUEN.	
"	30/8/16		Nothing to record.	
"	31/8/16		Lieut. W. Bridge returned to HESDIN.	

W. Lister 2/Lieut.
Officer i/c Nucleus at Base.
1/3rd Battn. Monmouthshire Regiment.

woas / stray / zzz

www.ingramcontent.com/pod-product-compliance
Lightning Source LLC
Chambersburg PA
CBHW080923230426
43668CB00014B/2184